Marketing Basics
for Designers

Marketing Basics for Designers

A Sourcebook of Strategies and Ideas

Jane D. Martin

and

Nancy Knoohuizen

John Wiley & Sons, Inc.

New York • Chichester • Brisbane • Toronto • Singapore

Illustrations by Don R. Martin, II

Don has a BA in fine art from Rollins College and an MBA in marketing from the University of Colorado. He does freelance art as an adjunct to his business career in marketing and sales.

This text is printed on acid-free paper.

This publication is designed to provide accurate and authoritative information in regard to the subject matter covered. It is sold with the understanding that the publisher is not engaged in rendering legal, accounting, or other professional services. If legal advice or other expert assistance is required, the services of a competent professional person should be sought.

Library of Congress Cataloging-in-Publication Data:
Martin, Jane D., 1943–
   Marketing basics for designers : a sourcebook of strategies and
ideas / Jane D. Martin and Nancy Knoohuizen.
      p.   cm.
   Includes bibliographical references and index.
   ISBN 0-471-11871-0
   1. Interior decoration firms — Economic aspects — United States.
2. Design services — United States — Marketing. I. Knoohuizen,
Nancy. II. Title.
NK2116.2.M37   1995
729'.068'8 — dc20   95-13176

Printed in the United States of America
10 9 8 7 6 5 4 3 2 1

Contents

Acknowledgments   *ix*

Designers Interviewed for This Book   *xi*

Introduction. *1*

CHAPTER 1   **Finding Your Niche in the Market**
Focus Your Marketing for Better Results. *5*

EXPLORING NICHE POSSIBILITIES   6

CHOOSING A NICHE   12

WHAT MAKES A NICHE WORK?   17

HOW TO DIFFERENTIATE YOUR DESIGN SERVICE   26

CHAPTER 2   **Mapping Your Marketing Goals**
How to Write a Marketing Plan *28*

WHY DO A MARKETING PLAN?   29

INVOLVE OTHERS IN PLANNING   29

WHAT SHOULD YOUR MARKETING PLAN LOOK LIKE?   31

CONTENTS OF YOUR MARKETING PLAN   36

HOW TO USE YOUR MARKETING PLAN   49

TIME MANAGEMENT   50

CHAPTER 3   **Setting Your Fees**
             How to Price Your Services *55*

             WHY PRICING IS MARKETING   56
             KEEP YOUR MARKETING MESSAGE CONSISTENT   57
             ARE YOU SELLING SERVICES OR PRODUCTS?   58
             HOW TO SET YOUR FEES   59
             HOW TO TALK TO CLIENTS ABOUT MONEY   65

CHAPTER 4   **Building Relationships and Referrals**
             Making Word-of-Mouth Marketing Work for You *70*

             WHY ARE MARKETING RELATIONSHIPS IMPORTANT?   71
             CREATING PARTNERSHIPS FOR MARKETING   72
             NETWORKING   81
             AND DON'T FORGET TO ASK YOUR CLIENTS   86

CHAPTER 5   **Breaking the Ice with Prospective Clients**
             Building Visibility and Credibility *89*

             MARKETING IS A PROCESS   90
             HOW TO BE VISIBLE TO THE RIGHT PEOPLE   91
             CREDIBILITY: BUILDING YOUR REPUTATION   97
             "BUT HOW CAN I BE AN EXPERT WHEN I'M
                JUST GETTING STARTED?"   121

CHAPTER 6   **Building a Relationship with Prospective Clients**
             Marketing Methods That Get Results *125*

             MARKETING IS A RELATIONSHIP-BUILDING PROCESS   125
             PRESENTING A CONSISTENT IMAGE   126

TANGIBLE TOOLS OF THE MARKETING TRADE   127

ADVERTISING   147

PROMOTING YOUR SERVICE TO PROSPECTIVE CLIENTS   150

IDEAS FOR STAYING IN TOUCH WITH PROSPECTIVE
   CLIENTS   163

CHAPTER 7   **Selling Design Services**
Client Interviews and Sales Presentations *166*

WHAT IS DIFFERENT ABOUT SELLING DESIGN
   SERVICES?   166

OUR DEFINITION OF SELLING   167

FOCUS ON CLIENT PROBLEMS AND DESIGN
   SOLUTIONS   170

STEPS IN SELLING YOUR DESIGN SERVICES   171

THE ART OF CLOSING: ASK FOR THE CHANCE
   TO GIVE YOUR BEST   189

HANDLING OBJECTIONS   192

WHEN YOU DON'T GET THE JOB   193

ABOUT COLD FEET AND SECOND THOUGHTS   194

CHAPTER 8   **Keeping Clients for Future Business
and Referrals**
Quality and Customer Service *196*

THE VALUE OF A GOOD REPUTATION   196

WHAT IS QUALITY?   197

DELIVERING CUSTOMER SERVICE   199

QUALITY SERVICE AS A COMPETITIVE ADVANTAGE   206

WHAT DO YOUR CLIENTS REALLY THINK?   206

MAKE COMPLAINTS CONSTRUCTIVE   210

YOUR CLIENT LIST IS VALUABLE   212

CHAPTER 9   **Forty Marketing Ideas to Get You Started**. *219*

APPENDIX A   **Starting Your Own Interior Design Business**
A Checklist for Evaluating Your Entrepreneurial Skills *225*

APPENDIX B   **Tips for Using Technology** *231*

References   *239*

Index   *249*

Acknowledgments

Many people have shared in the creation of this book. It is a pleasure for both of us to recall our conversations with all of you — so many stimulating ideas and so much good humor. Throughout this process, one of our greatest pleasures has been the growing web of connections we made as people offered to help and suggested more people to call. We thank all of you for sharing your thoughts so generously.

Thanks to Margie Coel, Rosemary Menconi, and Cynthia Leibrock for helping us in the earliest stage to figure out what this book should be and how to get started in searching for a publisher. Amelia Edwards and Rosemary Menconi reviewed our book proposal and gave us helpful suggestions. We are grateful to the students and alumni of the Interior Design Institute in Denver for their enthusiastic participation in our initial focus groups to research this book idea.

Joe Pryweller with the American Society of Interior Designers (ASID) answered countless questions and cheerfully supplied suggestions — and telephone numbers — of the many excellent marketers interviewed for this book. And our heartfelt thanks to these designers who shared their ideas and experiences with all of us. The list on the next page gives their names and businesses.

Aleta Daley, our agent, has been a great representative and support. Linda Bathgate has been a delightful editor, patient with our questions and always supportive.

Thanks to Andrea Covington, Judy Johnson, Amelia Edwards, Alicia Werner, and Susan Miner for their support. Thanks to Tevis Morrow who helped Jane make the leap to computer literacy in time for this project. And to Bob Kaslik who doubled our RAM and solved the inevitable computer glitches.

Both of us thank our families for enjoying and enduring this process with us. Special thanks to Moka, Ginger, and Buffy — our pups — for dragging us on long walks in the Colorado foothills while planning this book.

To Bob, my thanks for so many things — among which are your support these months, the many clarifying discussions about marketing, and for keeping me smiling.

Nancy Knoohuizen

To my husband, Don, and sons, Don and Rob, for their encouragement, excitement, and support for our book.

Jane D. Martin

Designers Interviewed for This Book

Linda Blair, ASID, of Linda Blair Design, Inc. is located in Scarsdale, New York.

June Towill Brown, ASID, of June Towill Brown Interiors is located in Studio City, California.

Corinne J. Brown, ASID Allied Member, of Roche Bobois is located in Denver, Colorado.

Mary Ann Bryan, ASID, of The Bryan Design Associates is located in Houston, Texas.

Nancy E. Chilton, IIDA, of Hue, Inc. is located in Nashville, Tennessee.

Nancy Clanton, PE, of Clanton Engineering is located in Boulder, Colorado.

Helen F. Crockett of Pheasant Hill Interiors is located in Colorado Springs, Colorado.

Cheryl Duvall, FIIDA, of Duvall/Hendricks (now part of Griswold, Heckel, and Kelly Associates) is located in Baltimore, Maryland.

Amelia Edwards, ASID Educational Member, of Amelia Edwards Interiors is located in Donaldson, Tennessee.

Charles Gandy, FASID, IIDA, of Gandy/Peace, Inc. is located in Atlanta, Georgia.

Rita Carson Guest, ASID, of Carson Guest, Inc. is located in Atlanta, Georgia.

Mark Hampton, of Mark Hampton, Inc. is located in New York City, New York.

Ellen C. Jeffers, ASID Allied Member, of Pheasant Hill Interiors is located in Colorado Springs, Colorado.

Sarah Boyer Jenkins, ASID, IFDA, of Sarah Boyer Jenkins and Associates is located in Chevy Chase, Maryland.

John Kelly, ASID, of John Kelly Interior Design is located in Philadelphia, Pennsylvania.

E. Suzanne Leary, ASID, of R. M. Leary Company is located in Denver, Colorado.

Pat Leifer of Pat's Draperies is located in Boulder, Colorado.

Nila R. Leiserowitz, ASID, Associate AIA, of Perkins and Will is located in Chicago, Illinois.

Sally Sirken Lewis of SSID (Sally Sirken Interior Design) is located in Los Angeles, California.

Dennis McNabb, ASID, of Urban Archaeology is located in Houston, Texas.

Peter Miscovich, Senior Vice President and Director of National Accounts for ISI (Interior Space International) is located in Los Angeles, California.

Douglas Parker, AIA, of Steelcase is located in Grand Rapids, Michigan.

Kathey E. Pear of Pear Commercial Interiors is located in Boulder, Colorado.

B. J. Peterson, FASID, of B. J. Peterson Interior Designs is located in Los Angeles, California.

Trish Reddick of Interior Trends is located in Nashville, Tennessee.

Bruce Simoneaux, AIA, of Steelcase is located in Grand Rapids, Michigan.

Deb Springer of Springer Graphics is located in Boulder, Colorado.

Deborah Steinmetz, ASID, of Steinmetz and Associates is located in New Orleans, Louisiana.

Ambur Stevens of Decorator Den is located in Boulder, Colorado.

Michael D. Temple, IIDA, ASID, of M. Temple Interior Design is located in San Diego, California.

Gary Whitney of Whitney and Whitney is located in Houston, Texas.

Roger Yee, editor in Chief of *Contract Design* magazine, is located in New York, New York.

Marketing Basics
for Designers

Introduction

Marketing focuses on the human side of your business—your clients. The best way to think about marketing is as the connection between what you can do and what your clients need. It is the process of building relationships with clients that ensures you will be in the right place at the right time when they need your service.

Design is the creation of a harmonious whole, tailored to the context and needs of each client. Each element of a design is chosen for its contribution to the whole—combining function, beauty, and effectiveness. Good marketing is also a design. This book shows you how to create your marketing design by selecting the marketing methods most appropriate to *your* context and needs.

Marketing Basics for Designers demonstrates the wide range of marketing techniques from which you can choose. There is ample flexibility within the role of marketer for you to find a style that is right for you. So relax—*you can be a good marketer and remain yourself*.

You already know that marketing is important. You know it will be one of the keys to the success of your interior design business. In this book we hope to show you that marketing can also be creative and fun.

WHO WILL BENEFIT FROM THIS BOOK

Interior designers planning for or starting your own interior design business: This book provides helpful information for getting established through marketing and building your client base. It will be valuable to students still in design school as well as to those of you presently working for a design firm but dreaming of going out on your own. *Marketing Basics for Designers* will help you assess your marketing skills and your own work style to decide if going independent is a good choice for you.

Interior designers with established businesses: Interior designers already in business will find many helpful tips and new marketing ideas. If you find that your market has been shifting with changes in the economy or if you are trying to expand your scope beyond a limited loop of personal referrals, this book can help you analyze your situation and provide new, creative ideas to expand your business through better marketing.

HOW WILL IT HELP YOU

This is a sourcebook of marketing ideas for small interior design businesses. It is written specifically for *you* — to help you solve your marketing problems. You will find all the basic techniques of marketing, illustrated by first-hand experiences from working designers. You'll see what has worked for other designers — and why.

Marketing Basics for Designers is designed as a resource for marketing ideas. We invite you to browse and sample these ideas, then choose the ones that best fit your style and needs. In these pages you will meet all kinds of interior designers who have worked out their own ways to market their services. Their stories and ideas will inspire you and stimulate your creativity as you plan your marketing strategy.

This book will also give you the "how-to" details you need to carry out these marketing ideas. You will learn how to get started and how to follow through on marketing projects. And you will learn how to measure the effectiveness of a marketing idea — in getting clients and building a profitable business.

Marketing Basics for Designers will show you how to

- Choose a successful market niche and build your reputation as an expert in this niche.
- Budget time for marketing even if you work alone.
- Write and use a marketing plan.
- Set fees that establish your position in your market and provide adequate profit margin.
- Build a network of relationships with other professionals that generates referrals and a valuable word-of-mouth reputation.
- Develop credibility and visibility to become known as an expert in design.
- Create memorable — and cost-effective — portfolios, business cards, brochures, and other marketing promotion tools.

- Learn the secrets of comfortable and effective selling styles.
- Keep clients coming back with more business for you.

WHO IS WRITING THIS BOOK

Jane Martin has been an interior designer for 15 years, working in Boulder, San Francisco, and Nashville. She has an AA degree from Stephens College, a BS degree from Indiana University, and has an interior design degree from Watkins College of Art and Design in Nashville. She is an allied member of the American Society of Interior Designers (ASID). Jane focuses on residential design. In her professional career, she has had the dubious pleasure of starting her own successful business in a new location three times. This book is designed to pass along to you the marketing lessons Jane has learned the hard way through much trial and error.

Nancy Knoohuizen is a professional researcher and writer with a Master's degree in Private and Public Management from the Yale School of Management. She has experience in marketing consulting services and in planning and marketing with small business startups. Nancy is intrigued with the emerging issues in professional services marketing, and consults with professional services on marketing and practice development.

We bring you the benefit of having listened to many interior designers' ideas about marketing. They've told us what works for them. And what doesn't. This wealth of practical experience is the core of *Marketing Basics for Designers.* We believe the key to good marketing is not just "learning the process" or "following the rules." The key is focusing on your client—observing, listening, and using your knowledge and skills to respond to client needs.

OUR VALUES

We believe that long-term success is as much a result of integrity and of valuing the unique humanity of each client as it is of good marketing strategy and techniques. That integrity and attention to the individual lift the mechanics of marketing to a higher level of business excellence.

We believe in the value of cooperation, even with design colleagues who work in the same field. Sharing ideas and pooling knowledge in the long run creates more for all. We believe in looking for mutual benefits in all aspects of working together in business—with clients, suppliers, other professionals, staff, and other designers.

In researching this book, we held a focus group of interior designers in the Denver area to talk about marketing. As we sent out invitations, we wondered whether designers would be willing to share their effective marketing ideas with potential competitors—we weren't even sure people would be willing to get together to talk. So we were amazed at the number of busy professionals willing to take time from their schedules to share ideas about marketing. When we got them together we found them so eager to talk and share that we could barely sneak in our own questions. This demonstrated to us the design profession's open acceptance of the value of learning and growing together.

Above all, we wrote this book with a belief in *you*. We believe you have the energy, creativity, and intelligence to run a business and market your services effectively. This book is a tool for you—a workbook and a sourcebook of ideas to trigger your creativity. Read and use it, but trust your own ability and ideas. You are the best judge of what will work for you.

Finding Your Niche in the Market

Focus Your Marketing for Better Results

NANCY CLANTON *is a nationally recognized expert in illumination design. Based in Boulder, Colorado, she serves clients all over the United States who consult with her to solve difficult lighting problems. She has just finished consulting on lighting for the Kansas City Zoo. It's an environment-conscious plan—very appropriate for a zoo—that lights primarily with daylight and uses materials from renewable sources. Now she's turning her attention to an exciting new project: a master plan for minimizing "light pollution" in the Grand Canyon. Her ultimate goal with this project is to redesign the exterior lighting so that we can experience the Grand Canyon at night lit only by the Milky Way.*

NANCY CHILTON *helps medical facilities in the Nashville area stay competitive by presenting a fresh and attractive design image. She is successful in getting work with such large national health care corporations as Surgical Health Corporation and Ornda Corporation because she understands and meets the needs of these corporations. Currently, she has multi-year contracts with five area hospitals to do a phased design update of hospital interiors.*

What do these two interior designers have in common? They've both built a successful design practice in a *market niche.* A niche is a design specialty that focuses its services to meet the needs of a specific group — or *segment* — of the total market.

Marketing based on a niche or segment is more efficient than unfocused marketing because you don't waste time and money telling your story to people who aren't interested. Instead, you zero in on the potential clients most likely to need your service. Narrowing your focus makes marketing easier, faster, and more profitable. Serving a niche also helps you to focus on what clients want and need from your design service. Base your marketing on demonstrating to target clients how your design service is different, and why it is the right choice for meeting their design needs.

In This Chapter

This chapter will walk you through the process of finding a market niche that is a good match for you. Designers who have established market niches for their services will share what makes their niches work. These examples will help you think through your own unique combination of knowledge and skills and match these to a market niche.

This chapter will show you how to

● Evaluate and select a niche.

● Analyze whether a niche will work well for you.

● Research the market and your competition.

● Differentiate your design service.

EXPLORING NICHE POSSIBILITIES

In choosing a niche you are selecting a recognizable *segment* of the total interior design market. Niche marketing is also called market segmentation. Your segment will be a client group with a set of characteristics in common. This client group will have common needs and similar motivations in seeking design services. Specializing in a niche allows you to focus on communicating with and serving this special group of clients.

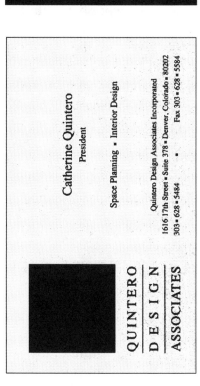

FIGURE 1-1 *Niche marketing by interior designers. Catherine Quintero, Quintero Design Associates: Space Planning and Interior Design. Pat Leifer: Pat's Draperies. Dennis McNabb: Urban Archaeology. Card design by Dawn Wolf, Graphic Decisions. Jo Anne McDowell: Philanthropy by Design.*

Your niche must reflect your strengths as a designer and must have enough potential clients for you to build a business. But, given those conditions, possibilities are as open as your imagination. Try brainstorming a list of market niche ideas. Here are some market niches designers have positioned their businesses to serve.

Art Galleries	Zoos
Bed & Breakfast Inns	Children's Hospitals
Casinos	Airports
Mortuaries	Resort Condominiums
Kitchens	Fitness Centers
Home Offices	Draperies and Window Treatments
Jewelry Stores	Theaters
Ski Resorts	Office Space Planning
Residential Remodels	Handicap Access
Residences for Seniors	Environment-Friendly Design

The segment of the market you choose as your niche represents your *target client*. Listing the characteristics of this client group will give you a profile of your target clients. And knowing this profile gives you the best foundation for effective, targeted marketing.

If you already have experience working with this segment — or if you yourself are part of the segment — you have the advantage of knowledge gained personally. Knowing your clients simplifies marketing because you already know client needs and preferences.

Think through what you know about your target clients.

- How do they understand design?
- How do they make decisions?
- What key observations have you made about this group?

Then work through the six factors discussed below to round out your knowledge.

Evaluating Market Niches

The first step in evaluating a niche is to separate your segment from the rest of the market. In working through the questions in this section, you are compiling a *target client profile*. The following six factors can be used in analyzing what distinguishes your target client group from other groups:

1. Type of Client   The first decision designers face in choosing a market niche is whether to focus on residential or commercial design. This decision requires segmenting by type of client: consumers or businesses. Consumers are clients who both purchase and live with your design. Business clients typically have a buyer who is purchasing design service on behalf of the whole business. Some market niches may pose variations or combinations of consumer and purchasing agent.

Ask the following questions about the clients in this niche:

- Who will make the purchasing decision in this niche?
- How will this factor affect your ability to communicate and work with this client group?

2. Demographics   Demographics are the language of the census, political polls, and mass marketers. Demographic information includes such categories as age, gender, occupation, income, education level, race, ethnicity, religion, and family status. Analyze your segment to see which demographics will help you understand what makes this group distinct. Use demographics to answer the following questions:

- What are the demographic characteristics of the people in this group?
- What do these people have in common?
- Which characteristics are *not* important in distinguishing this group?

3. Attitude and Lifestyle   Attitude and lifestyle characteristics fill in all the human information leached out by the impersonal results of demographic research. Attitude and lifestyle characteristics include interests, attitudes, habits, abilities (and disabilities), personality traits, and personal style. These characteristics rarely define clear boundaries of a segment, but they can be helpful factors in rounding out your understanding of your target client group. Ask such questions as

- What personal attitudes or interests characterize this group?
- What aspects of their lives do they care about most?
- What personal characteristics do these people share as a group?
- How do these characteristics and preferences affect their motives for seeking design service?

4. Location   Geographic location is important in deciding whether or not a market niche is feasible. You should decide if you want a local or regional practice, or if you are willing to travel to serve a national or international client group. Choosing a niche like zoos or airports is going to put you on a lot of airplanes, while choosing to design residential remodels or retail stores makes it more likely that you can sleep in your own bed most nights.

- Where will you find this group of people?
- Are there geographical boundaries that define your segment?

5. Problems or Needs   A group of people who share the same problem or need is one of the best market niches you can find. The trick is to define additional factors that characterize the segment so you'll be able to locate these people. An example of a niche defined by need is residential design for senior citizens. Ask such questions as:

- What needs or problems do these clients have in common?
- What common problems can be solved through design services?

6. Industry   Commercial designers usually begin with industry distinctions in analyzing a market segment. The group of clients to be defined is composed of companies rather than individuals, and companies are grouped by industry. Interior designers have already established some design categories by industry — such as health care, financial, legal, and hospitality. These categories are useful distinctions, but there are other ways to analyze commercial niches. The main characteristic is what type of space this industry requires and how employees and customers use this space. Ask the following questions as you analyze your market segment:

- Are the companies typically large or small?
- What product or service does this segment share?
- How do people doing the work of this industry use their work space?
- What are the other characteristics this industry demonstrates?
- How do these characteristics affect motives for seeking design services?

Analysis of these six factors will illustrate what distinguishes your market segment from others. The results of your analysis become your *target client profile*. See Figure 1-2 for an example.

Know the Benefits of Your Design Service

You'll find that you get to know your target clients well in the process of this niche analysis. Your goal is to understand your clients well enough to *be able to think and feel as they do*. Once you have completed the basic analysis, use these questions to fill out your understanding of this group of clients:

GMB Interiors Boston, MA	*TARGET CLIENT PROFILE* Target Market: Senior Citizens
1. Type of Client	• Assisted living residential housing developments for senior citizens; senior citizens will be the users of design. • Purchasers of design services are developers of housing projects. • Purchasers understand the basics of senior housing needs but will need some education about the benefits of good design in creating an environment for safe independent living.
2. Demographics	• Retirement age (65) and over; most residents in 70s and 80s. • Some couples; most residents will be single, predominantly women. • Financial ability to purchase or lease a unit.
3. Attitude & Lifestyle	• Senior citizens are looking for safety and protection of health. • Desire for community and meaningful social and leisure time activities. • Balancing family relationships with independence.
4. Location	• Northeast states of U.S. in the beginning; may expand services nationwide at later time.
5. Problems or Needs	• Safety and maintaining health—design needs for safe and easy walking, lighting, and manageable furniture arrangements. • Community space for socializing. • Space for inside exercise and activities. • Access to services within the facility. • Maintain health and independence with goal of staying out of nursing home. • Assistance with daily life while maintaining independence and personal dignity.

FIGURE 1-2 *Example of a target client profile.*

• What words would you use to describe this segment?
• How would the people in this group describe themselves?
• How would you know if you were part of this segment?
• What are the desirable benefits in design services for this segment?
• How do people in this segment define design?
• How do they feel about design?

You'll use this knowledge to communicate the *benefits* of your service to people in your niche through your marketing. We will be talking about the importance of stressing your benefits throughout this book. Benefits state the value of your service—from the client's perspective. Benefits are your answer to the client's primary question: *What's in it for me?*

CHOOSING A NICHE

A successful market niche is a combination of two factors:

1. Your unique expertise and interests as a designer.
2. A market with enough clients who are willing to pay for your expertise.

These two factors represent two ways of finding a niche. Some designers prefer to stay rooted in what they know they most want to do. If this way of evaluating market niches makes the most sense to you, base your niche decision on your expertise. Others find it useful to analyze the market first, looking for opportunities to match their design skills to identified market needs.

In the following sections, we share examples of niche choices made in both ways. The key is to remember that *both* factors must be part of your evaluation of a market niche. To make a decision on a design specialty based only on what you want to do or only on what the market wants is folly.

Base a Niche on Your Expertise

One way to choose a niche is to start with you—your interests, unique talents, or special knowledge. Follow your inner compass by providing the service you most enjoy. When you're doing something you love you'll automatically do a great job for your clients.

Let your unique passion guide you to your design specialty. When you limit the scope of your design service to designing humane and functional hospitals for children, parents, and caregivers, or to remodeling kitchens, you build expertise much faster than a designer whose focus is general.

Ellen C. Jeffers and her mother, Helen Crockett, have a residential design business in Colorado Springs that differentiates its service from other residential designers through an emphasis on antiques. Both partners have strong expertise in the history of design and the decorative arts. They have lots of antiques in their family. Helen grew up in England and traveled widely. When Ellen lived in New England she became interested in learning about and collecting American antiques and folk art before their value was widely recognized.

So it's natural for them to use their knowledge of fine antiques in their design work. "We try not to force people to use antiques," says Ellen. "We try to give people something classic that will last and not be trendy. We like to mix them in for an eclectic look." Ellen and Helen find that this knowledge of antiques can help establish a relationship with potential clients, because people warm to appreciation of their antiques: "You say, 'Isn't that a wonderful fall front desk?' and people appreciate that you recognize what they have."

Dennis McNabb, ASID, of Houston, Texas, shared with us the story of a designer who designs day care centers. She got started through her interest in day care facilities. She was curious about designing for day care and set out to learn about it. She talked to her friends, to people with children, and she did research—reading about day care issues and investigating various facilities. She found out which day care centers were most respected in her area and started talking to the directors. She told them she was an interior designer who knew nothing about day care but was interested in learning about the business.

She would ask to come in and talk to the staff and the director. And she would ask what their design problems were, learning about their space and design requirements. The day care workers were happy to share their knowledge with her. And, after a while, they began to call her with their problems with space or design and ask for her help. When she wavered, saying she wasn't an expert on day care and had not really designed centers, their reply was: "You showed the wherewithal to research our business. So we know from experience with you that you'll go out and do a good job for us—you'll research these things and find the best solution." And that is how she built her business in day care design.

Amelia Edwards, ASID Educational Member, has built her design business around her knowledge of historic preservation. She worked for museums, serving on boards and often contributing her expertise for free, to establish her credibility and build her reputation. Amelia does interior design for people who are buying and renovating historic homes in Nashville.

John Kelly, ASID, has based his Philadelphia business on his fascination with boats. His niche is designing the interiors of sport fishing and motor yachts. "It came from my love of boats. It is timing and marketing—being in the right place. I am very good at creating small spaces—good at using every ounce of space available: length, width, and height." (See Figure 1-3.)

Base a Niche on a Market Opportunity

The other approach to choosing a niche is to focus on the market. Design specialties that focus on law offices, health care facilities, or hotels have chosen niches based on market opportunities.

The most profitable market niche is one that serves a new market opportunity or gap where existing designers aren't responding to a group's needs. New markets are often created by external changes — demographic changes, technological advances, or legal requirements like the American Disabilities Act (ADA). Think about groups with special design needs not yet being served well, such as senior citizens or people with environmental concerns. Or look for an existing niche that is large enough to break down into smaller segments.

Nancy Chilton's design business developed in response to a market opportunity in the health care field. Nancy has a successful business updating the design of interiors of outpatient facilities or specialized departments within hospitals — primarily in health care facilities owned by large corporations.

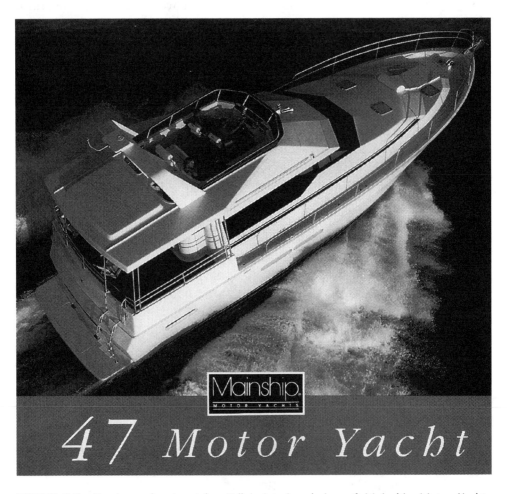

FIGURE 1-3 *Brochure showing John Kelly's interior design of Mainship Motor Yachts. Photographs by Nathan Williams Photography.*

Port Lounge & Entertainment Center   Office / Communication Center   Galley

Master Stateroom

Master Head

Forward Stateroom

Forward Head

Dining Table, Galley & Main Salon

Galley Pantry

Utility Room

*M*OST MOTORYACHTS ARE NOTHING MORE THAN HIGH-CUBE BOXES. STYLING IS SECOND TO SPACE, AND UTILITY IS LOST TO ACCOMMODATIONS. THE NEW MAINSHIP 47 MOTORYACHT BREAKS THE RULES. NOW THERE IS A MOTORYACHT THAT NOT ONLY LOOKS GOOD; IT PERFORMS WELL. PERFORMANCE CAN BE MEASURED IN SPEED, SEA KEEPING ABILITIES, AND DURABILITY. MAINSHIP TAKES PERFORMANCE ONE STEP FURTHER. PERFORMANCE IS MEASURED ON HOW WELL THIS YACHT DELIVERS ITS ATTRIBUTES TO YOU, THE OWNER.

THE MAINSHIP 47 MOTORYACHT WAS DESIGNED AND ENGINEERED WITHOUT COMPROMISE. IT'S DEDICATION TO DELIVERING OVERALL UTILITY TO ITS OWNER IN SUMPTUOUS COMFORT IS THE STANDARD TO WHICH MOTORYACHTS WILL AIM FOR IN THE FUTURE. THE MAINSHIP

DESIGN TEAM STARTED WITH A FRESH APPROACH TO DESIGN THIS YACHT IN THE WAY OWNERS WANT TO USE THEIR BOATS, NOT THE WAY MOST BUILDERS WANT TO CONSTRUCT THEM. FROM THE KEEL UP, THIS YACHT IS DEDICATED TO ITS OWNERS. THE LATEST IN TECHNOLOGY AND MATERIALS WERE COMBINED TO CONSTRUCT THE STRONGEST AND MOST DURABLE YACHT AFLOAT. THE MARINE SYSTEMS FROM THE TRIM TABS TO THE RADAR ARCH WERE SYSTEMATICALLY THOUGHT OUT, RESEARCHED, AND SOURCED TO PROVIDE THE BEST IN BOATING. THE MACHINERY SPACES WERE DESIGNED AND ENGINEERED FOR EASE OF MAINTENANCE AND PRACTICALITY. INTERIOR LAYOUTS FOLLOW THE FUNCTIONALITY OF A YACHT THIS SIZE.

THE GALLEY, FOR EXAMPLE, IS AFT IN THE SALON, SO TRAFFIC IS KEPT DOWN AND ACCESS IS MAXIMIZED. DURABLE, BUT ELEGANT, MATERIALS ARE UTILIZED NOT ONLY IN THE GALLEY, BUT THROUGHOUT THIS YACHT. LIMED OAK, CORIAN® AND BRASS COMPLIMENT THE RICH CARPETS, FABRICS, AND ULTRA SUEDE HEADLINERS. THOUGHTFUL TOUCHES SUCH AS A DISHWASHER, WASHER-DRYER AND COMPLETE ENTERTAINMENT CENTER ARE ALL STANDARD, AS ARE TELEVISIONS AND VCRS IN EACH STATEROOM.

VISIT YOUR NEAREST MAINSHIP DEALER AND SEE THE 47 MOTORYACHT FOR YOURSELF. MAINSHIP — THE STANDARD IN STYLE AND VALUE.

FIGURE 1-3   *(continued)*

As hospitals have had to become more competitive to remain profitable, they have found that attractive and functional interior design is one factor that draws physicians and patients. Older facilities need to refurbish their interiors to keep pace with the competitive environment. Hospitals need to present a modern state-of-the-art image and replace the old "generic hospital" look with one with a regional character.

Nancy has built her niche doing this kind of redesign for hospitals. She currently is working with five hospitals to update their interiors in a series of phases over 3 years: first patient rooms, then corridors, and so on. She's successful because she understands her clients' business and she keeps her focus on solving their problems. Nancy says, "I have business because I'm very cost conscious. Because if the corporation doesn't make money, they won't redo facilities; they have to make profit quickly. So I meet all budget requirements. I'd like to say that my interiors are so much better than everyone else's, but it's not true. I keep in mind my client base and the end-users, what they will relate to. I might love a $90 fabric, but the client might not see the difference — and the cost would cut into their profit."

Another market opportunity, currently the focus of new design products and services, is the growing trend toward home offices. The use of offices in the home is on the rise across the country as patterns of work continue to change. Companies in urban areas are turning to telecommuting employees to reduce automobile travel in crowded cities and to reduce their high occupancy costs. In addition, the corporate downsizing trend is increasing the number of self-employed people working from their homes.

Interior designers can help smooth this shift by creating solutions to the often frustrating problems posed by setting up a functional full-time office at home. To work efficiently at home, people have to have adequate workspace, storage, desks, lighting, and other equipment in correct scale to the space available — all of this designed to provide a pleasing and productive place to work. Providing this service is a great niche opportunity for designers interested in both office and residential design.

The October 1993 issue of *Interiors* led with an article on the new market opportunity for interior designers in serving the special residential design needs of senior citizens. Citing the expected demographic change in the United States to an older society as the baby boom generation moves into retirement, *Interiors* commented on the extent to which designers seem unprepared to respond to this change in design needs.

The next few decades will no doubt see the development of new living arrangements for senior citizens. Designers who understand their needs and have creative design solutions will be the pioneers in this niche. Senior citizens need living spaces that are safe and functional yet promote independence and dignity. These clients want to hire designers who have done their research; for example, designers who know that senior citizens need more than twice the interior light than they did for the same level of vision at age 20.

WHAT MAKES A NICHE WORK?

The key to choosing a successful niche is taking the time to think it through. Pausing to think about what kind of business you want to have and who your best clients will be can save you much future grief.

We all know of businesses that found a lucrative niche through coincidence, or designers who followed a lucky hunch into a successful specialty. But the problem with luck is that you don't know whether it's good or bad until the end of the story. And, after the fact, many hunches turn out to look more like wishful thinking than intuitive insight.

So we urge you to give your exciting niche idea the benefit of research and analysis to determine its true business potential. Do some of the simple research described below before plunging in. Then you can put your whole-hearted energy into developing your business because you know you've based your decision on solid information.

Asking the Right Questions

Asking the right questions can help you gather the information you need to evaluate the potential of your market niche. You want to choose a niche that has the best chance for success.

The following questions are a basic guide to help you weigh the pros and cons of a niche. If you aren't sure where to go to find the answers to these questions, see the next section on how to do simple market research.

1. Are there enough potential clients in this market segment to support the level of business you need? Before choosing a niche as the basis for your business you need to be sure there are enough potential clients to make your business profitable. The discussion above on factors that define market segments has helped you identify the characteristics of your target clients. Now you need to find out if there are enough of them — in the right location — to maintain your business.

For example, if you are researching the potential for the home office niche, you want to know how many people currently work out of their homes. A market research firm that tracks this trend reports a national market of 41.1 million people now working from home offices. The size of this pool is certainly encouraging enough for you to research this niche further.

If you plan to limit your business to your local area, you should also estimate the size of the local home office market. Find out what percentage of employees in large companies in your area are telecommuting. Get figures on how many people in your area are self-employed and working at home (if you don't know where to look for this information, see the next section).

2. How does the future look for this niche: Is this a growing part of the market, or is it likely to shrink?   You can never fully predict the future but you should try to anticipate main trends that would affect your niche. The home office niche appears to be a trend that will continue to grow. The news is full of reports of cost cutting through telecommuting and downsizing in companies. This niche would seem to be one of the growth segments of the office design market.

Design for senior citizens, too, is a growing niche market. The demographic trend defined by large numbers of middled-aged people whose children are leaving home and who are looking toward retirement predict a future of growth. Designers interested in this niche should monitor this trend to learn the kinds of living arrangements and design services this group of people will want.

3. Are the people or companies in this niche willing and able to pay enough for your business to be profitable?   If your clients are consumers, you need to know the income level and the amount of disposable income of your target clients. It would also be helpful to know if these potential clients have used design services before. This information will help you estimate how much of your marketing time must go toward educating potential clients about design.

If your buyers are businesses, research how successfully this industry is managing the current climate of rapid change and economic fluctuations. Are these companies able to afford quality design? Are they willing to pay for it — how well do the business decision-makers understand the benefits of good design? The answers to these questions are important indications of whether or not you can ask for and get the profit margin you need.

4. What investments must you make to get established in this niche?   You need to know how expensive it will be to enter this niche. Do you have the technology this client group will expect and need? Will you need additional training to serve this niche? Do you have adequate staff and studio to serve these clients? What are the clients' expectations about how large your business must be to serve them properly?

How much marketing investment will it take to establish a share of this niche? This depends on how much competition there is and how urgent the client need is for design services.

5. Can you identify any big obstacles to getting into this niche? Some market niches are profitable because there is little competition *and* formidable barriers that block new businesses from becoming competitors. Find out as much as you can about the competitive environment of your market niche. Ask the following questions:

- How high are the costs of getting established in this niche?
- Will it be difficult to gain a reputation or establish a position as an insider to serve this niche?
- How long will it take to get established in this niche?
- Will you need hard to get special knowledge or relationships?

Try to find out if you would need hard-to-get information before you could expect to get work with clients in your niche. In some specialized markets, there may be key organizations or groups with which you must have contacts before clients will accept you as knowledgeable enough to help them. And you may need to have knowledge of and access to key products, suppliers, or craftspeople to work successfully in a particular niche.

An example of a need for specialized knowledge is in the environment-friendly design niche. Designers working in this niche are satisfying clients' desires for interiors created with products chosen to protect clients' healths and minimize harm to our environment. But getting and keeping up to date on information about potential hazards and available alternative products can be an obstacle to building a business in this niche for many designers — just learning everything you need to know can seem like a full-time job. One interior designer, Victoria Schomer, has dealt with this potential obstacle creatively by starting the *Interior Concerns Newsletter* to share current information about alternative products that are environment-friendly and nontoxic.

6. Who is the competition in this niche? Find out how many other designers are focusing on this niche. Be sure to include the more general design businesses that sometimes work for clients in this niche. Find out as much as you can about the work these designers do — try to learn how their clients feel about them, what services still aren't being supplied, or what isn't being done well. Find the answers to such questions as

- How many other interior design businesses are now serving these clients?
- What reputations do they have?
- Is this niche dominated by a few companies?

- How do clients in this niche feel about the design services they have used? If clients are unhappy with the finished product or with the customer service, you have an opportunity to provide a better alternative.
- Would these clients pay more for excellent, totally headache-free service?

(For more information on researching your competition, see *Tips for Researching the Competition* later in this chapter.)

When Nancy Chilton started her own business to focus on a niche in health care design, she knew her competition well enough to plan her unique approach to win clients. She built her client base by being more cost conscious than her competitors, which allowed her to keep her fees down. Nancy focused on retaining clients by providing good service and building an excellent word-of-mouth reputation. This strategy saved her marketing budget dollars, and she translated these savings into lower prices for clients.

7. How difficult will it be to establish the credibility and visibility you need to get clients in this niche? Think through how you will establish a name in this niche. Ask such questions as:

- What kind of information about or demonstration of your service will build credibility with this segment?
- Where do you need to be, speak, or publish to be visible to these people?
- How difficult will it be for you to accomplish this?
- Whose opinions influence these people — what kind of testimonials will boost your credibility?

8. Do people in this niche need your service? A successful design business must fill a real need for clients. Research how people in this segment feel about design. Think about how design relates to their needs. Ask the following questions:

- Do these people know they need design services — or must you educate them?
- How important is this need in relation to their other needs?
- How would the people in this group describe their design needs?

9. How do you feel about this market niche? Don't forget to ask yourself some of the more subjective questions that can also be critical to choosing a successful niche.

- Do you genuinely believe your service meets the needs of this group?
- Will you enjoy working with these clients?
- Will this niche allow you to do enough of the creative work that is important to your job satisfaction, or will it be too limiting for you?
- Will you still be excited and stimulated by your work in this niche in five years?

How to Research Your Niche Idea

If you have worked through the previous sections in this chapter, you already have a lot of information about your market niche. You also no doubt have gaps in your knowledge. In this section, we'll share the techniques of basic market research that will show you how to fill in those gaps.

Market research reduces the uncertainty involved in choosing a niche. The more you learn about your market niche and the competition, the better you'll be able to make decisions as you plan how and where to get started. But keep your wits about you as you research. There is so much information available these days that it's far too easy to get overwhelmed — and forget what your questions were in the first place.

We advocate spending the minimum time and effort to get only the information that is relevant for you. Concentrate on *intelligent* information gathering. Write down your questions before you begin research. Then let these questions be your guide to picking a path through the swamp of data out there.

Keep your judgment and sense of proportion handy. The extent and depth of your research should be consistent with your situation and your needs. Less weighty choices call for less research. If a solo designer is considering adding design for bed and breakfast inns to his/her residential design business, simple research into needs and opportunities in the area will probably supply enough information to decide. But a firm that is considering basing its entire business on a niche like ski resorts should research all aspects of the niche extensively.

If you continue to think analytically about your niche as you research, you'll know when you have enough information. When you do, stop. And get on with planning your niche and marketing your services.

The Market Research Process

Use the market research process as a jumping-off point for asking questions and learning as much as you can about your market niche. Be creative and have fun. There are any number of ways to learn about your market niche.

There are three basic steps in doing market research:

1. Define your questions. Rank your questions according to their importance to your decision. Which information do you need? Which information
is less critical? that is, things that are nice to know but aren't crucial to your
decision.

2. Look for answers in information that is already available. Much useful information on demographics, market trends, and the size and growth of
specific industries has already been collected and compiled. In research terminology, this is called *secondary research.*

Secondary research sources are published reports of surveys and research
studies. Many agencies and organizations compile market research findings
and make this information public.

- Government agencies
- Trade, professional, and technical associations
- Business and industrial organizations
- Chambers of Commerce and other local business associations
- Suppliers and product manufacturers
- Commercial market research companies

3. Talk to people in your target group. After you've learned as much as
you can from secondary sources, take your remaining critical questions
directly to people in this niche. Asking questions of real people is called *primary research.*

There are four general methods of gathering information from people in
your niche.

a. Mail or telephone surveys

b. Personal interviews

c. Focus groups

d. Observation: Watching how people live and work in this environment

It is important to take these steps in the order given. Gathering primary
research is time-consuming and can be expensive. So it pays to find out what you
can from available sources before starting your own research. The information you
get in your search of secondary sources will narrow and focus the remaining questions to be answered in primary research. Secondary research can also help you
identify people and companies that would be good primary sources.

SUGGESTIONS FOR SECONDARY MARKET RESEARCH

1. Determine what you would like to find out about the size and growth potential of your market niche and ask your local reference librarian to suggest the most useful sources for your research.

2. Government publications, published surveys and forecasts, and special industry studies can help you learn about your market niche.

3. Census data can help you determine the size of a potential market niche in your chosen geographic area. The *Census Catalog and Guide* can help you decide what census data is appropriate and how to locate what you need.

4. Several U.S. government publications compile valuable information on current industry trends and future projections.

   > *U.S. Statistical Abstracts*
   > *Survey of Current Business*
   > *Business Conditions Digest*
   > *U.S. Industrial Outlook*

5. For some market niches, the best way to get insider information on the industry is to join the appropriate trade associations and read their journals. Trade associations often publish industry surveys or other special reports that can help you learn what is important to people in your market niche. Libraries have directories of trade journals and/or associations, such as: *Bacon's Publicity Checker*, Bacon's Media Directories, Chicago, Illinois; *Encyclopedia of Associations*, Gale Research Company, Detroit, Michigan; *Standard Periodical Directory*, Oxbridge Communications, Inc., New York, New York.

6. Skim general business magazines for articles or even special issues on your market niche. Subscribing to a clipping service can save you time. Such a service can review business magazines and newspapers to gather information on your market niche.

7. Large suppliers or vendors may have marketing data they would be willing to share with an interior designer not competing for the same business. Such companies have often done useful surveys or market studies.

TIPS FOR RESEARCHING THE COMPETITION

1. Who are your competitors? What services do they offer? Who are the leaders?

   - Don't neglect the obvious—check the phone book. Look up interior designers and see what specialties designers advertise. But keep in mind that not all interior designers list their business in the yellow pages.

   - Get to know people in local chapters of design associations—International Interior Design Association (IIDA) and American Society of Interior Designers (ASID); ask them which designers are currently working in your specialty.

   - Look around for completed design projects in your specialty and talk to clients about the project. You can find out who the designer was as well as the names of other designers considered for the project.

2. What are the reputations of your competitors? What are their strengths and weaknesses?

   - Ask around in local design organizations; listen carefully to shop talk. You can learn a great deal from your colleagues just by asking questions and listening carefully.

   - Ask suppliers and installers for their assessments of specific designers; they can give you an invaluable insider's view of the way these designers work.

   - Check out competitors' work for yourself. Get the names of some design clients of competitors and go to see their work. Talk to the owners, telling them you are interested in their design. Find out if

Doing Primary Research

Once you have general knowledge of your niche from secondary sources, refine your understanding of this niche by talking to as many people involved in the industry or the specialty as you can: trade association officers and staff, buyers and suppliers, salespeople, and editors of industry publications.

Attend a trade show or conference to meet people and get a sense of their concerns and how they do business. Create an opportunity to observe how people use their space—look for problems or design issues your service could address. Ask potential clients what their design needs are and what kind of design service they would like.

they're pleased and if the design has functioned well for them. Talking to actual clients can give you the best information about client expectations and whether they are being met by current designers.

3. What do your competitors charge?
   - Do some research over the phone. Call your competitors and ask what and how they charge.
   - Ask questions about fees in your local design organizations.
   - Ask clients of completed jobs if they would be willing to tell you the fees they were charged.

4. How do your competitors market their services?
   - Get copies of brochures and other marketing information from your competitors. Study these examples carefully and compare competitors for differences. Keep a file of these resources.
   - Ask clients who have worked with your competitors how they found out about them. Ask about brochures, letters, portfolios, and other marketing materials to see if anything was particularly memorable or influenced their decision.

5. How do people in this market niche feel about the designers who currently serve them?
   - Get out and talk to people in your niche. Find out how they talk about their design needs and check out how well designers are meeting those needs.
   - If you can afford to invest the time and money, a survey or focus group can give you valuable information about the problems and perspectives of the people you hope to work for in this niche.

If you're considering a major commitment to a new market, you will benefit from more formal primary market research: surveys or focus groups. We suggest hiring a market research firm to conduct your surveys or focus groups. You can do this research yourself, but you'll get more reliable results using professionals with experience in conducting and interpreting these studies.

For less crucial decisions, you can get useful information through a simple informal survey or by gathering clients from your niche for a focus group discussion. Just be careful in interpreting and applying your results beyond the effectiveness of your methods. See the *Reference* section at the end of this book for resources on forming survey and focus group questions and conducting your own primary research (sources listed under the *Market Research* heading).

The box on *Tips for Researching the Competition* provides an example of doing primary research. We've listed the basic questions you will want to answer about the competition in any market niche, with suggestions for finding the answers.

HOW TO DIFFERENTIATE YOUR DESIGN SERVICE

Differentiating your service is important to your success in a market niche. Being different is the way you stand out from your competitors. Good differentiation is based on the clients' perception of you—how they see your design service as both distinctive and valuable. Clients must recognize your difference.

Remember that your service must answer the client's main concern: *What's in it for me?* People want to know that spending money for your services will improve their business or the way they live. The benefits of your service must be important to your clients.

Outline for yourself the benefits your clients would receive in choosing your design service. Ask yourself such questions as:

- What do my clients think is important in choosing a design service?
- In what ways can my design service be more responsive to clients?
- What *unique benefit* does my service provide clients?
- How do I hope my clients describe the value of my service?
- Is my differentiation of my service linked to client needs?

Nancy Clanton's lighting design service is an excellent example of differentiating by emphasizing benefits. Nancy's firm has become a nationally recognized expert on lighting design solutions by focusing on understanding lighting from the clients' perspective. "We consider ourselves visual designers for the visual environment—pulling together what people see instead of just putting up lights."

This focus on her business's benefits is what establishes her firm's leading position in the lighting design niche. Her solutions feature overall energy usage reduction and use of materials from renewable resources when appropriate. One of Nancy's competitors acknowledges that her firm's work combines the perspectives of engineers and artists, resulting in a unique blend of concern for the visual environment and for energy conservation: "The reason

Clanton is unique is that they feel as comfortable doing an interstate highway interchange as doing a five-star restaurant."

Another way to differentiate your service through benefits is by giving clients the option of purchasing only the specific services they need. Pat Leifer's business in Boulder, Colorado, focuses on draperies and other window treatments. This niche strategy works well for her because it serves those clients who don't want help with the whole interior. By working with Pat they can get just what they need, quickly and easily.

Show the Client That Your Service Is Different

You have chosen your niche and identified your benefits. You've found out what matters to your clients. Now you want to create a marketing design that will differentiate your business and motivate clients to come to you. But you can't just *tell* them about it, you have to *show* them.

Slogans and glossy marketing materials won't differentiate your service. Nor will merely telling the client about your professional qualifications and your technical proficiency. You have to demonstrate your difference and live your benefits. Focus your attention on the client and know their needs. Demonstrate that your business is about serving those needs.

Ideas to Remember from This Chapter

- Focusing your design business on a market niche gives you an easier, faster, and more cost-effective way to market your design services.

- You can build a successful business based on a market niche you've chosen: (a) to showcase your unique design expertise, or (b) to develop a good market opportunity.

- Simple research into market potential and your competition can help you make an informed decision about the feasibility of building a successful business in a market niche.

- Identify the *unique benefits* that will differentiate your design service in this market niche—remembering that good differentiation is based on how your clients see you.

CHAPTER

2

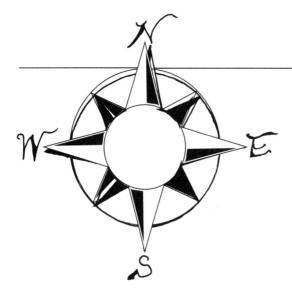

Mapping Your Marketing Goals

How to Write a Marketing Plan

Planning is thinking about your business and having a record of this thinking process. Through planning you connect your business goals with the marketing required to generate the jobs you want. Your marketing plan becomes the map that guides your marketing activity.

In This Chapter

In this chapter you'll learn how to create and use a marketing plan. Suggestions for effective planning include

- Creative marketing plan formats: bubble diagram, planning outline, or writing a letter.

- How to develop your marketing plan—and what to include.

- Ways to use your plan to improve your marketing results.

- How to improve your time management to have more time for marketing.

WHY DO A MARKETING PLAN?

In writing this book, our motto has been that you are always the best judge of what you need. The best — and only — reason to do anything we suggest in this book is because it helps you and your business. But we urge you to try a marketing plan if you haven't yet developed one, because we know that planning helps you get where you'd like to be. A plan can help you think more clearly and market more intelligently. Remember, when you're feeling lost, there's nothing quite so comforting as a good map.

View your marketing plan as a *process*; don't think of it as a *product* — an end in itself. The plan is a way to visualize your marketing design coming to life.

A marketing plan helps you to see marketing as a coherent and integrated design. Without a plan, it's easy to fall into reactive marketing — a string of random, unconnected marketing activities. Remember that marketing is most effective when your efforts work together, building your marketing impact to end up with more than the sum of the parts. Planning allows you to enhance the impact of your activities through piggyback marketing. With careful planning, everything you do — publishing an article or preparing a proposal — can be recycled and used again, for other clients or in another form.

Another plus for planning is the chance to weigh the costs and benefits of different marketing methods. A plan ensures that you know the limits of your resources and use them in the most effective way. In a small business you have to be selective. You can't do everything. The planning process ensures that you make the wisest choice among alternatives.

As you plan, remind yourself that this marketing plan is for your business to *use* — write it to help you and your staff market your business. Don't be intimidated by planning. And don't worry about how your plan will look to someone else. There is no "right" way to write a marketing plan.

"I'm very skeptical of fancy business plans," says Kathey E. Pear of Boulder, Colorado. "They don't have a basis in reality. People tend to justify what they want to do, and they can make it all look good on paper. These plans have no real influence on business. If the plan isn't for yourself, for your business to use, it has no value. We do elements of a marketing plan. The practical parts — budgeting and sales forecasts."

INVOLVE OTHERS IN PLANNING

Everyone in your business who is involved in marketing should be included in the planning process. Discuss your mission and goals with your staff as well as your partners. Take advantage of everyone's ideas and plan marketing methods that use the specific talents of your people. Also, involving everyone in planning builds staff commitment for implementing your marketing design.

Find ways to get support if you work alone. Getting started in planning can seem an impossible task for a solo designer. Discuss your marketing ideas with others to get an additional perspective.

You may find it helpful to get help with your planning from consultants. But we don't advise hiring a consultant to write a marketing plan for you. Having someone else write your plan is rarely a success, because you can't turn over the strategic thinking about your business to an outsider — no matter how qualified. Marketing planning is thinking, and you're the person best qualified to do the thinking about your business.

"Four years ago I had a marketing consultant come in to work with us," says Houston residential designer Mary Ann Bryan, ASID. "It was a learning experience for everyone. It cost me about $40,000 to learn that we still have to do it ourselves. Once I figured that out it was very basic stuff."

But there are occasions when you can benefit from consultant help. Call on consultants when you need specialized advice, when you're stuck on a problem, or when you're overloaded and need help. Remember, though, that consultants can't help you without clear direction. Know the results you need and give consultants clear tasks and goals.

The following are some of the categories of consultants who can focus and accelerate your marketing planning:

- Facilitators: If you want to take a day to develop a marketing plan with your staff, a facilitator can help you end up with a better product. You (and your partners) are relieved of running the meeting and managing the discussion. Instead you can focus on thinking and contributing.

- Direct marketing consultants: If you're thinking about investing in direct marketing but know nothing about it, a direct marketing specialist can help you find the best mailing lists and develop a feasible direct mail plan. Interview consultants to find someone with experience appropriate to your business.

- Market researchers: If your market research needs go beyond what you can do for yourself, it's wise to bring in a market research consultant. Decide in advance what specific information you need and be prepared to direct their efforts. Hire market researchers if you want to conduct a survey or conduct formal focus groups.

- Public relations consultants: Public relations specialists can help you set a plan for getting more exposure and better publicity. They can focus your efforts for faster results. These specialists usually have established contacts with the media who can help you get more articles and press releases published.

WHAT SHOULD YOUR MARKETING PLAN LOOK LIKE?

What image comes to mind when you think about writing a plan? A long document, dull and official-looking. Small print, neat margins. Lots of words and columns of numbers. *Boring*, right?

Wrong. There is no sacred format for a marketing plan. Your plan could be an outline or a list. It could be a timeline or a calendar. Or a diagram. All you need is a record of your planning to guide your marketing through the year.

Experiment until you find the planning style and format that is most helpful for you. The key is discovering a way to plan that lets you put down your ideas just the way you think, because your plan needs to make sense to you and the people who work with you. You're not doing this for anyone else.

Be prepared to change and update your plan regularly during the year. Staying flexible is as important as having a plan. Keep your eyes on your market. If your market changes, your plan should change, too.

Here are three quite different ways to approach writing your marketing plan. Experiment with these formats to find a style that complements the way you think and work. Be creative—*not* boring.

1. Bubble Diagram   We adapted this visual planning method from the bubble diagrams that designers use in working through a design project. Bubble diagrams work well for many designers because they are visual and tactile. And creating bubble diagrams is also fun.

This format encourages planning as a coherent strategy. The links between the bubbled ideas illustrate how marketing goals and methods are interrelated. The visual format encourages seeing the plan as a whole, not as separate parts.

Use the following simple steps to create a plan through bubble diagrams:

- Start your bubble diagram with one of your goals in the center.

- Think what steps—or subgoals—would be required to reach this goal and fill in bubbles with these steps. Flow out as you work, linking these bubbles to your goal.

- As you work out from your goal, keep asking yourself: How will I do this? Attach marketing methods and ideas that come to mind in each area, filling out the bubbles until the outer bubbles list relatively simple, immediate steps you can take to get started toward this goal.

- Estimate marketing costs for each method in your bubble diagram and weigh the costs and benefits of the methods you have included. Then revise the diagram, if necessary, and attach dates and names for implementing the plan.

Below is a sketch of the bubble diagram process based on a marketing goal of securing four new jobs to remodel medical practice offices.

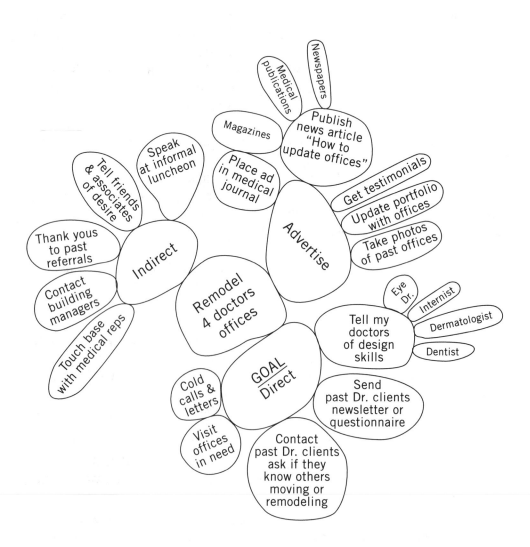

FIGURE 2-1   A bubble diagram marketing plan.

2. Planning Outline   The outline is the most familiar plan format for most of us. It's not as much fun as drawing bubbles, but some of us do think most clearly with an outline. Using an outline structure organizes your ideas under clear categories. And it's easy for others to understand.

But an outline should be a supporting structure for your ideas, not a prison. Guard against tensing up when you develop your outline plan. Use simple clear language and short sentences to represent your ideas. Avoid business jargon and use the present tense and active verbs.

- The main categories of your plan become the primary ideas in your outline, designated with Roman numerals. (In the next section of this chapter we've included a list of suggested categories for a plan. Use this list or modify it to fit your situation.)

- Under each category, make a list of your ideas. Keep breaking ideas down into more lists, getting more specific with each subcategory.

- Include short narrative sections to clarify ideas when necessary and to spell out what you intend to do.

The following outline plan example illustrates how to develop a marketing plan using the outline format.

3. Letter to Yourself or a Friend   If neither of the above formats stimulates planning for you, try clarifying your ideas in a letter. In his book, *Growing a Business*, Paul Hawken suggests a similar approach for writing a draft business plan. Relax with a cup of coffee and write to an imaginary friend. Tell your friend what your business means to you and what you hope to accomplish through marketing. Then explain the things you plan to do this year to achieve those goals.

This approach activates your thinking in a relaxed, natural way. When you write a letter, you tend to use clear simple language instead of getting bogged down in business language. You also explain *why* as well as *what* when you write to someone who doesn't know the design business. Explaining how your business works encourages thinking about marketing strategy.

Once you've written this letter, you'll have the core of your planning done. Go back over it to add dates and cost estimates to the marketing methods you have described.

Another way to use the letter format is to write a letter to yourself from the vantage of the completed marketing year. Writing from the future looking back lets you visualize achieving your goals. Explain to yourself what your marketing goals were and how you achieved them.

FIRST CHOICE DESIGNS
Marketing Plan–1995

I. **Mission Statement**

A. My mission is to help clients create a beautiful home or office environment which reflects their personality, treasures and lifestyle. The design will be artistic, balanced and honest. Integrity is most important in all my relationships.

II. **Goals**

A. Remodel four doctors' offices.

B. Design the entire interior of four residential jobs.

C.

III. **Description of Market**

A. Physicians in Boulder in private practice—approximately 300.

B.

C.

IV. **Strengths & Weaknesses and Opportunities & Threats SWOT**

A. Internal Strengths

B. Internal Weaknesses

C. External Opportunities

D. External Threats

V. **Action Plan**

VI. **Budget**

The following example imagines looking back at the results of a successful marketing plan.

January 1, 1996
Dear Jane,

    What a great business year I've had! Last January I sat down to look at my mission and I realized I'm tired of running around with all these small jobs. I wanted to focus my energy on fewer jobs to have more time for all the other things in my life. I wanted to make more money on the jobs I take.

    I thought , so what jobs have I really enjoyed lately? Designing the doctor's office. So I set as my goal to do four remodels of doctors' offices here in Boulder.

    I really had fun doing this. Remember that I'd talked to Dr. Jones once about my business? It occurred to me that his office is in the same building as Dr. May. So the next time I was in the building, I stopped in to remind Jones. And he said—what good timing, I was just thinking it was time to update this place. And right there I got a job. This worked so well I scheduled time to go around the building introducing myself and leaving my packet. Which reminded me I needed to update the enclosures for my packet, getting some new material for marketing to the doctors.

    Then I made a list of all the doctors I know in Boulder, scheduling time to call them and be sure they know I'm a designer, find out if anyone's thinking of remodeling. I made appointments for all my regular checkups—I thought I might as well tell them I'm a designer while I'm there. I started planning how to get more visible to doctors. Did a press release that brought me good publicity for creating such a contemporary and professional look for Dr. May. I got reprints of that article and sent it with an FYI letter to my client file.

    Next I hosted a breakfast meeting of my CEO group on site in the doctor's office, showing other professionals my work. That led to . . .

Use these ideas as a starting point and go on to invent your own planning style. But write *something* down to record your marketing plan. If you do nothing else, write your marketing goals on a white board in your office where you'll see them every day.

CONTENTS OF YOUR MARKETING PLAN

What should you include in your marketing plan? Only information that is useful to *you*. Below, we've listed the categories most businesses find useful for planning, but that doesn't mean that each piece of information will be relevant to you. Customize and create the marketing plan that works for your business. It's much better to create a simple, brief plan that you actually use, than a thick binder gathering dust on your shelf.

"I do a strategic plan and review it a couple of times a year," says B. J. Peterson, FASID, a Los Angeles residential designer. "Once a year I alter it because of changing facts. It's a written plan, where you have a mission statement, a vision statement, goals, objectives, and tactics. It's very important to write things down and be very specific."

If you haven't developed a marketing plan before, you may choose to start small and simple. You can build on this foundation in the future if you find that more comprehensive planning will help your business. If the planning process seems too intimidating or too time-consuming, at least make a simple list of your goals—and start marketing.

Here is an excellent example of a very simple plan—courtesy of Linda Blair, ASID, a residential designer in New York.

1. Place at least three rooms in newspapers or magazines.

2. Photograph two to four new jobs (at $1200–$1400 each!).

3. Do two to three mailings.

4. Write six articles.

5. Give three to six talks.

Some design firms find it helpful to include more information in their marketing plans. Cheryl Duvall, FIIDA, describes the comprehensive marketing plan her firm in Baltimore develops every year. "Our marketing plan would include a list of targeted industries and the type of work we want to do, based on the desires of the people who work here and a look at the historical data on past jobs—knowing where we have lost money and made money, so we hopefully avoid the losses and go after the moneymakers. We would include [in the marketing plan] targeted companies and targeted people within these companies. These could be people we know or companies we read a lot about in the papers.

"We include a methodical plan for touching base with our current clients, because a lot of current clients will repeat business in the future. The plan identifies each person who works here as representing us to different organizations and boards (such as the International Facility Management Association [IFMA] or the Society for Marketing Professional Services [SMPS]). We also plan how to promote our designers, both in press releases and in terms of writing articles and speaking. Overall, this information is what I think most firms see as a marketing plan."

WHAT TO INCLUDE IN YOUR MARKETING PLAN

The following items are included in most comprehensive marketing plans. Each item is explained more thoroughly in the next several pages of this chapter.

1. **Mission Statement:** Your statement of the purpose and philosophy of your business.

2. **Goals:** The business results your marketing will achieve.

3. **Description of Your Market:** Who and where your clients are.

4. **Strengths & Weaknesses and Opportunities & Threats:** Your analysis of the internal and external environment in which you do business.

5. **Action Plan:** The marketing methods for public relations, promotions, advertising, market research, and selling you will use this year.

6. **Budget:** Estimates of marketing expense and revenue for this year.

Consider taking a retreat — a day or an afternoon away from the office— as a way to begin your marketing planning. It gives you a break from the routine and encourages more creative thinking.

Mission

The best marketing plans are guided by a clear understanding of the mission of the business. If you have not yet done so, take the time to write a mission statement. Clarify for yourself why you have your design business: What is your purpose?

Think through the answers to the following questions in drafting your mission:

- What are my personal goals and how does my business reflect them?
- How do my design goals affect my business goals?
- What is the *purpose* of my business: Why am I running this business anyway?
- What matters most to me in doing this business day after day?

Be sure that your business mission is congruent with your personal mission. Seeing your business in the context of your whole life can help clarify what your business goals should be. Think about the values that you hope to live in your business. Dennis McNabb reminds us that "your personal mission and your business mission need to be parallel. Getting them together makes you less confused."

JANE'S NOTE

I started my planning session and review of my mission with this diagram of the "big picture" of my life (Figure 2-2). Both personal and business missions need to merge to reflect the proper balance. It's sometimes a struggle to achieve that. Design work is very time consuming, and putting small projects together often takes as long as putting the big ones together. We've all run ourselves ragged on lots of small jobs. While it's necessary when beginning a business, I've found I need to grow beyond the small jobs to achieve a personal balance in life. In order to have time for travel with my husband, occasional golf games and walks with the dog, and availability for friends and children, I'm growing my business in the direction of larger projects.

Because of my time commitment to this book project, I've said no to many small projects and referred them to other designers. I'm surprised how much better I can stay focused on the bigger jobs, have time to market, and still have some personal time.

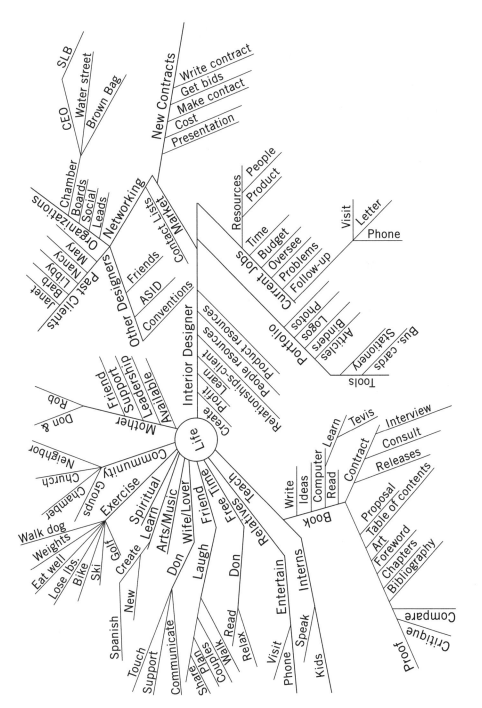

FIGURE 2-2 Jane's diagram of life choices.

PERSONAL MISSION
Jane D. Martin

My mission is to be a balanced person, enjoying and having time for my family and friends, my health and recreational activities, and my business. Integrity is of prime importance in my relationships. And creativity, personal growth, and beauty are the joys of my life.

Once you are clear on the role your business plays in your life, jot down your thoughts about the mission of your business. A good business mission aims for achievement and excellence. Your mission statement should be both realistic and motivating. The words you use should be personal and direct. You're writing this for yourself, so be honest.

Included below are three examples of mission statements from designers.

First Choice
D E S I G N S

2230 Knollwood Drive   •   Boulder, Colorado 80302   **Jane D. Martin**
(308) 440-0517

MISSION STATEMENT

My mission is to help clients create a beautiful home or office environment which reflects their personality, treasures and lifestyle. The design will be artistic, balanced and honest. Integrity is most important in all my relationships.

Jane D. Martin

Jane D. Martin

FIGURE 2-3   Mission statement of Jane D. Martin, First Choice Designs.

STALLWORTH STUDIOS

MISSION STATEMENT

"Architectural interiors not only shelter their inhabitants but soothe their souls"

Stallworth Studios sees its central mission as service to the client. We are dedicated to providing high quality design services that yield results meeting or exceeding our clients goals and expectations.

Stallworth Studios is a full service firm specializing in architecture, interior architecture and design, space planning, programming, and corporate communications. We place high priorities on delivering creative and successful design services; attention to detail; quality control; and the ability to meet clients schedules and financial considerations.

Stallworth Studios' goal is to remain a company of creative vision; providing the very best results for our clients.

300 M STREET S. W. SUITE N110   WASHINGTON, D.C. 20024-4019   202 488 3838

FIGURE 2-4   *Mission statement of Shauna P. Stallworth, Stallworth Studios.*

BETHUNE/GOODHUE & ASSOCIATES INC
DESIGN CONSULTANTS

FAX 303•698•1235
1284 south clayton, denver 80210 303•698•1133

BETHUNE/GOODHUE & ASSOCIATES, INC. MISSION STATEMENT

Our Mission is to provide our clients with exceptionally innovative design solutions that appropriately meet their unique needs.

To accomplish our Mission we commit to work as a team, seeking synergistic solutions that optimize the diverse strengths and contributions of all team members.

We pledge to encourage leadership, personal growth, cooperation and mutual respect. We commit to honesty and integrity in all communications.

Juli Goodhue, ASID
President

FIGURE 2-5   *Mission statement of Juli Goodhue, Bethune/Goodhue.*

Michael Temple of San Diego describes the importance of thinking through your mission in deciding what kind of design business you want: "I believe that first of all you have to sit down and decide what kind of firm you want. Do you want to be an independent designer alone in an office with a part-time assistant [which is where I am now] — completely controlling your own destiny and the work you are doing? Or do you want to be one of five designers in a little firm, with a couple of assistants, each one of you responsible for your share of the income? Or do you want to be something else? Each choice requires a different scenario and a different perspective. If you're not going to be satisfied with your income or it's not going to be enough to meet your needs, you're never going to be happy with the business. And that's going to reflect on how you treat clients and how successful you are."

Define Your Market

Defining your market is simply writing down who your clients are and where you will find them. Including this information in your marketing plan ensures that you stay aware that finding and pleasing your clients is the main purpose of your business. Estimate the size of your market and how much of that market you hope to bring to your business.

If you worked through the questions in *Chapter 1: Finding Your Niche in the Market* on researching a market niche, you have already defined your market. Just summarize this into a concise description of your market—or several markets—and keep it with the rest of your marketing plan. If you have not yet researched your market, the section in *Chapter 1, What Makes a Niche Work* (page 17), will guide you through this process.

Set Marketing Goals

Marketing goals are the results you will achieve through your marketing plan. Goals should be simple, doable, and dynamic. They establish the context for the rest of your marketing design. A goal is a directional marker, a guideline for moving your business where you want to be.

You might set goals to improve your visibility or to increase the numbers of jobs in a specific area. Or you might set a goal of improving your marketing ability or getting better market research. A good goal focuses on a measurable outcome you would like to see in your business. Good goals also allow you to evaluate whether you have achieved them or not.

Goals should be challenging but obtainable. Set goals with which you are comfortable. You need to be able to imagine yourself achieving them—set yourself up to succeed.

"Set a goal for three months, six months, and one year and look back on these goals," says Linda Blair of Scarsdale, New York. "It will help you focus on the direction you want to go in your business. Target *x* number of times you are going to get out in front of the public. You can start small—you can say, I'm going to appear before the public eight times, and two will be giving a little talk. Then the next year you can increase it."

Goals focus on marketing results, not methods. Marketing methods are what you do to make your goals happen. Your choices of specific methods will be included in your marketing action plan, which is described below.

In formulating your goals, think through both long- and short-term expected results. Estimate how long it will take to achieve each goal. Also consider who and what may be affected by your pursuit of this goal. For example, if you set out to increase your volume of projects, you may need more staff to handle the added work.

Strengths & Weaknesses and Opportunities & Threats (SWOT)

A SWOT analysis is a window looking simultaneously inward into your business and outward at the external factors that influence your business. When developing your marketing plan, take inventory of your business's internal strengths and weaknesses and the opportunities and threats you expect to find in your external environment. Spending a few minutes with SWOT can put your marketing goals in clearer perspective. Your action planning will be more focused if you've taken time for this honest appraisal of your business environment.

Nila R. Leiserowitz, ASID, Associate AIA, of Chicago, describes the way SWOT analysis is used in her firm. "Every year we write a marketing plan and it's very extensive. It identifies the amount of sales projected, and all plans are based on what we projected. We look at what we forecasted for last year and compare it to what we have actually accomplished. We separate it into the different markets we're in: corporate interiors, health care, financial institutions, and other. We also write up our strengths and weaknesses, then write down what we think are the strengths and weaknesses of our competitors—who we have been losing to and why. Then we go to forecasting the types of projects we'd like to market for the upcoming year and how we are going to market them."

Take a few minutes to list your personal strengths and weaknesses in marketing your business. Or do this with a bubble diagram. Then analyze the strengths and weaknesses of your business as a whole. Switch to the client perspective on your business and list what your clients would say are your strengths and weaknesses in serving their needs.

Consider the following questions in analyzing *strengths and weaknesses*:

- Are you encountering any problems in meeting client needs and delivering promised services?
- Do you need additional staff to help you get jobs done well and on time?
- Do you need to learn any new skills?
- Do you need additional equipment or more technology?
- What are your best skills? What are your worst skills?
- What are the unique benefits of your business?
- What is your reputation with clients?
- Do you feel you are getting the right clients and the right jobs?

Now survey the *opportunities and threats* facing you in your external business environment. This is a great exercise for stretching your vision into the future.

Learn to recognize marketing opportunities. Be aware of how current trends could affect you in the future. Ask yourself questions similar to the following:

- What changes do you foresee in your competition? Do you expect any new competitors? Compare competitors in pricing and quality of service.
- What is the long-term economic prospect for your region?
- Is the number of prospective clients increasing or decreasing in your chosen geographic area and/or niche?
- How does the national economy affect your business?
- How do economic trends like consumer demand affect your business?
- What social and cultural changes will have an effect on your business? Consider such trends as telecommuting, globalization of business, growing environmental concerns, and new health and safety issues.
- What is going on in the legal and regulatory environment that affects the design industry—ADA, certification and licensing, changes in health care?
- What technological changes affect your business?

Use the SWOT analysis diagram below to summarize your business's strengths, weaknesses, opportunities, and threats.

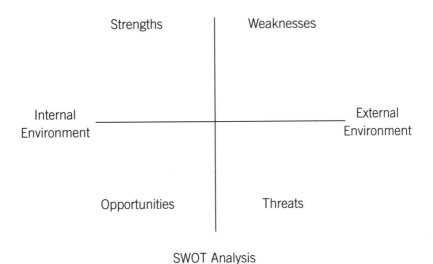

FIGURE 2-6 *SWOT analysis diagram.*

Action Plan

The action plan lists the specific steps required to accomplish your marketing program for the next year (Figure 2-7). To write this part of your plan, select and schedule the marketing methods you will use to achieve your goals. The remaining chapters in this book present a broad selection of marketing methods from which to choose.

The basic questions to be answered in writing your action plan are similar to the classics of journalism: *who, what, where, how, when,* and *how much.* No matter what format you've adopted for your plan, get into the habit of covering each of these categories. Your action plan needs to consider the information you need — about your interests, skills, time available and budget — to select the best marketing methods to reach your goals.

Your aim in marketing is to reach your target clients for the least cost. So you should choose the most effective marketing methods for the least drain on your resources. You can't do this without having cost estimates to compare. As you complete your action plan, estimate the real costs of your planned marketing activities. And, as far as is possible, estimate the revenue you expect for your marketing investment.

Budgeting and Cost Projection

Budgeting is nobody's favorite task. Designers are no exception. Along with other creative professionals, many designers are "quant-phobes." Quant-phobes are intimidated and bored by numbers — and usually avoid them.

If you feel insecure about or dislike working with numbers, you probably tend to avoid budgeting. If this describes you, resolve to demystify budgets. Learn to make the budgeting process useful to you.

Your budget completes your marketing plan. The budget projects the expenses and revenue expected from each of your marketing methods. Once you have this information, it is easy to compare your marketing alternatives and choose those that give the best results at the least expense.

The most practical way to learn budgeting is to learn by doing. Start now to build your own financial marketing data. List your marketing methods in your action plan and write in your best guess of what each marketing activity will cost. Then track your expenses for these activities religiously for the next year. At the end of the year, compare your actual expenses with your estimate, and you'll have the basic data you need to project your marketing budget. Keep track of your questions as you develop your budget and notice where you find the answers. This procedure is part of the gradual process of learning how to research the information you need.

MARKETING ACTION PLAN

	WHAT	HOW	WHERE	WHO	WHEN			HOW MUCH		RESULTS
					PREPARE	START	FINISH	BUDGET	ACTUAL	
Goal	A.									
Method	1.									
	2.									
	3.									

FIGURE 2-7   *Marketing action plan.*

If you would like more help with budgeting, here are some other ways to learn.

- Set up a consultation with a good accountant.
- Look for training sessions sponsored by professional associations.
- Read resource books on marketing and business planning.

Once you know how to budget, you'll have to answer the critical question: How much should I spend on marketing? We posed this question to designers whom we interviewed. Designers who have an established business and are marketing for an ongoing practice typically spend 5-10% of their annual gross income for marketing. Those who are starting a new business will necessarily have a larger proportion of marketing expenses as they work to build their client base.

These percentages should only be taken as a rule of thumb—a general guideline to a reasonable level of marketing expense for maintaining a healthy business. What really guides your marketing budget is your own business growth strategy. You should invest more heavily in marketing when you want to develop a new market or change your business focus to include more jobs that are more professionally satisfying for you.

One budgeting mistake designers frequently make is forgetting to count their time as a critical resource. In costing out your marketing plan, always include the cost of your time—as an hourly rate or as a percentage of your salary. Adding the cost of your hours to your projections really brings home the importance of good time management, as well as avoiding time-consuming marketing activities with dubious potential for new clients and added profit.

List all marketing costs in your budget.

- Designers' salary — hours allocated for marketing
- Support staff salary — hours allocated for marketing
- Materials
- Postage
- Telephone
- Travel
- Entertainment
- Contract and consultant fees

JANE'S NOTE

I look at every job's profit and the profit on every item. Then I try to determine which jobs and which products—furniture, draperies, blinds, carpet and rugs, or wall covering—are the most and the least profitable. I evaluate the time spent on different clients and products. My bookkeeper prepares a computer printout, and I review this monthly.

HOW TO USE YOUR MARKETING PLAN

Even the most thoughtful and comprehensive plan is meaningless if it isn't used to guide your marketing. So keep your plan in view, not tucked into a file. Create a time every week to look at your plan and schedule the week's marketing activities.

Schedule a regular time to evaluate your progress and adapt your action plan as needed. As we stated earlier, a good marketing plan is a process. Be prepared for it to change and evolve as time goes on.

You need to monitor and evaluate your success in reaching your marketing goals. *Monitor* your progress in accomplishing the tasks listed in your action plan. Also *evaluate* the results of your marketing activities. Keep track of the source of your jobs and their profitability. You'll be grateful for this information when you develop your next marketing plan. You'll know what works and what doesn't for your business. Remember to analyze failures as well as successes.

Establish a simple system for monitoring and evaluating your marketing progress. Your system should record the marketing information that will allow you to answer the following questions:

1. Did you do the marketing activities you planned? Did you accomplish them on schedule? *Monitoring* involves counting accomplishments: how many presentations made, proposals submitted, direct mail promotions sent, calls made, and so on.

2. How effective were your marketing methods? *Evaluation* means analyzing the numbers of clients and jobs and revenue generated by your marketing methods: the number of prospective clients reached, the number of new clients under contract, the amount of business from new and old clients, profitability of new business, and so on.

3. What is your return rate from your marketing investment? Monitor your actual marketing expenses and compare total expense to the revenue generated by marketing activities.

Celebrate your progress. As you evaluate and monitor your marketing activities, take time to appreciate your marketing achievements. Celebrating results is a part of planning that too many of us forget. Stop to acknowledge your accomplishments — before writing your next *To Do* list.

TIME MANAGEMENT

Managing your time effectively is critical to your marketing success. Don't fall into the trap of postponing planned marketing tasks because you're too busy with jobs. Learn to manage your time well and make time for marketing.

If you are a solo designer, good time management can be your lifeline, because marketing when you're busy is always difficult in a small business. This is why your marketing action plan is so important. When you're swamped with work and deadlines are looming, keep your action plan in front of you. Make the time to do one small task a day that makes progress towards your goals. Hire temporary help to send a mailing when you don't have time yourself. Set aside 30 minutes each morning to make follow-up calls before the phone starts ringing and your day gets crazy. But make the commitment to yourself not to let the marketing go "just until you catch up." Too many designers have done this — and found themselves with no work pending when the crush is over.

"Making time for marketing when you are very busy with jobs is the problem," says Cheryl Duvall. "It's a lesson we constantly learn — that when you are the busiest is when you need to be marketing. In fact, we just came out of a meeting this morning about all the work we need right now, because we didn't market as well as we should have when we were busy."

When you're busy, it is easy to think of marketing as taking time away from your work. Don't fall into this trap. Tell yourself every day that marketing *is* your business. "Don't begrudge the time you spend preparing for public speaking," says Linda Blair. "It takes time away from your routine of doing the design work and the installations and client problems and getting paid and all the things we need to do. But this exposure is so important. Furthermore, when you're successful is when you should market most heavily, even though it's when you have the least amount of time. The marketing prepares you for the down time."

Organize to Save Time

Set up your marketing activities in chewable bites, especially if you work alone. It's easier to make time for small steps forward that, taken all together, get you where you want to go.

Try keeping a big calendar for the whole year in your office where you'll look at it every day. Write in the marketing tasks that are scheduled in your marketing action plan. As you see events coming up on the calendar, arrange your schedule to have the time you need. Write in everything on this one calendar to avoid surprises.

1995 Calendar

Jan	Feb	Mar
• Complete Andrews • Newsletter (include current award, projects, photos, new employees • 10 'warm' calls based on networking • Contact past Dr. jobs • Marketing meeting to target markets	• Complete Dr. May • Contact other Drs. in same office park • Retreat-review market plan, mission stmt, target market	• Gift for Dr. May (plant for office) • Photo Dr. May, Andrews, Klout • Get testimonials and any referrals • Evaluation letter Dr. May • 10 warm or cold calls • Press release on Dr. May's new office • 1 week vacation
April	**May**	**June**
• Symphony Dance • Lunch with possible client • Article for medical journal written on Dr. May • Check personal wardrobe • Take class to improve public speaking	• 10 warm calls • 3 lunches from contacts • Enter tile contest in builders magazine • Place an ad in a medical journal for May, June, July • Marketing meeting • Give or make arrangements for a speech to 8 office mgrs.	• Newsletter on last 6 months • Get physical, eye exam, dental visit, and ask for opp. to update their office also ask for referrals and information on who is retiring, moving, etc.

FIGURE: 2-8 Marketing calendar.

Organize your marketing materials to minimize the time required for marketing. Keep copies of your materials — marketing packets and enclosures, brochures, and marketing letters — filed together in your office so you don't waste time finding what you need. Have a file of previous materials and models. It's much easier to write a new marketing letter or a newsletter if you have examples to compare and to stimulate your ideas. Set up templates for your standard marketing items — such as proposals, letters, and newsletters — as files in your computer. When you need to prepare new marketing materials, use the templates to tailor your communication to fit each situation.

Cheryl Duvall's design firm in Baltimore has an excellent system to organize and streamline their marketing efforts. Cheryl shared these helpful suggestions for getting organized for marketing.

1. Set Up a "Promo Station" "The promotional work station in our office is the home of everything we need to put together an answer to a request for proposal or information. When we're chasing a job, we can go out there and find our brochure, our portfolio, project descriptions, and case studies from previous work."

2. Photography Binders "This is just a series of binders that hold any professional photography we have done. Slides, photographs, negatives, 4 x 5 transparencies, and photos from any competitions we have entered. This is where we find the photography that supports what we do."

3. Library and Topic Resource Files "We try to keep resource files on hot topics in the industry — such as the environment or carpal tunnel syndrome — as well as topics important to our market. For instance, under Law Office Design we would find files and articles we have seen on law office design or any statistics on secretary-to-lawyer ratio and these sorts of things."

4. Standardization "We use a standard computer template for proposals so that when we answer proposals, we are building on what we've done before, not reinventing the wheel. We have a short-form project description that describes briefly what our projects have been. We also have a longer, more detailed description to include when it is more appropriate for the proposal we are chasing. We've also standardized our board format and developed a presentation checklist that speeds up our preparation for presentations."

TIPS ON TIME MANAGEMENT FOR MARKETING

How To Work Smarter—Not Harder

- Review your action plan every day or every week. List weekly or daily goals and rank them by importance.

- Take time to *think*. Keep your marketing creative and don't miss new opportunities.

- Break your goals into small tasks that you can accomplish in 15 or 20 minutes. Squeeze these marketing steps into your days—no matter how busy you are.

- As you put your plan into action, take notes on how much time you spend on each step. This information will help you schedule more realistically and plan ahead.

- Overcome creeping procrastination. When you start postponing a project that seems overwhelming, pick out a place to start and do one small thing. Keep doing this until you build the momentum to finish.

- Plan for some quiet time without interruptions to work on marketing. Pay attention to the pattern of your days to find your best time.

- Group similar activities to save time. Do a batch of errands at once. Save phone calls and do at one time. Take an afternoon to catch up on paperwork.

- If you're distracted and can't focus, stop for a few minutes to analyze what is bothering you. Take time out to deal with whatever it is so you can get back to work.

- If you're too busy to keep up with marketing and your jobs, get others to help. If you have staff, delegate. If you work alone, hire temporary help to get it all done.

- Learn to do the most important things and let the small stuff wait. Know what your priorities are. Ask yourself, what can't wait—and what can.

Ideas to Remember from This Chapter

- A marketing plan is a map to guide your marketing efforts through the year.

- The only rule that counts regarding how to write your marketing plan is that you should write it in a way that makes sense and is useful—to you.

- A comprehensive marketing plan should cover these six areas: mission, goals, market description, SWOT, action plan, and budget. But feel free to write a simpler plan if a comprehensive plan doesn't fit your skills or context.

- Budgeting for marketing is important in order to be able to analyze costs and benefits of marketing methods and make an informed choice among alternative methods.

- Effective marketing for small businesses demands good time management and organization.

Setting
Your Fees

How to Price Your Services

Pricing—what you charge and how you present your fees to clients—is a key element of your marketing success. Services like design are intangible. Quality is subjective and hard to define. This means that value and quality exist in the client's perspective. So your fee functions as a signal to clients: It tells them how good you think you are.

In This Chapter

This chapter shows you how to set your fees to communicate your marketing strategy. This discussion will help you

- Know what your fees communicate to your clients.
- Determine the pricing strategy that fits your situation.
- Decide which method of setting fees is right for you.
- Establish—and get—your profit margin.
- Talk to clients about money—painlessly.

WHY PRICING IS MARKETING

Your fees help to establish your position in the marketplace. Make sure that your fee structure is clear and understandable to your clients. Always communicate your unique benefits to your target clients in order to justify the return on your time that you want.

In setting your fees, avoid the two extremes: pricing too low or too high. Make sure your clients take you seriously and are prepared to respect your work. If your prices are too low, you'll lower your credibility. Most clients will assume that your design quality will match your low fees. You'll also diminish your profit from each job, which dooms you to scramble continually after too many low-paying jobs. When you sell a service, remember that your inventory is finite. You can't sell more time than you have. So don't underprice your most valuable resource—your time.

The other extreme is pricing yourself out of the market. If your fees are too high, clients will take their business elsewhere. Find out what your competitors are charging, and use this information to gauge the acceptable price range for your market. Find out how your clients attribute value to design. High prices are acceptable to clients if they believe they are getting appropriate value for their investment.

JANE'S NOTE

My fees are very competitive with the people in our area whose work I respect. My fees are fair but not so low I get jobs I don't want. When I first started my business, I had lower prices and I took low-profit jobs I won't accept now. People who were shopping for the best price would have me come out to measure a whole house for mini or duette blinds. No designer is going to make enough for the job to be worth their time in this situation. However, when first starting a business, it's a way to get your foot in the door and hope to build a relationship, leading to additional business.

Know Your Pricing Strategy

Use the following five considerations to think through your pricing strategy and decide on the price range that is best for your service:

1. Your Financial Needs   How much do you need to earn to live and keep working? Pricing has to be realistic. When you're establishing your business — or if you hit an unexpected dry spell — you may need to take some low-paying jobs to pay the bills. Accept this, but tune up your marketing so you can get your fees back up to a more profitable range.

2. Point of Price Resistance   There is always a point that is really too high for all but a few clients. You'll have to do some experimentation to find it. Pay close attention to client responses. When you start seeing solid clients walk away from your proposal, you know you have hit the point of resistance. As you establish your price level, give yourself permission to experiment with pricing. Quoting a fee to one client doesn't mean you're locked into that fee for all future clients.

3. Competitors' Fees   Make sure you know the fee range designers in your area or your specialty are charging. Find out what your competitors charge and how they structure their fees. How much spread is there between the lowest fee and the highest? How do these designers differentiate their services to correspond to their fees?

4. Reaching Your Target Clients   Set your fees to reach the clients you want. Keep your fees in the price range your target clients are willing and expect to pay. Pricing that is lower or higher than client expectations can make your target clients uneasy about choosing you. Price your services high enough to discourage the jobs you *don't* want.

5. Your Professional Status   Your professional status is the sum of your experience, years in the business, success with past clients, recommendations, and reputation. Professional status can give well-established designers the edge in winning clients, because status increases client confidence in choosing a designer. If you're new to the business, counter the status advantage by pushing hard to build your credibility. Or find a unique market niche with less competition that will enable you to ask for higher fees. Remember that ability and fresh ideas count as well as professional status.

KEEP YOUR MARKETING MESSAGE CONSISTENT

Your fees are communication. Remember that what your clients perceive is more important than your intent. Do you know what your pricing level and your method of charging communicate to your clients? If not, talk to some former clients and find out.

Keep your fee range consistent with the benefits of your service. Clients will pay higher fees for services that deliver what they need. Be prepared to show clients the *benefits* of hiring you. Start by knowing what your clients want from design. Find out how important such benefits as the following are to your target clients:

- Comfort
- Convenience
- More efficient office space
- Style
- Lower occupancy costs for businesses
- Security and safety

Be able to spell out the value clients can expect from your design. Learn to be wary of discount thinking. It can be tempting to drop your fees when you feel threatened by the low prices of discount sources selling direct to clients, or to try to gain a competitive advantage by positioning your prices lower than competitors, while claiming to deliver the best service. But all discounting does is confuse your clients with conflicting marketing messages. It's smarter and safer in the long run to establish your position with fees based on benefits and value to the client. And believe that you're worth it.

ARE YOU SELLING SERVICES OR PRODUCTS?

Be clear on what you're selling. Are you selling products or a service — or both? If you're selling both, how do you make this clear to the client?

Cast yourself in the client role and imagine how baffling it can be to figure out what you're paying for in some design projects. Some of the design industry's charging methods — taking percentages of cost or retail prices, markups, markdowns, fees for concepts, fees for purchasing — seem arcane to outsiders. Remember that confusion breeds mistrust. Take the time to explain your fee structure. "I've defined the parameters of my design firm, what I want to do and accomplish," says Michael Temple, a residential designer in San Diego. "Now I basically do three major projects at a time and turn down smaller jobs. I charge a flat fee based on a time line, and I pass the net savings on to the client. I sell service, not products. Trying to compete as a product salesperson these days doesn't work for an interior designer.

"If I just say — 'you're paying me these prices, I'm making my profit here and that is how you're paying me' — the client feels gouged and doesn't understand. Instead, I sit down at the very beginning and explain that there are different ways I can charge. I tell them— 'this is the way I work and this is the reason why. When you hire an interior designer, one way or another you are going to pay for the service—whether it's through a markup on product or an hourly fee. I prefer to tell you right up front that this is the cost for me to be a creative mind and for the execution of the project. It's going to cost you *x* amount of money and I project *x* amount of time to do it. For this fee I will do *a, b,* and *c* for you, and the rest is passed along to you in saving in the purchasing part of it.'"

People find it hard to assign value to the intangible, and your time and skills are intangible. It is up to you to explain and demonstrate to the client the value of your knowledge and experience. Michael Temple says that residential designers are struggling toward charging for service as contract designers have done for years. But it's hard to make this change— "mainly because it is so intangible to walk in and say, 'I want you to pay me for my creative skills and technical knowledge even though you don't understand all the technical knowledge that goes into a project. You're buying a concept— not a thing you can touch like an automobile.'"

Part of your pricing strategy must be client education in the design process. We hear a constant lament from designers that the public doesn't understand interior design. So it's up to every designer to demonstrate to the public why design has value. "Designers are now focusing on the value of the services they offer and not on the value of the goods," says Deborah Steinmetz, ASID, whose firm does interior planning in New Orleans. "So a lot of designers are getting into this purchasing fee—where you are very open and up front that purchasing is a service and the service costs money. The rest of it is fees based on our expertise. It's a harder sell for residential design. People are oriented to think of how much the chair costs instead of how much time you invested in finding it. They don't see the value apart from the merchandise."

HOW TO SET YOUR FEES

There are many different ways to set your design service fees. Mary Knackstedt lists sixteen methods in *The Interior Design Business Handbook*. Each method has evolved to fit certain contexts. What is the right method for setting your fees?

Use the following three considerations to simplify the decision and clarify the underlying issues in establishing your prices:

1. Start with the *message* that you want to give your clients, and choose the method that makes this message most clear.

2. Choose a fee structure that maximizes your profit and is simple to manage for project management and accounting.

3. Maintain adequate flexibility for inevitable contingencies.

Working through the pros and cons of each of the sixteen methods in detail is not in the scope of this book. For our marketing discussion, these pricing methods can be grouped into four distinct types:

1. Fixed Fee: Charging a lump sum for the total completed project.   The easiest type of fee to market to clients is a fixed fee for a total project. Clients understand paying for results and would prefer an agreement based on project outcome than on time billed. The client is more able to accept paying for the design process when it isn't separated from the total project. In addition, the fixed fee provides the comfort of knowing what the bill will be at the end.

From the designer's perspective, the fixed fee is also a winner if you can accurately predict what your costs will be in the project. The project needs to be an area in which you have a lot of experience. If you have good records of costs from past projects, you should be able to project an accurate estimate of time and materials for the job.

2. Time: Charging for the designer's time, usually through an hourly or daily rate.   To be successful at getting paid directly for your time, you have to link the results the client wants to your time spent on the project. Charging a design concept fee is one straightforward way to charge for your design time on a project. This works because the client can see the results of your time—the completed project design and management plan. The fee is a fixed

---

JANE'S NOTE

There are situations when charging for time is the clearest method to use. I like charging by the hour for some projects. It gives me flexibility and consistency. One of my favorite things to do is to plan the space with a client in a new home. I charge by the hour to arrange pictures and accessories. This is often the best way to help clients who have moved into a new home and are deciding what to use and what to buy. This service sets me up to help when these clients want to purchase new things or if they want to make major changes. I set my hourly fee high enough to ensure that clients are serious and want my service. Then they don't waste my time.

charge within the larger project framework that ensures you are paid for your more intangible design work.

3. Percentage of Cost: Making your profit by charging a percentage of the materials' cost of the project. The practice of billing for products with a profit markup for the designer isn't immediately intuitive to the client. The message to the client is that the product is the most important part of the transaction. This message devalues the importance of your design skill and knowledge. The percentage of cost method is used by designers because it is well understood and convenient — for designers. But it is neither for the client.

Remember that a client who hasn't encountered this charging method before may find it difficult to understand your part in the project. If you use this method to set your fee, take the time to explain thoroughly to the client.

4. Square Footage: Charging a fee inclusive of all project costs multiplied by the number of square feet in the project. Charging by the square foot is the norm in certain industries. Design jobs in office design, hospitality, and retail tend to be priced this way.

It is important to set your fees in the form your clients expect. For example, Deborah Steinmetz quotes tenant development jobs on a square footage basis because that's how the developers want to see it. But she cross-checks these quotes by estimated time at the appropriate hourly rate as well as a percentage of the total project value.

Most designers like to figure a project estimate using several alternate methods, to check for errors and to see if a different method seems more profitable. Look for possibilities in combining charging methods — you may be able to build in more profit without an apparent fee raise. And you may find a new fee structure that better conveys your service message to your clients.

B. J. Peterson makes her fees very clear to clients. She charges either an hourly fee or a design fee. "With merchandise, I do cost, plus a service charge. The service charge is for facilitating the order and taking the responsibilities that come with it. A client has to realize that the service charge does not just mean time spent ordering and sending it in. I have a sliding scale for the service charge based on the difficulty, and I explain all this to the client as we go along."

Know how your competitors structure their charges. If your clients seem comfortable with this method, it may be best for you to conform. But explore the issues carefully and talk to your clients to find out how they feel about it. You may be able to come up with a structure that is profitable for you and makes better sense to your clients—perhaps by using a creative mix of several different charging methods. If so, your different fee structure can become a way to differentiate yourself from your competition—through being more responsive to client needs.

What Is Your Profit Margin?

To run a profitable service business, you must ensure that your fees include an adequate profit margin. Just covering your salary and your business costs isn't making a profit. Your profit is your reserve for the times you can't bill your time to specific projects. The profit margin compensates for the time you spend marketing and managing your business.

Beware of the pitfall of running your business as if your time doesn't count. Too many professionals fail to account for the full cost of doing business. Time, which is your most valuable resource, is too often undervalued —particularly for marketing activity.

HOW TO GET HIGHER FEES

If you are trying to change your position and aim for a higher profit margin, Linda Blair suggests raising your fees in increments. Every six months, raise your fees so much per hour or per job. This allows you to test response to your changing fees. And practice asking for a higher fee without apologies. Also, you might begin charging a design concept fee if you do not already do so.

In raising fees, you have to raise the perceived value of your service. The best selling position is to offer something that clients can't get from another designer. Focus on ways that you can differentiate your service and be perceived as unique. When you are the innovator you can set the fee range—at least until others imitate and create competition. Develop a niche position or pull various services together into a new combination, marketing this as a new package of benefits to the client.

The other basis for differentiating your service is through a reputation for doing what you do better than competitors. This is marketing on the basis of perceived quality of service and a stance of trying harder, striving to please clients.

Figure out what the annual break-even point is for your business—how much revenue you need to cover the costs of your time and all your business expenses. You'll also need to figure the break-even point on each project before you can make an accurate project estimate. Make a habit of figuring out what your profit will be for each job you quote.

Your break-even analysis will give you the minimum amount you need to earn in the next year to stay in business. Use this figure to experiment with different fee structures. See how much time you need to bill at what hourly rate to earn your target profit, or how many projects you need to do at what total amounts.

"I asked myself: In order to make this paradigm shift from being a glorified salesperson to becoming a designer that is paid for services, what do I need to earn?" says Michael Temple. "Start with that bottom line. I figured what I wanted to earn in six months. Since there is only one of me, I figured having three jobs going at once for six months each would be the ideal situation. I can balance three jobs and be in all different places and keep these people happy." From this thinking he was able to lay out what his minimum project should be—and has not accepted any jobs under that amount. He has gone on to raise his fees based on the concept of a flat project fee paid for a service. In charging the flat fee, he is careful to explain how it is figured on a time estimate at an hourly rate. Once clients understand, they are comfortable with the flat fee.

Creating Accurate Cost Estimates

If you're just getting started in a design business, you won't yet have past projects to draw upon in estimating project costs. But you can start building this information right away. Talk to other designers to get an idea of usual costs in your area.

Another clue to getting accurate estimates is to do a project estimate as a separate step in your project (Figure 3-1). Do this as a free service to the client or charge a small fee. Doing an extensive estimate in the beginning allows you to plan more accurately.

One of the benefits of a small design business is having low overhead costs. This can give you an advantage in submitting a competitive estimate for a project. Just be sure that you account for all your nonbillable costs in figuring your overhead.

"People bemoan the fact that the design industry cannot make money," says Houston designer Gary Whitney. "But it *can* make a lot of money. What counts is what you spend it on. I used to think if you were big you were successful. I never made the connection that it's not how much you make, but

JOB COST ESTIMATE FORM

	Cost Item Description	Quantity	Unit Cost	Total Cost	Markup %	TOTAL
Design Concept Fee						
Hours						
Furnishings/ Materials	1. 2. 3. 4. 5. 6. 7. etc.					
Purchasing Fee						
Subcon-tracts						
TOTAL						

JOB SUMMARY

Client Cost _____

Total Cost _____

Profit _____

Profit Margin _____

FIGURE 3-1 Cost estimate form.

how much you keep. Millions of dollars of revenue and millions of dollars of expense do not a profitable business make. But hundreds of thousands of dollars of revenue and no expenses make a nice business."

HOW TO TALK TO CLIENTS ABOUT MONEY

Be straightforward when clients ask about your fees. Explain your range of project costs — how you charge and why. Explain the value the client gets for that amount. You don't need to apologize for charging for your services. Remember that clients expect you to provide a professional service and charge professional fees.

Residential designers in particular often have trouble knowing the right way to approach clients to discuss the project budget. You need to know your clients well enough to maintain good rapport while being clear and direct about fees.

JANE'S NOTE

I've recently begun to use the word investment *when talking to clients about the cost of large items — "the investment in this sofa is $5,000." This has been helpful to me. Clients also like to hear that their plan functions, will give them pleasure and enjoyment, will last, is durable, and has good style or design. They also love it when they can feel your excitement about how great their space will look.*

Timing

Clients deserve advance notice of costs. But talking about money too soon can jeopardize your sale. Sometimes, at the beginning of a preliminary interview, a client gets too anxious at not knowing the cost and can't talk about anything else. But if you quote an estimate at this point, the client may back off, because you have not yet had the chance to lay the groundwork that illustrates the value behind the cost. On the other hand, if you try to hedge — postponing the fee issue — the client may lose confidence and trust, seeing your reticence as insincerity.

Think about this issue from the client's point of view. It's hard to feel at ease if the person who wants you to buy won't tell you what it's going to cost. People may not even know enough to put a range to it. If you won't discuss it, you can seem evasive and unsympathetic.

Be willing to give the client a possible range of costs. Quoting a range early also allows clients to get used to a higher figure than they might have planned. Then explain that you need to work out an estimate based on the needs and issues discussed today with the client. But set a specific time — and make it soon — to bring back the estimate. If you show consideration in helping clients deal with their early anxiety about cost, clients will be more relaxed when you get to the critical stage of quoting a precise fee.

Another common problem of timing for designers is waiting so late in the discussion that the introduction of cost feels like a jarring intrusion to a developing friendship. So it pays to work out your own style and strategy for talking about pricing, one that fits with your overall marketing image. It's a part of your sales technique. It needs to feel right to you so that you can be comfortable, thus putting clients at ease.

You should also be prepared with a strategy for giving fee estimates or ranges to prospective clients who are information shopping. You can give your hourly fees and explain how materials are purchased. Or you may have a service package for a job of a certain time length that could be given a cost range.

Use Proposals and Written Cost Estimates

It is good marketing to prepare a proposal or project description for your client that gives a detailed breakdown of the costs involved. Using such a document helps the client appreciate and understand the costs for design time, project management, and carrying financial responsibility for purchasing.

"Our design fee is based on the scope of the project," says Sarah Boyer Jenkins, ASID, IFDA, a residential designer in Chevy Chase, Maryland. "Very seldom do I quote what it is going to be on the spot. I follow up with a written proposal, and then I call them after they have received it to be sure we both understand."

Do yourself a favor by explaining carefully to the client all that they get for the total project fee. Most people don't understand everything that is required for good interior design — it's up to you to do some educating. A written proposal attached to the contract that itemizes project phases and outlines the work entailed makes the project clearer. Also, you can take the jolt out of a big fee by showing the work and the fee broken down into smaller amounts for specific phases. Use the proposal to restate the *benefits* the client will get from your work. Many clients who might balk will be satisfied with the fee if you can do a good job of explaining clearly the results and benefits they can expect.

A softer way to present your project estimate is to call before you meet with the client. Repeat your understanding of the project and talk through your fee estimate. This approach allows a more flexible discussion. Clients will feel they have more opportunity to discuss the fee than if you bring a contract all ready to sign.

Ask for a deposit or retainer — to get the client into the project with you. It makes good financial sense, but it also brings the client psychologically into the project team.

JANE'S NOTE

The most important thing about talking about money is to put it in writing. I get signed contracts and make sure my clients can see in black and white the costs of purchases for them, the design charges, and the payment schedule. They sign these proposals. This way is professional and saves later confusion. If clients get a good value, their space works, and they know the costs ahead of time, there are rarely problems at the end of the project.

Be Sensitive to Cultural Differences

Your style must also fit your clients' expectations of how to talk about money. Be aware that there are cultural differences in discussing financial arrangements and that it's easy to offend without intending to. You need to be sensitive to clients' subtle clues.

In some areas, people believe it is impolite to ask about costs. They may want to know, but they are waiting for you to start the discussion. Some cultures require a session of polite social conversation before business begins. Others may judge you evasive if you don't state your business immediately. Learning about these differences will play a growing role as our business environment gets more diverse and more designers do international business.

JANE'S NOTE

In Colorado, I find most people want to know prices and talk about them easily. People are straightforward and ask when they want to know. When I worked in Nashville, however, cultural norms dictated a more subtle approach. I learned to build the relationship before discussing my fees.

If you have questions about social and cultural attitudes regarding your business, talk to designers who have lived in the area. Ask your questions ahead of time to save yourself embarrassment and to know how to put your clients at ease. Learn to be observant of the small interactions that make up social customs. Listen closely and modify your communication style to make clients comfortable. Good communication takes careful observation, listening, and practice. See the *Reference* section at the end of this book for resources to use in learning more about cultural differences.

Should You Negotiate?

Be prepared to handle a client's attempt to negotiate on price. Know before you meet with the client how much you want this job and for what reasons. If the client protests that they can't pay as much as you ask, be reasonable and flexible — but stick with the fee you have set for your time. The middle of a contract negotiation is not the time to experiment with different fees. It gives the wrong message to clients — and to yourself — to lower the rate for your time in negotiation. Doing this undercuts your value.

If a client objects to your fee for the job, work through the issue with the following three steps:

1. Find out how much the client can spend for the project.
2. Scale down the scope of the project to fit the budget without changing the fee for your time or for the total package; don't change the value, change the *amount* of value.
3. If this isn't possible, offer to refer them to someone else.

You never want to get to the end of the selling process and run into price resistance. That's one of the reasons for qualifying clients as you go and for explaining your fees carefully. By the time you have a contract to present, there should be no major surprises left for you or the client.

Ideas to Remember from This Chapter

- Your fees position your business in the client's perception; set your fees in the right range to attract your target clients.

- Your pricing strategy must be consistent with the rest of your marketing message to clients.

- The method you use to set your fees should

  a) Make your marketing message clear to your clients.

  b) Maximize profit and be easy to manage.

  c) Be flexible.

- Successful communication with clients about money matters requires a strategy: proper timing; clarifying expectations through a project estimate or proposal; and sensitivity to client feelings and needs in discussing project costs and fees.

CHAPTER

4

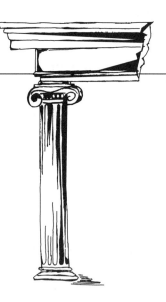

Building Relationships and Referrals

Making Word-of-Mouth Marketing Work for You

Your ability to build relationships with other professionals is a valuable marketing skill. Relationships are the foundation of word-of-mouth marketing.

JANE'S NOTE

Here is my calendar showing how many relationship-building opportunities can be squeezed into a typical busy week (Figure 4-1). Each of the highlighted engagements is an example of the way relationships with all kinds of people enhance my ability to market my design services.

On Monday I talk to former clients about their satisfaction with my work. Tuesday I build my referral potential with realtors by sharing design ideas. Wednesday evening I network with other professionals in the Chamber of Commerce Chief Executive Officer (CEO) Exchange program. Thursday I follow up on a possible new job that was a realtor referral. In addition, my bookkeeper and I share leads with each other at our weekly meeting. On Friday I lunch with a builder to discuss a proposed joint project and follow up on a lead from a friend in my CEO group.

	MONDAY	TUESDAY	WEDNESDAY	THURSDAY	FRIDAY
9	write P.O. & proposal— Sanger job	presentation at Wright-Kingdom Realtors Sales Meeting	call Anderson re job	order Matthews job	draft and work on projects
10					Bryce— ideas for her kitchen
11	Meeting— Sanger	lunch with Taylors— discuss progress on Breckenridge condo	Denver Design Center— gather resouces for clients	golf and lunch with golf group	lunch with builder re possible joint venture
12	call to followup on last week's installations— clients happy?				
1				consult with James and realtor about updating mountain home	
2		set up client appts. for next week			meeting of Hospice committee— planning dance
3	take samples to Johnson		draft space plan and fabric for Johnson	check progress— drapery installation	
4		haircut			call CEO's friend who is remodeling house
5	tennis group			meeting with bookkeeper—	
6			CEO Exchange Group meeting	remember to trade client leads	party at Brenda's — take cards!

FIGURE 4-1 *Jane's engagement calendar.*

In This Chapter

This chapter will show you how to build and maintain marketing relationships and partnerships. You will learn how to

- Develop joint ventures and agreements to share reciprocal referrals.

- Focus your networking activities to network effectively.

- Encourage referrals from former clients.

- Thank clients and partners for referrals in creative ways.

WHY ARE MARKETING RELATIONSHIPS IMPORTANT?

Your reputation as a designer is one of the main ingredients in generating referrals and getting new clients. Especially in service businesses like design, people feel reassured about working with you if someone they know recommends you.

Relationships with other professionals can help you extend your marketing by getting your message to prospective clients you can't reach on your own. If you're running a small design business, you don't have the luxury of a sales and marketing staff, and you can't be everywhere to do it all yourself. Relationships with key professionals who trust you and know the quality of your work can be a powerful "sales force" on your behalf when they meet a client who asks for a referral to an interior designer.

CREATING PARTNERSHIPS FOR MARKETING

To get a sense of all the possibilities open to you in building partnerships for marketing, jot down a quick list of the different professionals you work with in your design business.

- Suppliers
- Craft artisans
- Installers
- Furniture representatives
- Building managers
- Florists
- Lighting specialists
- Art dealers

Then add to your list professionals who work in related fields who could give your marketing a boost.

- Realtors
- Architects
- Builders
- Landscape designers

Keep this list in mind as you read through the following examples of partnerships that interior designers have developed for creative marketing.

Joint Ventures

Joint ventures are one type of partnership that can be effective in bringing you new clients. A joint venture is a project in which two independent businesses work together. Your work is interdependent but you maintain your separate business status. The idea of joint ventures is to plan and carry out projects with other professionals that will have mutual benefits.

Design firms occasionally form joint ventures with architects or engineers to provide full service for major projects. Establishing relationships prepares the foundation for opportunities to work together. Designers also form joint ventures with each other to complement one another's capabilities and connections. One design business that specializes in health care design in Washington, DC wanted to broaden to take health care jobs in Philadelphia. So they created a joint venture with a Philadelphia firm that specializes in space planning. The venture allows them to trade their expertise in different locations and do joint marketing.

Look for creative opportunities to get exposure for your work and to build partnerships. Be ready to take advantage of unique opportunities. "During an exhibition of paintings by artists from the Hudson River school in New York, I did an installation of eighteenth and nineteenth century furniture in the galleries to help create the *mise en scene* for the paintings," says Ellen C. Jeffers. "I then gave a gallery walk for the docents and discussed the pieces of furniture used."

For solo designers, joint ventures can be a rewarding way to work with others. Designers accustomed to working alone enjoy the camaraderie and creativity that can be part of a good partnership. Trish Reddick, a solo designer in Brentwood, Tennessee, told us about the benefits of her joint venture with a builder: "The very best part about working with this builder is that from the beginning we had a mutual feeling of admiration and respect for each other, for what each brings to the project. We have a shared vision of the quality of the project, the design integrity, and the expression of the client's personal needs and wants."

A designer in Denver who works for a retail store that sells quality international design products has found that joint ventures with other vendors can produce new business for both partners. Corinne Brown, ASID Allied Member, had established a relationship with a company that sells fine European linens and had found these products to be a good complement to her own products. This relationship led to shared sponsorship of a home show for the new product line in linens.

With the European linen vendor she arranged a private show in an elegant home and invited about fifty clients. The home show was a success, providing an inviting and informal way to get customers excited about new products and thinking about using them. Corinne was present at the event, ready to pick up on clients' interest and suggest ideas for redesigned master suites that would create a fresh look using these beautiful products.

JANE'S NOTE

As a residential designer, I know what a valuable resource realtors are for gaining access to new homeowners. One creative joint venture I had with a realtor was a collaboration on an open house presentation. This came about because I had laid the groundwork with Gail Palmer of Palmer Realty in Boulder Colorado. I respected the realtors in this company, and I had already built a relationship with them.

Palmer Realty wanted an interior designer to help prepare a home for an important open house showing. I contributed skills by rearranging the interior, creating more immediate visual appeal, and focusing viewers on the best features of the house. In return, I was featured in the realtors' advertising in local papers for the open house. I planned to be present during the open house to talk to viewers, hoping to get leads to future clients — or would have if the home hadn't sold several days before the scheduled open house! This project with Palmer Realty strengthened our relationship and the ability to give and get good referrals from each other.

Many designers have established long-term contractual relationships with builders. Designers take over the task of leading clients through the multiple design decisions about carpet, tile, fixtures and such that many builders find so daunting. In return, the designer gets work generated by someone else's marketing, a guaranteed fee for each client — *and* the chance to build relationships with clients that can lead to future work.

Trish Reddick has created a successful joint venture with a builder in Nashville, Tennessee. Trish provides design consultation for this builder's new construction. She is paid a percentage of the sale price of the house. "One of the best things about working with her [the builder] is that I do not have any risk. I specify and her company does the buying and installation.

"My job starts with the planning phase. We go over the plan together, then I take it and rearrange spaces, door openings, and windows, working with the architect if need be. We actually go and walk the lot, talking about the placement of the house and the mass and style of the house that should go on the property. It is a collaboration from the beginning. If you get a lot of input from designers and architects on paper, it saves the builder money — and she is very conscious of that."

Trish has found that this joint venture arrangement allows her to screen home buyers as future clients. "I also work with the builder on custom homes. In that case the homes are always presold, and I work with the client as well as the builder for all the specifications. We choose carpet, tile, wall coverings, and sometimes paint and trim, but in every instance I have ended up doing other things as well — furniture, window treatments, and accessories. It's a good screening process. Working with them lets me find out if I enjoy this client relationship and feel that these are folks who will allow me to do the very best work I can for them. The quality of work the builder does and the price range and area of town she is in has put me in the niche I wanted. This is really great for my business."

However, not all proposed joint ventures are this beneficial for both partners. It is important to evaluate each partnership opportunity carefully to ensure it is an opportunity for your business.

JANE'S NOTE

My experience illustrates the factors to be considered in this evaluation. I had been looking for a joint venture opportunity with a builder so I was initially enthusiastic when a young builder approached me about taking on the interior design decisions for a spec home. But after evaluating this situation, I decided that the benefits to my business were not strong enough to counter the potential liabilities of the joint project. Listed below are my reasons for saying no to this joint project:

*1. **Maintaining Quality Standards** The builder proposed giving me a budget amount for materials and installation of carpet, tile, counters, and hardwood floors. This amount would include my fee. Looking at his proposed budget, I saw that I would have to nickel and dime the product quality and the installers' fees in order to get my normal fee. I chose not to have my business name attached to a final product that didn't reflect my quality standards.*

*2. **Cash Flow Problems** The builder proposed one payment when all installation was complete. This meant I would front the expense of deposits to order materials and pay installers and could wait up to ninety days to be reimbursed. I decided the benefits of establishing this relationship—even considering future business potential—were not worth the liability of becoming the banker for this project.*

*3. **No Existing Relationships with Installers** In evaluating this project, I checked around town with other builders and called some installers. I found that construction was currently in a boom phase so installers were in high demand. Since I didn't regularly use these wood floor, countertop, and cabinet installers, I had no prior working relationships with them. I decided that having to wait around for an installer to make time for this project could too easily push me off schedule.*

*4. **Too Busy** At this time my business was buzzing and I had more than enough current work. With marketing in mind, I knew that I needed to build relationships that could lead to work in future, potentially slower times. But this* *project posed too many liabilities to justify taking time away from current clients. At a slower time, I probably would have pursued this joint project by negotiating with the builder to create a better balance of shared risks and opportunities.*

▣ ▣ ▣

Reciprocal Referrals

A more informal type of partnership focuses on agreements for reciprocal referrals and extends your marketing through the contacts made by other professionals. Such partnerships generally are less structured and take less of your time than joint ventures. But they can help you reach more prospective clients than would be possible if you had to rely on your own limited time.

Maximizing referrals has always been the backbone of marketing for residential designers. Commercial designers as well depend on referrals to bring clients in for more information. But waiting for referrals to happen is too pas-

---

TIPS FOR MAKING A JOINT VENTURE A SUCCESS

- Work out the idea thoroughly with your project partner before you plunge in. In any joint venture it's important that you both understand what you each will do and have reasonable expectations for the results. Common pitfalls are underestimating the amount of preparation time required to establish a joint project and failing to clarify each partner's expectations of each other and of the project.

- Before you get involved, check out the professional reputation of your proposed partner. Talk to other professionals they have worked with. You will be dependent on this professional for the outcome of the project—keeping on schedule, staying within the project budget, and working with the clients. So make sure this person can follow through and manage the details to produce a result to please both you and the client.

- Put your venture in writing. Some larger joint ventures may require the creation of a legal joint entity. Other projects can be done through agreement to form an association. But write it down and have both partners sign. Write down your respective roles and responsibilities and the timeline for the project. Make this a formal commitment.

sive for today's competitive environment. Creating partnerships with other professionals is an active and effective way to stimulate more referrals. These partnerships multiply the number of people who are recommending your service to potential clients.

Think about the other professionals you know whose work has natural ties to your design specialty. For residential designers these might be

- Landscape designers

- Architects

- Contractors

- Financing specialists for land development

- Realtors

- Real estate appraisers

- Schedule regular meetings or phone calls with your partners to ensure good communication. These types of collaborations can unfold over a long period of time with just a small amount of your time needed to keep the preparations moving toward an event months away. It's easy to let the preparation details and staying in touch get pushed back by the demands of current projects. Don't let this happen to you.

- Make sure you both benefit from this project. If the object is to have some time to meet and get to know prospective clients drawn to a special event, make sure that you both will have time with and access to clients.

- Evaluate how well the project worked for both partners after it's over. You need to have a way to know if this project brought you new clients or more visibility–or whatever your goal was for the project.

- Take care to nurture the relationship with your partner. No matter how this particular project works out for you, remember that your partner is watching your professionalism and your design skills, forming the impression that will become word-of-mouth marketing for you. It's up to you to make it a good one.

- Thank your partner for collaborating with you.

Be creative in imagining potential partners. One Colorado designer had moved to a town in the mountains and was establishing a new residential design business. She reasoned that people buying a new house in a resort town need two things: interior design and a hot tub. So she got to know the spa dealer in town, showed him some of her projects, and they agreed to refer each other to clients. It's been a very profitable partnership for both.

JANE'S NOTE

When I established my current business in Boulder, I made building relationships with realtors one of my top marketing priorities. I'd learned through previous business experience that realtors would be one of the most productive relationships for my residential design specialty. In addition, I knew that realtors needed to know and trust my work before being willing to refer, and they needed to see a clear mutual benefit to a reciprocal referral arrangement. Here is a step-by-step example of how I built a healthy partnership for referrals with Wright-Kingdom Realtors, Inc.

1. My first step was to survey the real estate businesses in Boulder. I planned to develop close relationships with two of these businesses—because I know I can't supply good referrals to more than two companies. I talked to about twenty realtors before selecting my two preferences.

2. Knowing that a previous relationship smoothes the path of creating partnerships, I chose Wright-Kingdom Realtors, Inc. because my husband and I had an excellent experience with them searching for our own Boulder home. In addition, the office manager was a respected former neighbor and friend. I took the partners to lunch and explained my business, suggesting ways I could help their salespeople.

3. The next step was meeting with the partners and key staff: the sales manager and the relocation specialist. I brought business cards, brochures, and a notebook-sized version of my portfolio to leave in the realty office.

4. With the sales manager, I planned a presentation for the Monday sales meeting, demonstrating some design ideas for preparing houses for showing that can boost sales.

5. I went on the realtors' caravan to see new listings and went through a "dog" of a house with them, showing how changes of interior design features could make a dramatic difference in visual appeal. These suggestions were a helpful service to the realtors and built their trust in my work. This trust became the basis for a long-term relationship. I have gotten good design jobs through referrals from Wright-Kingdom Realtors, Inc.

Pat Leifer is a Boulder designer who specializes in draperies and window treatments. In the 22 years she's been in business, she has developed good instincts for building reciprocal referral relationships. She has found that it doesn't pay to stray out of her narrow field of expertise. So when clients want new carpet as well as a new look for windows, she refers them to a carpet salesperson with whom she has already worked out an agreement. For a percentage commission, she works with the client to choose style and color, and the carpet company handles all the details of ordering and installation.

Pat's agreement with the salesperson ensures referrals — the company refers clients who ask about window coverings and she sends her clients who need carpet to this salesperson. Pat says that this partnership has been very good for both sides: "I get lots of jobs from him."

Pat has a similar piggyback marketing relationship with a furniture store. She talked with the sales staff, explaining that she doesn't like the hassle of selling furniture and that she would refer her clients to them. Since the furniture store staff knew nothing about window treatments, they were happy to start a referral trade. Pat left business cards with the store staff to make referrals easier for them. "This was a nice fit — they gave me lots of business," Pat says. "You can't just take, it has to work for both partners."

When you're brainstorming possible sources of referrals for your own business, make sure you consider even the less obvious sources among the people with whom you work.

JANE'S NOTE

I've gotten good jobs through a mutual referrals relationship with a graphics artist. Deb Springer and I both worked for a new boutique in downtown Boulder, marrying the redesign of the store space with the graphic image of the new business. Since then, we have continued to build our friendship as well as our sharing of referrals. It's always great when we get to work together on a project.

TIPS FOR FOSTERING INFORMAL PARTNERSHIPS

- Approach your prospective partners with *what you can do to help them.* Work out your ideas before you meet and be able to show them how the partnership will benefit their business. This approach is a better beginning than focusing on how this connection will help you get more client contacts.

- The referral agreement can be informal but be sure you stay in touch. Even if you have no specific referrals to make, take the time to check with your partner at regular intervals. It reminds them of your business and hearing a quick update on your partner's current business may jog your mind toward a possible referral after all.

- Keeping a partnership working over time requires that it produce mutual benefits. Good partnerships need a "win-win" attitude from both sides. If you find it's hard to keep this balance with your partner, this may not be the best working relationship to continue. Make sure you are giving enough business to your partner to keep the partnership equitable. And make sure you are getting enough referrals to make this a good use of your time.

- Follow through on what you promise to do, and do it well. Remember that you are demonstrating the way you work to people who can recommend you to clients you want.

- Get feedback from your partners on how well this relationship is working for them.

- Remember that maintaining a professional relationship benefits from the same attention to courtesy and consideration as your other relationships. Say thank you for referrals and recommendations and show your appreciation for someone's willingness to help you. Your thanks should be appropriate to the relationship. For some hints from designers on saying thank you, see *Creative Ways to Say Thanks* at the end of this chapter.

NETWORKING

Networking. These days it seems we hear the word at every turn. This business buzzword of the 1980s has come into common usage in all aspects of our lives, so much so that there are times when we confess to feeling "networked out," longing for simpler days when we went to gatherings merely to socialize or to learn something—and left the business cards at home.

In clarifying our ideas for this book, we talked honestly about our negative feelings about the excesses of networking. We concluded that it is still an important technique for word-of-mouth marketing. It remains one of the key ways to promote referrals. But there is good networking and bad networking, and *the key to good networking is knowing the difference.*

Bad networking is exploiting others, using them merely as a means to your own ends. You know you're on the receiving end of bad networking when the networker insensitively jams a card at you, demands suggestions, and then stops listening, scanning the room for someone more useful. *Good networking* takes time for mutual sharing of information and treats others with respect and consideration. And *great networking* adds the spice of good conversation—and with luck a dash of humor—and can create true synergy when both participants go away enriched by the encounter.

Defining Networking

In this chapter we are defining networking as time spent with other professionals for the purpose of giving and receiving information about prospective clients and opportunities. Networking can be as formal as leads groups organized specifically for this purpose or as informal as talking shop at lunch with several old friends who happen to be a realtor, a lawyer, and an accountant.

We are not including social or professional activities with people likely to be potential clients though this, too, is often called networking. The focus of this chapter is on building and benefiting from relationships with other professionals. You'll find lots of ideas for meeting and getting to know clients in *Chapter 5: Breaking the Ice with Prospective Clients.*

Where to Network

You want to build a network of professionals who are likely to know new clients who need your services. Think about your clients—the kind of work they do and their usual activities. Make a list of the services they use and professionals with whom they have frequent contact. Then think of ways you can create opportunities to meet and network with these professionals. Listed below are a few networking ideas that have worked well for other designers.

1. Join Organizations   The local Chamber of Commerce is probably the most logical networking forum for interior designers whose businesses serve local clients. Yet as we've asked and listened to designers, we've heard mixed reviews about results from Chamber of Commerce networking. The designers who have done effective networking through the Chamber have usually participated in a Chamber program that establishes a smaller group and meets over a period of time. Good leads or referrals rarely come from someone you've just met for the first time at a large reception. It takes time to get acquainted and to build a solid sense of how a professional works before most people feel enough trust to make referrals.

An example of successful networking through joining the Chamber of Commerce is the way E. Suzanne Leary, ASID, focused on the Denver Chamber's Ambassador Program. To promote membership retention, Chamber Ambassadors call and visit businesses to check on their satisfaction with chamber services.

This program created a great opportunity to meet potential clients for office design jobs. Sue says, "I had the opportunity to go to their offices and meet them on a one-to-one basis. I'd find out about their business and see if there was any neglect in design — they might need a chair or something. It was a good way for me to get my foot in the door, instead of doing cold calls, which I hated." Sue said that there was the added benefit of wearing ambassador badges at the luncheons and chamber events, which meant people would seek her out to ask about chamber activities, providing a comfortable beginning for conversation and networking.

2. Volunteering with Community Organizations   Community involvement is a wonderful way to combine a desire to become involved in an organization you care about with building a network of relationships. Volunteering

---

JANE'S NOTE

One of the best networking activities I do is the Boulder Chamber of Commerce CEO Exchange program. The group is ten people, each the head of his or her own small business. The program's intent is to pool expertise and help solve one another's problems, acting as an ad hoc board of directors for each business. As the group meets at a different business site each month, the members get well acquainted and trust one another, which is the formula for good networking. We meet for 10 months and then form new groups. This networking has led to many jobs through my CEO contacts.

your special skills or serving as a director on a nonprofit board—such as the symphony, educational council, or hospital board—can be an effective way to get to know other professionals. Nonprofits often look for professional expertise by nominating directors or committee chairpersons who have special knowledge.

The advantage to this type of networking is that you build high trust with these people by working together toward a common goal, making this the best possible environment for thoughtful and creative networking.

3. Joining Leads Groups Leads groups are organizations you can join for the express purpose of exchanging leads and information about potential referrals with other professionals. You pay dues and meet every week with a group of fifteen to thirty others. As a designer, you would be the only interior designer in your specific group. You have a chance to give a presentation of your services and show your work so others will know which referrals would be most likely to need your services.

Ambur Stevens joined such a group, *Leads*, one month after starting her business in Boulder. She has found it to be her most effective marketing tool. "*Leads* is responsible for my fast start because I had twenty-nine other women who were interested in my help or knew somebody," says Ambur. "It's a definite benefit."

4. Creating Your Own Networking Group If formal leads groups don't seem to fit your needs, you can create a less structured informal group of your own. This demands more time and energy from you in setting it up but it may be a better option for your situation. Make a list of professionals who would have contact with the same clients as you and call to ask if they are interested. Set a regular lunch or breakfast meeting and get started helping each other. You can limit the burden of managing the group by getting others in the group to share responsibility for inviting new members.

Another idea is to form a professional peer group to share referrals as well as helping and supporting each other with the inevitable questions and problems of running a small business. Pull together a group of professionals with similar—but noncompeting—businesses, such as:

- An engineer
- A contractor
- A real estate broker
- A light designer

Meet once a month. Give each person the spotlight for one meeting to talk about their business goals and marketing plans. The group members contribute their own expertise, passing along helpful advice as well as possible referrals.

How to Get the Most from Your Networking

Getting the most from your time spent networking means planning ahead and monitoring how well the activity is working for you. Set goals for your networking and plan time to follow up on suggested leads. The following are suggestions for working well with an established network.

1. Have a schedule for regular contact with your network. Mark this on your marketing calendar.

2. Give your network the key information about your business.

- Explain your business's mission.
- Describe your design specialty and your target clients.
- Describe the key benefits of your services.

3. Be clear and specific about what you would like your network partners to do for you.

4. Take time to learn about your networking partners' businesses. Ask good questions and take notes so you will have information to pass on to potential referrals.

5. Have a lead to offer when you meet with your networking partner.

6. Give your networking partners something specific to pass on about you. If you are planning an event to meet prospective clients or you have a special offer or promotion, make sure your partners have the information. If you have invitations or other marketing material promoting response, give copies to your network.

7. Use networking as an opportunity to stay up on what is happening in the community or on changes occurring in your target market. Listen for mention of opportunities you can use for marketing or for meeting prospective clients. If your market niche is office design, you need to stay aware of fluctuations in office occupancy in your area. Or a residential designer may hear of a developer looking for a designer to help with design choices for a new development of luxury homes.

8. Be generous in your promotion of others.

9. Look for opportunities to build more formal marketing partnerships with your networking partners, or for ways you can piggyback your marketing efforts with others. Networking can be the first step in building valuable marketing partnerships.

10. Keep track of how many clients you get through your networking activities. If this networking group is working for you, stick with it. If not, bow out gracefully and save your time for marketing activities that produce for you. It's important to remember that networking, like other marketing relationships, may not produce new clients for you right away. Be sure to allow enough time for evaluation before deciding that it's not working.

TIPS FOR EFFECTIVE NETWORKING AT MEETINGS

- Arrive early and stay late. Some of the best networking happens just before or just after a meeting.

- Have cards ready. Be sure to ask for the other person's card and take a minute to jot a note on the back to make sure you will remember who they are.

- Have your goals clearly in mind when you're networking with any group. Take the time to plan your introduction of yourself to give people the specific information they need to give you helpful leads. Saying "I'm an interior designer" doesn't give people as much to work with as something like: "I specialize in designing kitchens that are efficient and have that special feeling that makes them the place in the house people always want to be. If you know of anyone building a new house or planning to remodel—or even people who love to cook and entertain who would be interested in my service—I'd appreciate their name so I can contact them personally."

- Ask for the same kind of clear statements from your fellow networkers so you can give them leads and suggestions that will be most helpful in the shortest amount of time.

- Take the time for *good networking*. Having only a few sincere conversations is more effective than trying to work the room.

- Follow up with new acquaintances. Call them, go out to lunch, or send an article or other material that came up in conversation.

On Networking with Friends

For some of us, networking with friends can be difficult. It feels awkward and strained to ask friends to pass on leads for prospective clients. Yet we know that some of our best referrals have come from good friends. Because there is already mutual trust, respect, and a desire for each other to do well, friends are a good resource for referrals. A trade of good work for friends and good referrals from friends is a mutual gain for both.

We encourage you to let your friends know they can help you by suggesting prospective clients or making referrals. It is important to remember that friendship is first and leads are second. When you receive a referral from a friend, you need to thank them and let them know how much you appreciate it.

AND DON'T FORGET TO ASK YOUR CLIENTS

We don't have to tell you that clients who are pleased with your solutions to their design problems are the best source of word-of-mouth advertising you can have. But remember that there are three key parts to getting the most out of the good will that comes from a happy client.

1. Quality Service   Show clients that their satisfaction with the completed work is important to you. Insist on quality work from yourself, suppliers, and others who are contributing to the project. This insistence on quality often means following through on those last few tedious details even when you're already working overtime on new projects. Schedule time to follow up on each completed design job to make sure the client is satisfied—good endings can be as important as good beginnings. You will find more information on quality and customer service in *Chapter 8: Keeping Clients for Future Business and Referrals.*

2. Ask for Referrals   Too often designers assume that clients will automatically recommend them to others. And some do. But many more just won't think about it unless you make the request specific. Tell your clients that referrals are a key part of your business and ask them to pass your message along.

Some designers have developed ways to remind former clients that referrals are always welcome. "I find that just asking is my best marketing," says Dennis McNabb. "I just say—can you refer me to your friends? I enjoyed working with you so much. This is the kind of work I like to do and you are the kind of client I love to work with."

Mary Ann Bryan of Houston shared with us the advice given in a seminar given by Michael Thomas on referral-based marketing. "The theme is that you ask for referrals about five times during the project. When you sign the contract, you ask—you tell them that your business operates not on the basis of one job, but on the future work that each job will bring. And you do that five times through the job. I was convinced."

Another system is that used by a designer who sends a card to former clients with the offer of two hours of free design consultation for a referral. One realtor we know who also relies on client referrals has a clever system for staying in touch—she sends former clients a packet of forget-me-not seeds (Figure 4-2).

3. Say Thank You Say it often and say it as uniquely as you can. In the next section designers share their favorite ways to thank both clients and marketing partners for referrals.

Creative Ways to Say Thanks

Thanking all those who promote your business with good word-of-mouth marketing has been a recurring theme throughout this chapter. Expressing

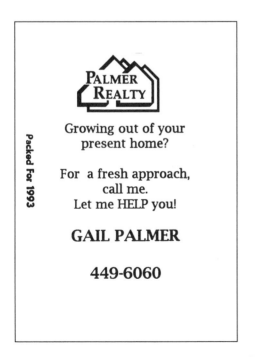

FIGURE 4-2 *Forget-Me-Not seed packet: client reminder sent by Gail Palmer, Palmer Realty, Boulder, CO.*

sincere thanks will keep your marketing relationships strong. To give you some good ideas we asked designers for their favorite ways to thank partners and clients for referrals.

- Express your appreciation with a thoughtful and sincere handwritten note.
- Thank them with a gift certificate to a local restaurant.
- Send flowers — it's a beautiful way to express your gratitude.
- Thank people for special referrals by taking them out to lunch or dinner at a favorite restaurant.
- Thank clients for referrals by surprising them with an accessory that is a special complement to their design project.
- A designer who loves to entertain does something very special to thank clients for referrals. She includes them in a dinner party at her home for other friends and says that people new in town are especially appreciative.
- The best way to thank a networking partner for a referral is to return the favor with a referral.

Ideas to Remember from This Chapter

- Joint ventures, reciprocal referral relationships, and networking with other professionals are valuable ways to extend your marketing reach to prospective clients.
- Good joint ventures with other professionals require careful planning, good communication, and mutual benefits for both partners.
- Reciprocal referral partnerships work best when you approach your potential partners with a clear statement of what you can do to help their businesses.
- Build a network of professionals who can help you stay aware of prospective clients and new project opportunities. The most effective networking techniques for most designers are joining organizations, volunteering and serving on organization boards, and leads groups or informal networking groups.
- Ensure that your clients will be a good source of referrals by providing quality service, asking clients for their help in referring prospective clients, and thanking clients sincerely for all referrals.

CHAPTER

5

Breaking the Ice with Prospective Clients

Building Visibility and Credibility

Build your *visibility* so prospective clients will know who you are and feel comfortable asking for your help. Build your *credibility* so they will recognize your authority on design. Visibility and credibility form the foundation for more targeted and specific marketing. Clients who have already heard of you will pay more attention to your marketing messages.

In This Chapter

This chapter shows you how to break the ice with prospective clients—how to establish the visibility and credibility that make the rest of your marketing easier. The chapter describes the many marketing methods you can use to build visibility and credibility. You will learn

- Tips for both residential and commercial designers on being where your clients are.

- How to build credibility by demonstrating your skills.

- How to build your reputation as an authority on design by publishing, speaking, and teaching.

- Tips on getting great publicity.

MARKETING IS A PROCESS

Marketing a design service takes many encounters before prospective clients are ready for a sales presentation. Conventional wisdom holds that it takes from five to ten contacts before the client is ready to buy. Everything you do to build trust in your competence and reliability furthers the marketing process.

Buying design services is buying an intangible — the belief that your expertise will solve a problem. Creating this belief requires building a relationship with your client. Visibility and credibility are the first steps in creating this relationship.

The purpose of the marketing process is to deliver your message to your target clients in the clearest and most appropriate way. Every aspect of your marketing should be tasteful, professional, and ethical — remember that your marketing reflects your business.

What Are the Steps in Marketing Design Services?

The diagram of the design marketing process illustrates the way the steps of the process add to your growing relationship with a prospective client. Every step contributes to the whole cycle of relationship-building. Developing visibility and credibility creates the foundation of trust that supports the client relationship throughout the full marketing process cycle (Figure 5-1).

1. Define your market and your target clients. Choose and define a market niche.

2. Lay the foundation for marketing by building visibility and credibility.

3. Get leads to prospective clients — through promotion and networking. Begin building your relationship with prospective clients to get acquainted and prequalify.

4. Meet with prospective clients to learn about their design needs and explain your services.

5. Discuss your analysis of the client's needs and present your solution — with a proposal or presentation. Close the sale.

6. Complete the job satisfactorily. Continue nurturing the client relationship with excellent customer service.

This chapter and *Chapter 6: Building a Relationship with Prospective Clients* describe the many methods that can be part of your marketing

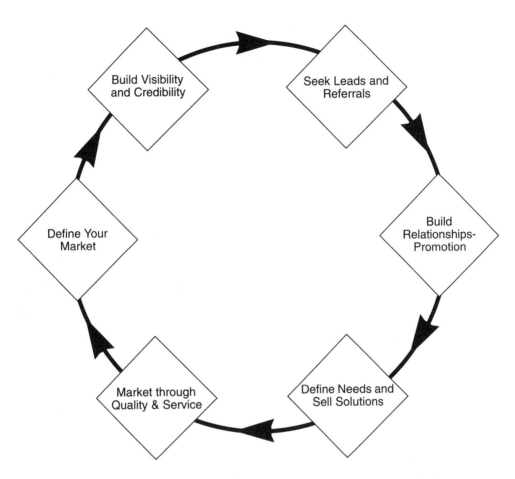

FIGURE 5-1   *Design marketing process: A cycle of relationship-building.*

process. We're not suggesting that you use every method listed here—this material is for reference and for stimulating your own ideas. So read on but don't get overwhelmed. Choose the methods that will help *you* reach *your* target clients.

HOW TO BE VISIBLE TO THE RIGHT PEOPLE

It is impossible to be accessible and visible to everyone. So you must use your time wisely and focus on your target clients. Learn everything you can about your target clients. Find out what they need to know about you. Ask yourself the following questions as you research your target clients.

- Where would you meet these prospective clients?
- What are their interests?

GETTING CLEAR ON MARKETING TERMINOLOGY

Before taking a closer look at marketing methods, let's get clear on the terms we are using. No one defines marketing terms in exactly the same way. We're presenting the parts of the process as they seem to make the most sense in the context of marketing design services.

Marketing is the entire range of activities you use to make your services available to your clients. It is the process of building a relationship with clients, ensuring that you are in the right place at the right time when they need your service. Advertising, promotion, public relations, publicity, and selling are all part of the marketing process.

Advertising is paying for time—on radio, TV, or other audiovisual media—or space—in magazines, newspapers, and other printed advertising—to deliver your message to clients.

Public relations is strengthening the positive image you and your business convey to clients. Public relations includes the way you dress and the design of your studio, community involvement, public speaking, publishing, publicity, and participation in trade organizations. The result of public relations is your total professional image to the public.

Publicity is using the news media to tell your story to clients. Publicity is often defined as free advertising, but it is much more than that. Publicity is everything outside of your control that your clients hear or see about your business. Though, as you will see in this chapter, there are ways you can encourage publicity that will relay a good message to clients.

Promotion is preselling prospective clients through direct communication about your services. Promotional activities cover all the tangible things you do to communicate the benefits of your service to prospective clients: direct mail, telephone contacts, fliers, informational events, and informal discussions.

Selling is the stage of marketing that brings you face to face with clients. It is the personal communication of your solution to the client's problems and your request for this job. The marketing process leads naturally into the selling stage. By this point, clients should have the information and confidence in your business they need to make their decision.

- What are they worried about? What are they excited about?
- What do they read?
- How much do they know about design services? What do they need to know about you and your business?
- How much educating will you need to do to show them how you can help?
- How would these clients prefer to learn about you and your business? What message — and in what form — would be most likely to reach them and convince them of your ability?

Always view the relationship you are building with prospective clients through the clients' perspective. As much as possible, learn to think as they do. Approach clients in the way they would prefer.

Residential Designers: How to Build Visibility

Residential designers know the value of socializing with people who are prospective clients. In social settings people are less guarded and more comfortable. And you are more comfortable if you're meeting people while doing things you enjoy. So be a joiner and a doer — play sports, join community organizations, book clubs, or the Chamber of Commerce.

It's also very important to appear accessible. Realize that prospective clients could be feeling even more insecure than you do. Many people feel intimidated by designers. Make it easy for them to talk to you and to choose you.

JANE'S NOTE

I do activities I enjoy. If I don't have specific work, I get out with people — playing tennis and golf. I'm active in groups and I keep meeting people. I ask people what they do — if you're interested in people, they will be interested in you. They usually respond by asking what I do, which makes a natural opening for me to tell about my design business. Enthusiasm and friendliness are contagious.

I try to join organizations where clients would belong. For several years I volunteered to decorate for Pizzazz, a hospice fund raising dance. As a result of these relationships, I'm doing the chairperson's house and two committee chair homes, and I've gotten many referrals.

Mary Ann Bryan, who has a residential design business in Houston, has analyzed where to meet her clients. "Our market is the client who has spendable income and the desire to make their environments work for them. Clients with this income are found in certain places. The visual ones are at the gallery openings, art museums, the fashion shows. They usually have a kinesthetic husband who is on the go, likes to be with people–out to lunch at the town's best known spot or at charity events. The auditory ones are out at the music stores or going to the symphony."

Join community organizations such as the Chamber of Commerce and the Rotary Club. Get to know people in local government. It's important for residential designers to be active in the community. The way to be well known is to work hard for issues you care about. Your energy and your sincerity make your reputation what you want it to be. "Get involved in everything that is going on, so your name is repeated over and over until people become aware and say, 'oh yes, I've heard that name — he's an interior designer.' I've gotten a lot of work that way," says Michael D. Temple, a residential designer in San Diego.

JANE'S NOTE

One of my best marketing strategies is to be a good customer of the local area where I want to do business. For example, I buy my clothes in Boulder at a small retail store. We eat dinner out at locally owned restaurants and get to know the owners. I use local dry cleaners, hairdressers, lawn care people, car dealers, service stations, florists, and other small retailers. I am good to them and they are good to me in return, both in word-of-mouth advertising and in becoming clients. Get to know people in your community and make sure everyone knows what you do. Show that you consider yourself part of the community.

It takes a different strategy to create high visibility over a larger geographic area. Designers with a market niche have the advantage of knowing where clients will be. John Kelly's niche is yacht interiors — sport fishing and motor yachts. He uses trade shows to meet clients. "My whole life is built around marketing. I usually attend every boat show with pictures of boats I have done, with or without having a booth for my business. I'm an amateur photographer so I take pictures of 95% of the jobs I do. You know, it's a great tool to meet people. It's good to be at a show where a couple of boats I've done are on display. I can show people how I select color, finishes, lighting, and how to accessorize a boat. All I do is tell people what I do. I think the more you get excited about marketing what you do the more excited people become—and they want to use you."

Residential designers with a national clientele still need to meet people and develop relationships. "Our clientele is national so being involved in national organizations like the International Interior Design Association (IIDA) and the American Society of Interior Designers (ASID) allows me to have contacts all over the country," says Charles Gandy, FASID, IIDA, of Atlanta. "Our involvement isn't just in professional groups—we're involved in churches, civic groups, a lot of organizations. The bottom line is people like to do business with people they like. I like for people to get to know me as a person first and a designer second."

Commercial Designers: How to Build Visibility

The goal for commercial designers is the same as for residential designers— to be where your clients are. And to show them that you understand them and their needs. But the focus of shared interests in commercial design is more on your clients' business than on social and leisure time activities.

Roger Yee, editor of *Contract Design*, points out that designers must learn to "partner with their industry—learn to think like hoteliers or educators or restaurateurs." He reminds us that the 1990s are a time of rapid change for virtually all industries.

Designers need to stay up on trends and be prepared to help solve the problems posed by these changes in the markets they serve. In a national ASID conference workshop—*How Designers Can Prosper from Today's Chaotic Business Environment*—Bruce Simoneaux, AIA, and Douglas Parker, AIA, both of Grand Rapids, Michigan, offered good suggestions for designers who work for corporate clients.

- Read business magazines and management books. Be able to refer to or quote from the current management consultant gurus.

- Keep up with the new vocabulary in the business world.

- Understand the kinds of organizational change being implemented in the business world these days. Use this knowledge to show how good design can be part of the solution in such movements as work group teams, creating high-performance teams, single versus shared offices, continuous process improvement, and quality management.

- Understand the problems facing companies: keeping up with technology, globalization bringing on the need to be in business 24 hours a day, environmental concerns, office health issues (such as air quality, ergonomics, or carpal tunnel syndrome). Also be prepared to discuss design contributions to solutions.

- Demonstrate that you can help anticipate the design needs of the future. You'll need to show that you understand the technological world of the "Nintendo generation."

If your design business focuses on an industry niche (such as health care, hospitality, and so on), you need to become a specialist in that industry. Know what it takes to do business in this industry. Talk, ask questions, listen, and learn. Read what clients read, know the language, know the issues and trends. Be prepared to tell potential clients what you know about their industry and their needs.

Deborah Steinmetz makes a practice of getting involved in organizations in which her clients are involved—the Institute of Real Estate Management (IREM) and the Building Owners and Managers Association (BOMA). "The client I got this morning was the direct result of a speech on space planning I gave for IREM two weeks ago. This new client was in the audience." Deborah emphasizes that it's important to be active, not just be a member: "For instance, we were the newsletter editors for the local chapter of IFMA."

Use niche organizations to become an insider. Join trade organizations and be active in them. Work your way into a leadership position if possible. You will be more visible and know the key people in the industry. Nancy Clanton has a nationwide market, and she has used her insider position in organizations to create a national reputation and credibility. She joined the Illuminating Engineers Society (IES) and worked her way into a board member slot. She volunteered in this society at the local level and was willing to serve as an officer or committee chair. Then she made it a point to go to meetings at the regional level and get involved. "Through such a regional commitment I was nominated to the board of directors of IES. They were tough to break into, but once I became a board member, I got the national reach. Then people consider you for speaking at national seminars and you're asked to join other key organizations. Once you get recognized at the national level for whatever reason, all doors open to you. It takes a lot of volunteer time to get to that point."

Speak and write articles for publications that serve your niche industry. You want to be the person these potential clients think of first when they need a designer. Nancy Clanton got the sponsorship of professional societies as a seminar presenter and speaker: "When you are on the American Society of Interior Designers or the American Institute of Architects approved speaking list, you have clout."

If you focus on an industry in which there are gatekeepers or certain procedures for acceptance, learn what you need to do to become an insider. Rita Carson Guest, ASID, specializes in law office design in Atlanta. She has found it useful to participate in legal trade shows, such as an expo sponsored by the

American Bar Association (ABA) and the Association of Legal Administrators (ALA). "We attended the expo to become an insider. We attend lots of ALA meetings, and we try to support them as a sponsor." At one trade show Rita's firm handed out a survey about how to choose a designer. They shared the results through an article, which brought the firm more publicity and exposure.

Nancy Chilton of Nashville has learned how to deal with corporations so bankers and lawyers will feel comfortable working with her. She shows them that she understands corporate structure and how things work. She says, "You have to be involved in the business world and come across as a businessperson. In Nashville there are a couple of restaurants where the businessmen eat. You have to show up there; take a local businessman along and you get introduced. And slowly you become a player in their world. Meeting on a personal level makes it easier to get in the office."

CREDIBILITY: BUILDING YOUR REPUTATION

Why does a client choose to hire you? Clients choose you because you provide a service that has value for them, and because they trust your skill and trust you to treat them fairly and with respect. A client can't make this decision without knowing something about your credibility as a designer.

Demonstrate your credibility in ways your clients understand and respect. The purpose of building your credibility is to

1. Get greater name recognition for you and your firm.
2. Educate target clients about you and your business, the services you offer, and problems you can solve.
3. Get acquainted with clients and establish a relationship.

The following are five key methods of building your reputation as an expert in design:

1. Demonstrate your design ability to the public by participating in show houses, model homes, and competitions.
2. Publish articles or write a book. Get photos of your work published in magazines. Publishing contributes to your credibility.
3. Use public speaking for organizations to reach clients and demonstrate your expertise.
4. Teach a course or a seminar—to other designers or to the public. Teaching establishes you as an authority on your topic.

5. Keep your name and your business in people's minds through good publicity.

The rest of this chapter shares ideas from residential and commercial designers on building credibility and visibility using these five methods. Use your imagination to extend these ideas to fit your situation. Think about how you would use these methods to reach the clients you want.

Demonstrating Your Skills: Show Houses

Build your credibility by demonstrating your creativity and ability to solve design problems. Show houses have long been a classic means of demonstrating talent. And designers know that show houses are a way to have fun with a creative project.

But doing a show house is also a way to spend a lot of money. We have heard mixed reviews — and a few horror stories — from designers about the effectiveness of show houses as a marketing method. The expense and heavy time commitment demand that you carefully weigh the pros and cons before signing on to do a show house. The critical question to keep asking is *What's in it for me?*

Using show houses as good marketing requires having a clear goal and strategy in fitting the show house into your marketing design. We talked to many designers about their positive and negative experiences with show houses. The following are the main lessons learned from their experiences.

1. Commit to doing it right. Be willing to invest your time and money to showcase your talent. "Show houses have worked for me," says Mary Ann Bryan. "I have had people call me for business as long as ten years later with my card taken at a show house. My only advice is to do it well. Don't do anything that limits your demonstration of ability. In other words, you need to spend the money and resources appropriate for the project. Don't do it if your money and resources aren't adequate. I've seen designers hurt themselves this way. Once you commit, you have to go the whole nine yards."

But don't waste your money either. Get help from suppliers — through discounts or loans of furniture and materials, borrow from friends, and arrange resales after the show. "I find part of the challenge is how much I can do for the least amount of money," says Michael D. Temple. "Most of the successful designers do it that way, too. I figure out which vendor will donate products or give a substantial decrease, who will loan me stuff — and I concentrate my design in those areas. The first home I ever did I dropped $11,000 before I knew what happened. I got it back, but just barely."

2. Investigate how well publicized the event will be—and how much publicity the designers will get—before you commit. Have your personal plan as well for creating good publicity from the show house. Be prepared to use photos or the show house catalog and magazine coverage in your own marketing communication with clients.

"When you have photos taken at a show house, do them in black and white as well as color," suggests June Towill Brown, ASID, Allied Member, of Los Angeles. "Some magazines only want black and white. And consider taking color slides—I do a lot of slide presentations in my lectures. Another thing to do is take a videotape of *before* and *after*."

JANE'S NOTE

I have only done one show house but I felt it was successful. A local architect redid an old Victorian home and made it into a bed and breakfast inn. He asked several local designers to do a room. He gave us each a budget that allowed us to do the room without additional cost—other than our large amount of time.

The reason it was successful for me was the free advertising. It was in the local newspaper, and our names were placed on permanent brass nameplates on the door to our room. But the best advertising was an invitation-only two-day open house. Each designer invited fifteen people. The architect and builder invited their friends and constituents. The designers were in their rooms for the open house. The final event was an elaborate catered party on the last evening. This show house gave me exposure and credibility in the community. I also got some jobs.

---

3. Use the event to reach past clients or targeted prospective clients. Share free tickets, take clients on custom tours of the show house, or do your own mailings to invite clients.

"If you do show houses, spend the extra money and invite as many people as you can in pairs, so they can bring a friend or a spouse when they come," says Linda Blair. "It's a lovely gesture to make for your past clients. Past clients are the number one base of all future business no matter what your marketing is—that's your strongest referral source. Sending pairs of tickets will make you the talk of your clients."

June Towill Brown of Los Angeles says that clients love having their designer in a showcase. For prospective clients, she suggests arranging to take them through the show house instead of just giving tickets. On their own, they might fall in love with another designer's room! Give them special attention and a private tour.

4. Commit to doing show houses repeatedly for maximum exposure and building your designer reputation.   Getting your name out there only once does very little. Publicity has to be continuous to be effective. Recognition stops as soon as the noise dies down.

"I have done them but they haven't been good for me," says B. J. Peterson, Los Angeles. "And I know why — those who are successful do show houses consistently, year after year. If you don't, it doesn't have the impact and you don't reach people when they need you. They forget from one year to the next that they loved the room you designed. I specifically know a handful of designers who get all of their business from show houses."

5. Use your imagination to create an opportunity with your room. Make it a demonstration of your ingenuity and your problem-solving work.

"I did my first show house and I got tremendous press from it. I was on the weekend *Today* show and in nine newspapers, including the *New York Times*," says Linda Blair. "It was the top floor of an old house, a space 50 ft x 25 ft with tall ceilings, all rafters removed. The owner wanted it turned into a combination English country sitting room and full-scale exercise equipment room, with a huge pool table as well. I had a disaster space and I made it positive for me. It turned out to be one of those sensational spaces."

Dennis McNabb recalls this story told by Carlton Wagner. "Carlton wanted to participate in a show house sponsored by the local ASID chapter when he was just getting started as a designer. They said, 'Well, we don't really know you; you don't have a track record. But we'll let you do the garage.' Carlton said OK and went out to look at it. He picked up the little button for the door and started punching it. As the door went up and down, he thought 'What can I do with this? What profession likes gadgets?' He realized that doctors love gadgets so he decided to design this space for them. He worked on the garage and put every kind of gadget he could think of in there. He had someone dress up in a maid's costume to lie on the bed, punching a button to make the walls go up and down and to run the other gadgets. He said the doctors loved it. From that garage showroom, he started building his business with the clientele he wanted. Just because he figured out a gadget or gimmick they could relate to."

6. Keep the "client" in mind.   You need to reach the people who come through the show house if you are to convert any of them to clients in the future. Make your work approachable and create a context in which it makes sense, so people can understand what you do as a designer. Tell a story or show how you solved a problem — *before* and *after.*

"When you do show houses you are marketing yourself," says June Towill Brown. "You're pinpointing the clientele you hope will ask you to do their homes. You have to design the room to have the most appeal. So people walk into the room and say — 'Gee, I could stay here. I love these colors — this is it!' Once in a while designers say they just want to have fun, do whatever they want and be really creative. Because, for once, they don't have a client.

"But they *do* have a client — all the people coming through the door. Designing in a show house with no regard for whether people can identify with it — to me, that's ridiculous! Brillo soap pads from the ceiling just to be innovative just is not it."

Sarah Boyer Jenkins gives this advice. "Whenever you participate in a show house, you must tell a story, not just do a pretty room. You must also tell the story in a publicity release for the press. We did a solar room in a show house back before solar was a household word. We worked hard and did a lot of research. We did dark tile floors, white walls, blinds with metallic linings, fans, and the furniture was all on legs for circulation. It was a great story and we got lots of publicity. Show houses have been great for me. One of my rooms was featured in the *House Beautiful* issue last year of the ten best rooms in the country. Every show house I have done for the last 4 years has been in a major publication."

7. Commit your time and energy to be at the site and meet people. Be accessible and use the opportunity to educate potential clients about design. Your goal should be to get the message to some of the do-it-yourselfers coming through that working with a designer can help them express their ideas.

"Many people say they've been in show houses but have never gotten any work. Well, you can't do just one, " says June Towill Brown. "And you have to be in the room at least 75% of the time — 90% would be even better. When people are coming through, saying, 'what a wonderful room!,' what better treat than to have the designer in there to say, 'Hello, my name is such and such, and I did the room this way for these reasons.' Suddenly it's not just a great room, it's a fabulous room. Because they understand the problem solving. Being there is the best selling tool there is, better than taking any ad."

8. Think like a marketer — never pass up an opportunity to get a list of names. Get lists of those who attend. Follow up with a mailing about your design business. If the list is really large, you can narrow down the names of those with real interest by including a qualifier — on offer of consultation or of sending more information if they respond with a request. Those who

Joseph Galas, ASID and Carolyn MacRossie, ASID

The breakfast nook was transformed into a romantic and fanciful setting, perfect for the enjoyment of leisurely breakfasts and intimate dinners by ASID interior designers Joseph Galas and Carolyn MacRossie. The room's unique geometric shape, rustic worn slate floor, richly detailed paneled pine walls, and distinctive wood-burning cook's corner fireplace presented the designers a choice opportunity to display their creative ideas.

Waxed pine panels were refreshed with oil to bring out the wood's warm honey tones. The herringbone patterned brick chimney breast and wall panels were painted a creamy French peach color to harmonize with the wood paneling. With the basics finished, the designers concentrated on arranging the many detailed layers of ornamentation which transform the space into a Bavarian woodland.

On the ceiling, a capricious hand-painted ivy vine twists and turns its way around the room. At the window, a charming rustic swag of twigs and vines festoons the elegant lace and hand-embroidered panels which soften both the light and the view. In the fireplace, birch logs, vines and

46

Design Notes

Junior Symphony Guild, Inc.
1994 Designer Showhouse

FIGURE 5-2 *Program of the 1994 Designer Showcase by the Junior Symphony Guild, Inc. A great place for the public to see your name and your work. Cover design by Scottie Button; drawing by Marilyn Rest. Courtesy of the Junior Symphony Guild, Inc., Englewood, CO.*

respond would be excellent targets for your focused marketing. See *Chapter 6: Building a Relationship with Prospective Clients* for more information on direct mail techniques.

9. Get your work published. "Show houses are wonderful for young designers starting out," says Mark Hampton of New York City. "They are

The Breakfast Octagon
Room 16

flowers form an enchanting thicket for a droll white rabbit.

The entrancing dining table promises a delightful dinner for four. Rustic handmade iron chairs sport designs of abstract forest animals. A striking green and white striped underskirt provides the backdrop for the wildly colorful tablecloth. For the table setting, a bright potpourri of handmade Majolica ware, glassware, metal and lace provides a distinctive meld of pattern, color and style. Cupboard and cozy corner shelves are richly ornamented with accessories which make this room delightfully appealing.

Resource List:

Ceiling Stencil	Fluzzies, Lynn Smyth, 692-9798
Four Iron Chairs	Myers Massie Studio, Vancouver, Mollie Polus
Upholstery	Country Club Furniture Shop, Inc., 388-6373
Table Settings & Accessories	The Perfect Setting, 759-1200
	4992 East Hampden Ave, Denver
Floral Designs	Thru the Woods, Dave & Georgia Mills, 799-4877
	9940 East Costilla Ave., Englewood
Fabrics: Floral Print	Kravat Fabrics
Striped Table Skirt	Country Life, Regency House
Window Lace	Henry Cassen, Decorators Walk
Wall Tapestry	The Rug Source in Denver
Sketch Artist:	Marilyn Rest

Carlson Photography

Design Team:

Joseph R. Galas, ASID
Harrison Interiors
Denver, CO
333-8761

Carolyn MacRossie, ASID
Carolyn MacRossie Interiors
Denver, CO
322-6357

47

very successful. They are expensive, but a lot of the stuff is recyclable in some way or another. Show houses often get published and they get seen by a lot of people. Show houses usually publish a catalog, which is a permanent document that people often keep. It's also a way you can do good work without having some dull client confining you at every turn (Figure 5-2)."

10. Get out with people and learn how they react to design.   Show houses offer you a chance to survey your market and talk to people about what they like. "The contact you have with the public is great," says Mary Ann Bryan. "It gives us a reality check on the market. Sometimes designers remove themselves from the real public. They need to be like their clients and know what they relate to. The show houses are a good way to get the feel of what people are interested in."

11. Have a clear marketing strategy for participating in a show house. Know how you will reach your target clients or achieve good publicity. Always be aware that a show house is a *marketing project,* not just another design project.

Rita Carson Guest found that her firm's publicity from a show house didn't help business because they didn't reach their firm's clientele. "We did our first — and last — show house. It was a living area constructed in a convention center, a project that raised money for the homeless. This was warehouse space with 40-ft ceilings, awful lighting, and concrete floors. We had to go in and build walls. Ours was the main showroom and we did a living area that won first-place awards. It was a lot of work and trouble for us — very expensive, even with some donations of materials. We found that the market that came to this type of thing were more people looking for ideas to do themselves rather than thinking of hiring a designer. We didn't get any jobs from it. The best thing it did was get us a lot of publicity. We won a national award, were featured in the local newspaper, and we were featured in two national ASID magazines by being a national ASID award winner."

12. Be prepared for the stress with a sense of humor.   You may have to work with difficult people who have very different motivations than yours — charity fundraisers don't see the project in the same way designers do. Be flexible, but make sure you get enough out of the project to make it worth your contribution.

13. Have patience — this is not quick-fix marketing.   Building credibility and name recognition takes place over years, not weeks. If you do show houses, your expectations have to be realistic about getting clients out of the event. You will benefit, but it probably won't be in time to pay the next studio rent check.

14. Be creative in thinking of new ways to do show houses.   One idea that came up in a discussion among designers about show houses was to take control of the project. Take the active role instead of accepting a mediocre situation as a passive participant. Instead of participating in a show house organized by the Symphony Guild or Junior League, designers could develop their own project to benefit Ronald McDonald House or a homeless shelter. You gain the headaches of planning and administration, but you also gain control of publicity — the critical piece for designers — and the good will of doing a community project.

CHECKLIST FOR A GOOD DECISION ON SHOW HOUSE PARTICIPATION

Show houses aren't right for everyone. Evaluate whether this is a good marketing strategy for you at this time. Always get clear on your reasons for doing it and check that your expectations are valid in this situation.

❏ Does the show house fit into my overall marketing design?

❏ Will this show house make me more visible and credible to *my target clients?*

❏ Is there adequate opportunity for good publicity for my business?

❏ Is there a budget to help me with my expenses? If not, can I afford the costs of doing a good job?

❏ Do I have the time available to demonstrate my best design ability?

❏ Will I have the opportunity to meet people at the show house?

❏ Will I get a list of names of attendees?

❏ Will my work be published in connection with the show house?

Demonstrating Your Skills: Model Homes

Designing a model shown to sell houses or condominiums is another good way to get your work in front of the public. Designers usually work out a contractual arrangement with a developer to do the model. "I started my business doing models for real estate projects," says Mary Ann Bryan. "I did the first condominium in Houston — I did two models for the developer. I must have had calls for ten years from those two models."

This demonstration of her design skills was excellent exposure for Mary Ann. She went on to design twenty projects in that condominium development, building her business and hiring other designers to complete the work.

Demonstrating Your Skills: Competitions

Investigate the competitions available in your design specialty. Many product manufacturers sponsor competitions. Professional design organizations also sponsor contests.

Plan your own publicity from your exposure through design competitions. Arrange to have press releases sent to local publications that are read by your clients. And make sure your clients know about any awards you have won. Send copies of publicity to your client list.

"Entering contests is a good way of getting free publicity," says B. J. Peterson. "It's important when you enter a contest to make sure that they do in fact have a publicity system set up. It doesn't do you any good to win an award if no one knows about it. Many local ASID chapters tie in with a local magazine which agrees to publish the winners."

Deborah Steinmetz finds that entering projects for award competitions elicits good will from clients. "If you win, it's an opportunity to share the success with the client. The client is really happy that what you did for them is appreciated by other people. They like to tell others and often will display the award. Watch for local and national ASID competitions. Every building association has an awards program. You can list the awards you have won on your resume."

"We try to keep track of all the major design competitions and their approximate deadlines along with the submittal requirements," says Cheryl Duvall. "That way we can keep a lookout for them and be ready in time. Sometimes you get notification of a design competition that is due in a month. That might not be enough time to schedule a photographer and get exactly what you want. If we know up front what is coming, we can plan for it better."

Show houses, designing models, and competitions are particularly good for new designers, because recognition isn't dependent on experience or past projects. This is something you can do well even if new to the business. It's a good way to build your reputation and get photographs of completed work for your portfolio (Figure 5-3).

Writing Articles

A published article with your byline conveys instant expert status to the public. Write an article about your design specialty for the local newspaper or for a relevant trade publication. Or write an article about a design project and submit it with photographs to your local city or regional magazine.

"If you like to write, this can be a great marketing advantage," says Mark Hampton, who enjoys writing. He started writing articles for *House and*

Bryan, Eilers and Walker Win ASID/Houston Chronicle Award

First Place, Residential:
Over 3,500 square feet

The 10th anniversary of the ASID/Houston Chronicle Interior Design Awards competition proved to be a banner year with a record 102 entries and 32 winners, also a new high. Winners for 1994 were announced at the gala ASID Awards Night ceremonies September 8 at The Majestic Metro theater

Ten first place awards were presented in tne eight categories, with two ties. and 22 honorable mentions. Announcement of the prestigious design awards followed the presentation of the American Society of Interior Designers' Gulf Coast Chapter awards.

Judges for the 1994 design competition—all from New Orleans—were Deborah Steinmetz, ASID National Director, IBD, of Steinmetz & Associates, John Burgin Barousse, ASID, of J Burgin Barousse Interior Design. and Judith Andre Verges, ASID, of Verges Associates Interiors.

The winning interiors are featured in the September 11 issue of Texas Magazine in the Houston Chronicle

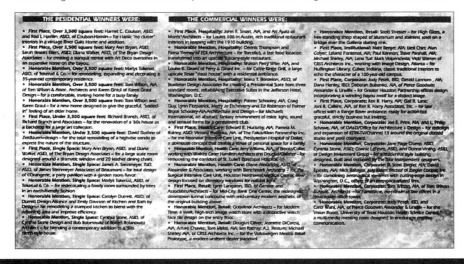

FIGURE 5-3 *The Bryan Design Associates' publicity for winning the ASID/Houston Chronicle Interior Design Awards. Reprinted from the Houston Chronicle, September 8, 1994.*

Garden about ten years ago. "I continued and published a couple of books, and those have had a big effect on my career. You know, the public's interest in our field is huge. I'm astounded by it every day. Local newspapers thrive on well-written pieces from designers working in the field."

Don't spend time on an article that won't reach potential clients. But you can and should use reprints of anything you write for additional marketing.

JANE'S NOTE

My work has been published in Colorado Homes & Lifestyles *and* Nashville. *I make myself photograph and send a possible article once a year. It's part of my marketing budget. Before and after articles make a great easy format with photos.*

Tips for Getting Published

1. Set goals for writing and publishing articles — an article every year or six months. Set aside time frequently to brainstorm possible topics for articles. This practice will get you into the habit of thinking about what people would like to learn about design or about your business.

2. It is easier to get published in local publications than in national trade or general interest magazines. So start small and local, then send reprints of these local publications — or a list of your publications — when you submit a manuscript to a national magazine. You have a better chance at getting a piece published if you have a publications record.

3. Short, to-the-point articles have the best chance of getting published. Two to four double-spaced typed pages is a good length.

4. Publication possibilities include
   - Local or weekly papers
   - Local free newspapers or other free shopping publications
   - Trade publications in your niche
   - Local business magazines
   - Local home and lifestyle magazines
   - National home and lifestyle magazines

5. Reach your target clients with your publications. "We try to write articles specifically for our target markets," says Rita Carson Guest. "We provide information and photos of local offices we have done for the local legal daily paper, the *Fulton Daily Report*. So they will publish our photos with an article on law firms recently opened. We've also done an article for the *Atlanta Business Chronicle* on *How to Keep Office Space Up to Date.*"

6. Call or send a query letter — a short letter describing your idea — to the editor before you send your article. Sending a query letter gives you the chance to change or add to your piece to make it more appealing to the editor.

7. Propose a column in a newspaper or magazine widely read by the clients you want.

8. Use the best photographs you can get. Magazine editors will be more likely to run your story if you furnish a set of striking professional photos free to the magazine. Each magazine will have its own required format for photographs. Know these details before you arrange to shoot your project. "The primary tool that can help market your business or you as a designer is magazine publicity," says Mark Hampton. "There is no comparable agent that can do for you what having your work published in magazines does. The way to get published early in your career if you don't have connections is to hire someone to take a few very good photographs of a good job or even your own house — even if you have to prop it up with extra things for the photos. Send those photographs off to magazines. I do know that magazines have always been dying for material. If you can send them attractive pictures, I think they always respond to that."

9. If your goal is to get photos of a design project published, take the time to write up all project details and, if possible, create an interesting story to accompany the project.

10. Before sending a piece to a trade magazine, become familiar with the type of articles and style of the publication. You want your first impression to the editor to be positive. Be as professional as you can in all dealings with editors to create a good impression, and everything you submit should be of high quality.

11. For double punch, run an ad in a publication in which you have a feature article.

12. If writing is not one of your skills or you don't have time, you can hire a writer to produce articles for you. Or get someone to edit your article for you before you submit it. Mary Ann Bryan says she has recently hired a writer. "I think it will make a world of difference. We work with the writer, brainstorming to come up with a story. We write the story first, then work out the photography. The writer has experience working with the magazines, so she knows how to work with the photographer and set up shots just like the magazines do. We don't do any photography until we have the story and know we can get it placed for free publicity."

For more help with writing articles, see the resources listed in the *Reference* section at the end of this book.

JANE'S NOTE

I published a story in the local newspaper—Changing Your Home for Different Seasons. *The most difficult part was finding the right person to contact at the newspaper. When I finally talked to the Home Editor, he said yes. The editor would like me to write articles regularly.*

The published article was 7 x 9 in. in the Sunday Home section. If I had taken out a similar retail advertisement, it would have cost me $545. I plan to use this article for additional marketing. I'll copy the article on a good-quality bond paper and include it in my portfolio. In addition, I'll send it to selected clients (Figure 5-4).

Giving Speeches

Public speaking demonstrates both your professionalism and your approachability. Speaking gives prospective clients a good look at you. Just seeing someone in person often makes it easier for a client to call you.

Pick your audience carefully—too many professionals make the mistake of only speaking to each other at professional organizations. It takes more effort to cultivate the contacts to be considered as a speaker in other contexts, but this is when public speaking will produce the most benefits.

Any number of topics would be the basis of a good speech. Your best choice will be a combination of client interests and your unique expertise.

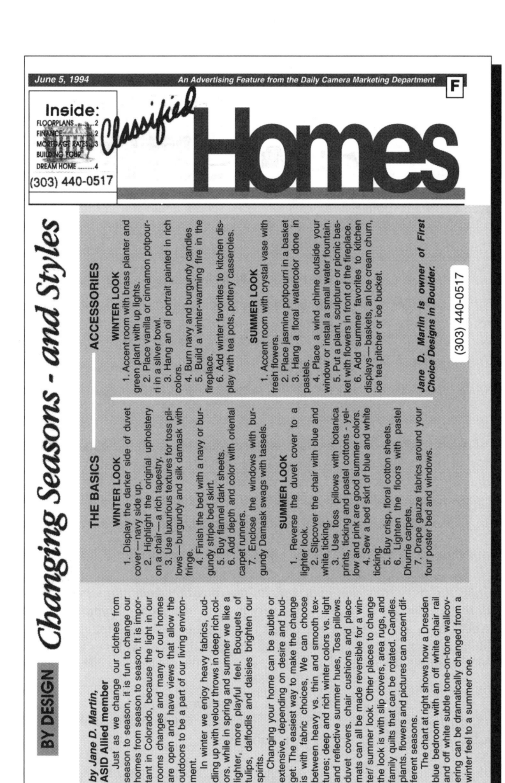

June 5, 1994 — An Advertising Feature from the Daily Camera Marketing Department — F

Inside:
FLOORPLANS.........2
FINANCE.............2
MORTGAGE RATES...3
BUILDING TOUR
DREAM HOME.......4
(303) 440-0517

Classified

Homes

BY DESIGN

Changing Seasons - and Styles

by Jane D. Martin,
ASID Allied member

Just as we change our clothes from season to season, it is fun to change our homes from season to season. It is important in Colorado, because the light in our rooms changes and many of our homes are open and have views that allow the outdoors to be a part of our living environment.

In winter we enjoy heavy fabrics, cuddling up with velour throws in deep rich colors, while in spring and summer we like a lighter, more playful feel. Bouquets of tulips, daffodils and daisies brighten our spirits.

Changing your home can be subtle or extensive, depending on desire and budget. The easiest way to make the change is with fabric choices, We can choose between heavy vs. thin and smooth textures; deep and rich winter colors vs. light and reflective summer hues, Toss pillows. duvet covers. chair cushions and placemats can all be made reversible for a winter/ summer look. Other places to change the look is with slip covers, area rugs, and family quilts that can be rotated. Candles. plants. flowers and pictures can accent different seasons.

The chart at right shows how a Dresden blue bedroom with an off white chair rail and off white subtle tone-on-tone wallcovering can be dramatically changed from a winter feel to a summer one.

THE BASICS

WINTER LOOK

1. Display the darker side of duvet cover—navy side up.
2. Highlight the original upholstery on a chair—a rich tapestry.
3. Use luxurious textures for toss pillows—burgundy and silk damask with fringe.
4. Finish the bed with a navy or burgundy stripe bed skirt.
5. Buy flannel dark sheets.
6. Add depth and color with oriental carpet runners.
7. Enclose the windows with burgundy Damask swags with tassels.

SUMMER LOOK

1. Reverse the duvet cover to a lighter look.
2. Slipcover the chair with blue and white ticking.
3. Use toss pillows with botanica prints, ticking and pastel cottons - yellow and pink are good summer colors.
4. Sew a bed skirt of blue and white ticking.
5. Buy crisp, floral cotton sheets.
6. Lighten the floors with pastel Dhurrie carpets.
7. Drape gauze fabrics around your four poster bed and windows.

ACCESSORIES

WINTER LOOK

1. Accent room with brass planter and green plant with up lights.
2. Place vanilla or cinnamon potpourri in a silver bowl.
3. Hang an oil portrait painted in rich colors.
4. Burn navy and burgundy candles
5. Build a winter-warming fire in the fireplace.
6. Add winter favorites to kitchen display with tea pots, pottery casseroles.

SUMMER LOOK

1. Accent room with crystal vase with fresh flowers.
2. Place jasmine potpourri in a basket
3. Hang a floral watercolor done in pastels.
4. Place a wind chime outside your window or install a small water fountain.
5. Put a plant, sculpture or picnic basket with flowers in front of the fireplace.
6. Add summer favorites to kitchen displays—baskets, an ice cream churn, ice tea pitcher or ice bucket.

Jane D. Martin is owner of First Choice Designs in Boulder.

(303) 440-0517

FIGURE 5-4 *Design article written for the* Boulder Daily Camera *by Jane D. Martin. Reprinted from the* Boulder Daily Camera, *June 5, 1994.*

How to Get the Most Out of Giving Speeches

1. It is easier than you may think to get an invitation to speak.   Write a letter to the program director of your target organizations, volunteer to speak, and give topic suggestions. Be sure to include the advantages to the audience of hearing your presentation. Follow your letter with a phone call if you haven't had a response.

JANE'S NOTE

I've found that many groups are looking for speakers: Chamber of Commerce, women's groups, service organizations, or church groups. I spoke at the Association of College Women, the Newcomers Club, and high school home economics classes. I got jobs through all.

Kathey E. Pear describes how her firm pursues speaking opportunities. "One of our best marketing ideas was to send out a letter with a little bit about me and the company, Pear Commercial Interiors, with a list of topics, saying, 'Kathey E. Pear or someone from her company will be available to speak on these topics.' We listed such topics as ergonomics and air quality. There were some things on the list we felt we'd have to research first. But our marketing consultant said, 'Oh yes, you'll rise to the occasion.'"

2. Find out before you approach an organization how many people you will reach.   Decide if this is a good way to spend your time. If you are asked to speak by an organization you haven't approached, ask questions about the audience to make sure you will speak to potential clients. Investigate how much publicity there will be.

3. Keep in mind that your goal is to reach prospective clients or a high prestige group that builds your expert status.   Know how you'll use this speaking engagement for your own publicity.

4. Most organizations schedule speakers months in advance.   Know the schedule and get your offer in front of the program director in time. Get familiar with the organization's interests. Know what speakers and topics they have had in the past.

5. Find out how long the program director expects you to speak and stick to that. The right length is 15–30 minutes. Practice to be sure your speech will fit your allotted time.

6. Be ready with a picture to include in the organization's newsletter or meeting announcement.

7. The best topics will be related to your business so you are demonstrating your knowledge and expertise. But your audience will be turned off by a sales pitch. Just give people solid information on a topic of interest to them.

8. Have well-designed handouts with your logo and business information so attendees carry something home about you. Or hand out reprints of a recent article.

9. Write your own introduction, making sure to include the key information you want potential clients to remember about you. This makes it easy for the person introducing your speech and ensures that the introduction will be a good one. If no one from the organization plans to introduce you, take the time to welcome the attendees yourself and share your introductory information.

10. Use discussion periods with attendees to find out about client problems. This technique can give you good feedback about client needs.

11. Don't hurry away after your speech is over. Stay to talk with people. Get business cards from the people who stay to talk or ask questions.

12. You can qualify potential clients at a speaking engagement by asking for a response. Get the names of those interested in getting a brochure, the next issue of a newsletter, or a reprint of a relevant article. Have those interested sign a list or give you their business cards.

13. Ask for a list of names of attendees or a copy of the membership roster. Another way to get a list of names is to have a drawing for a giveaway of some kind, having everyone put business cards in a bowl — then you keep the business cards for your mailing list. Or you could pass out a short survey on a subject relevant to your topic, asking for names and addresses from those who return it.

14. Plan ahead to piggyback your marketing efforts. Speeches can be recycled into an article or you can print copies on your letterhead and mail them to clients or prospective clients.

15. Keep practicing and getting feedback on your public speaking skill.
Take a class or join Toastmaster's International, form a support group of colleagues working on public speaking, or tape yourself and listen carefully.

"I give talks and I became a good speaker, but I didn't start out one," says Linda Blair. "As president of the local ASID chapter I had to give a lot of talks. I opened the Design Center in Washington with Donghia and Jack Lenor Larsen. I was a terrible speaker and I vowed never to go through that again.

TIPS FOR A GOOD SPEAKING PERFORMANCE

- Prepare your speech well ahead of time, planning the sequence and content to be clear and easy to follow. It may help you to write out the whole thing, but, if you do, be sure you read it aloud as you are writing. It should flow as a talk, not sound like a written article. Use short sentences and make the organization of your thoughts very clear.

- Don't read directly from your notes. Practice until you can speak with confidence from an outline or note cards with key words.

- Have your speech planned for the amount of time allowed and keep track of your time as you speak. If you start running over, be able to move ahead to your planned closing remarks.

- Plan how to involve your audience with questions, visuals, or audience participation. Learn to "read" your audience, to know if they are paying attention or getting bored or restless. If you have handouts, give them out at the end of your speech so your audience isn't reading instead of listening.

- Use your own style instead of trying to copy another speaker you admire.

- Make eye contact with your audience. Look at individuals and try to include everyone in the room.

- Approach your audience with respect for their time and intelligence—how would you like someone to tell you about this topic?

- Your dress should be professional and appropriate to your audience, but make sure you are physically comfortable. Practice your stance and gestures. Your audience wants you to be relaxed and natural so they can relax and listen to what you have to say.

I became a good speaker by taking some courses and taping myself. Now I'll give talks on anything. I speak for the profession and for myself and that is a very strong form of marketing because you reach out to people."

Teaching Classes or Seminars

Teaching is another avenue for establishing your credibility. Teaching others about your specialty or sharing some of your expertise confirms you as an authority in your subject.

If you are careful to select the right teaching opportunities, you may also reach potential clients. Most organizations send out a catalog of course offerings. Your name in the catalog is free advertising about your expertise sent out to this organization's mailing list.

Be creative in thinking up a list of organizations that could sponsor classes for you. The most common are schools or training programs sponsored by trade organizations. One of the most approachable teaching opportunities is adult education classes in community colleges or local community adult education programs.

Write a letter to the department head or program coordinator at the school and propose what you'd like to teach. Colleges and universities usually have previously contracted with teachers for standard courses, so you'll have a better chance if you propose something different.

Nancy Clanton, a lighting design specialist in Boulder, teaches in University Continuing Education classes and does seminars for engineering and technical societies. "As you know, if you are an instructor for a technical seminar, you are seen as the expert in the field. This is how I do my marketing."

June Towill Brown teaches classes to keep her name as a designer in the public eye. She has taught classes on interior design for the public through the extension program at UCLA for the last 17 years. She teaches a class in avoiding costly mistakes in interior design. She also teaches design students at UCLA — on cost estimating and project organization.

Rita Carson Guest's firm in Atlanta has found it useful to participate in legal technical seminars. "One was *Legal Tech*, a seminar Price Waterhouse put together, that had lots of speakers on technical topics concerning law firms. I was one of the speakers, and I got calls from prospective clients. It worked."

Getting Good Publicity

Publicity is getting your name and news about your business to the public. Publicity has more clout than paid ads because you aren't able to dictate the

PUTTING ON YOUR OWN SEMINAR

When you sponsor your own seminar, you'll market the seminar as well as present it. To ease the management burden, collaborate with other designers or professionals to share the work. Or do this as a joint venture—with a continuing education program, another school, or organization.

- Choose your seminar topic carefully. Your topic should be of interest to clients and lead to client interest in hiring you. So a do-it-yourself class in design is not a great choice for marketing your service.

- Charge a fee—people will take the seminar more seriously and assume it has value. Or consider doing a seminar as a fund raiser for charity. This is a good way to build your credibility while building community good will.

- Commit to careful planning and attention to the details of space and presentation. A high quality product is essential. An informal seminar can be in a studio setting; a more formal seminar will need appropriate space.

- Plan good publicity to advertise your seminar. Send out fliers or a letter to your client list.

- Plan your follow-up with attendees. Get them on your mailing list. Also, you should plan more personal follow-up with qualified prospective clients.

- Know your costs before heading into this—good budgeting is important to keep expenses under control.

message. Everything that potential clients see and hear through news media about your business is publicity—good or bad. The best insurance against bad publicity is conducting your business in an ethical and professional manner.

The people who have good luck in getting favorable free plugs for themselves and their businesses are those who understand how the news media work. They know how to cooperate with the system and help the people who produce the news.

It's true that many publications are looking for stories and news to fill their publications. But it's not true that they will be willing to print anything you give them. When you're trying to get good publicity, think about your request from the standpoint of the editor you're approaching. Lead with what makes this item of interest to his/her publication. And always be courteous and professional.

Tips for Getting Good Publicity

1. Know what is news and what makes an interesting story. Present your news with an interesting angle. Be sure it will tell a story about you that will genuinely interest others. Newsworthy topics are current or unusual. The definition of news may be different for various publications because they target different audiences.

2. Learn to observe your business with the eye of a publicity expert. There are many opportunities to turn events into news: a new contract, a party to celebrate a big installation, milestones or anniversaries, hiring new staff, or election to a leadership position in a trade organization. Winning an award is a perfect opportunity for publicity.

"I market everything I do," says Linda Blair. "For example, I was just fortunate enough to do a Lifetime cable show on how to buy a sofa. So I placed a story in our local newspaper that comes out on the Friday of the show. The article says *Blair on Lifetime TV discusses how to buy a sofa* — and I get this big play on the second page, all free. It doesn't matter if people saw the show because I got this play from it in the paper. I xerox the article and every time I give out my new packet I include it."

Cheryl Duvall says, "Doing good press releases requires a regular schedule and someone responsible for it who can think like a news reporter — pay attention to things that could be news and press releases. Good stories might be getting a new client or a new contract." Have good black and white photographs available of everyone on your staff.

3. Think about the possibilities of creating newsworthy events. Some examples are community service projects, speeches or seminars, or taking a stand on a controversial issue.

4. Don't limit your publicity efforts to the local newspaper. Consider all the news media available.

- Daily newspapers
- Radio
- Television
- Cable television channels

- Trade journals
- Consumer magazines — particularly city or regional
- Free local newspapers

5. Cultivate good contacts. Make the effort to meet the editors and writers of your local newspaper and magazines.   "I make it my business to know all the editors, both national and local, and they use me as a resource," says Charles Gandy. "Even though I may not give them the story, I can tell them who to call. So they keep calling me, and, eventually, the call will be a story they can do about me. It is constant. I think a third if not half of my time is spent in marketing. It is all soft sell. It's getting to know people as human beings first."

Kathey E. Pear says "I figured out the difference between public relations and advertising. I hired a PR consultant and she said — you can get publicity for free. Publicity is more credible and not slanted in your favor. You get better over time at recognizing opportunities that are there all the time." Kathey suggests getting to know the editors of your local paper or business journals and letting them know what your expertise is. You need to tell them the topics you can contribute. "I could be considered an expert on a variety of topics — people doing a story could call me for my opinion, quoting me in the story."

6. Community projects are excellent sources of publicity.   "Community service is a great way to do something for the community while letting people know that interior designers are not just about 'pretty'," says B. J. Peterson. "You educate the people you're doing the project with — hospice or a clinic or Ronald McDonald house. And then they understand that designers are about health and safety, and they are about how spaces function and how people use them. This kind of project can also be good free publicity for you. Newspapers and magazines are always interested in these kinds of projects. You have to follow through yourself to make sure the word gets out and the pictures get taken.

"For instance, there was a project that a group of eight of us in Los Angeles did several years ago called the L.A. Free Clinic. We entered it in a design competition and won. We also entered it for President Bush's 1000 Points of Light awards and won. So, if you do something like this, you have to let people know you did it."

7. Be creative and capitalize on unexpected publicity opportunities. Kathey E. Pear says that getting good publicity means being ready to respond to an opportunity — you have to be quick thinking and ready to act. "There was a Rudolph the Reindeer statue stolen from a Christmas display at the city-county building in Denver about five years ago. When I heard about it, it dawned on me that this was a good chance to build good will — and positive publicity — by helping out. I called the TV news people and offered to replace the statue. I got interviewed for TV and by the newspapers, and it created good will. It was a vague business reference in the publicity, but I got a lot of phone calls." There was a happy ending in this case as the statue mysteriously reappeared before the replacement was made, so Kathey's check wasn't needed. But her offer was remembered as a quick response to fill a community need.

June Towill Brown suggests being ready for unexpected publicity opportunities by carrying a camera loaded with black and white film. "When I was teaching in Japan I had my photograph taken with the principal, with the name of the school as a backdrop, and I can use that photo for PR."

HOW TO WRITE A GOOD PRESS RELEASE

A press release is a short news story or feature about your business distributed to editors of selected news media. To get the attention you want — and to get your release published as a news story — it needs to be newsworthy, have an angle, and tell a story. Your press release should show why this story has value for the editor and the publication. (See Figure 5-5 for format.)

- Check your mailing list — correct names are important. Be sure you have the correct title (Business Editor, City Editor, House and Garden Editor, and so on), but avoid sending a press release to a title without a name.

- Write the release well. Make it concise and interesting. Be sure all the pertinent information is included.

- Get out your news release in plenty of time for it to be accepted by your release date.

- Many press releases are boring and bland. Give yours some backbone — have something to say or a controversial perspective.

- Try formatting the body of your release to draw the eye and focus attention. Use bullet points or boxes.

COMPANY NAME

ADDRESS

CITY, STATE, ZIP CODE

HEADLINE

SUBTITLE

For Immediate Release

Date:

Contact: NAME

                 COMPANY NAME

                 PHONE

(City)   *BODY OF TEXT*

FIGURE 5-5   *Press release format.*

Study the following example of a press release and try drafting one of your own.

MGB Design
16 Peach Street
Boston, Massachusetts 02123

MGB Design Creates Team Space

For Immediate Release
Wednesday, May 03, 1995

Contact: *M. G. Buffington*
MGB Design
617-554-9964

[*Boston*]—Widgets, Inc., has partnered with MGB Design to transition Widgets' staff from private offices to a more efficient and ergonomic "team space" environment. The new design reorganizes the company's work areas to support its new focus on product development teams.

MGB Design is a contract furniture dealer, offering a full range of commercial interior services, including space planning and project management. The company has a showroom in Boston. MGB Design, headquartered in Boston, serves businesses throughout the Northeast.

FIGURE 5-6   Example of a press release.

"BUT HOW CAN I BE AN EXPERT WHEN I'M JUST GETTING STARTED?"

Let's pause for a short break. We know from talking to designers that some of you may be feeling intimidated right about now. We frequently hear the question: How can I put myself out there as an expert when I don't yet have years of experience to promote? If you are feeling this way, first relax and understand that this is a normal reaction. There's nothing wrong with you for feeling a little shaky. But also realize that your prospective clients don't need to hear about your doubts. They need the reassurance that comes from your ability to solve their problems.

And this is one of the times it won't help you to think about your competition. If you're new in business, you can talk yourself out of the running if you focus too much on other designers' years of experience compared to your months. Instead, focus on your knowledge and your skills — and how these can help your client.

Whether you are new to the business or have years of design experience, the key to claiming credibility is to commit yourself to being the best designer you can be. This means constant learning and continuing to build your knowledge and skills.

"I have had a long and blessed career and I've spent my entire adult life seeking designers and places they have done; in Europe and the United States there are great houses and gardens that are open to the public," says Mark Hampton. "I have known many great designers and all have spent their time traveling to see all the beautiful things in the world. I think if you want to make yourself a designer who has authority, you must develop your own taste and talent. I think people in the design world are just like people in any other profession. The more they know, the more respect they will get — and the more seriously they will be considered by their clients."

Know the Benefits of Your Expertise

Know the benefits of choosing you as a designer. This means understanding the particular expertise you offer a client, and knowing how to say it clearly and directly. A clear statement of benefits keeps the focus on your strengths — and away from your status as a newcomer. In addition, knowing your source of expertise is a tremendous confidence booster. Instead of trying to say "I'm the greatest" you can focus on your knowledge and how that will help the client.

Practice describing yourself and your business with positive words. Let the news out that you are good. Be ready to tell people the benefits of hiring you as a designer. When you introduce yourself, it's important to be able to come across as an expert in 15–20 seconds.

Without a market niche or specialty, designers sometimes find it hard to communicate benefits clearly. "I have a value-added list of things I think I do best," says B. J. Peterson. "Things I do that other design firms don't do as well — or at all. It's a typed list, and I include it in my publicity packets and my brochure for prospective clients. I review and update this list every year." Make a list of the benefits of your design service and turn it into a value-added list to share with clients.

JANE'S NOTE

When I introduce myself to potential clients, I say: "I help people focus on what makes an environment enjoyable, and then I work with them to create it. Doing this well is fun and rewarding for me."

Mary Ann Bryan says her firm's approach to residential design is not to strive for the reputation of trend-setter — the innovator who pushes for a highly individual look or style. She states the firm's benefits this way. "Our expertise is in helping people create an environment that brings out who they are — an environment that they feel comfortable with and can afford. We are known as problem-solvers. We have the ability to balance things, to work within the paradox posed in balancing money, beauty, and function."

Deborah Steinmetz's firm specializes in interior planning in New Orleans. The designers have created a data bank of building plans that they make available to building owners and managers. This detailed information is already created in computer aided design software (CAD) and can be import-

---

HOW TO BUILD YOUR CONFIDENCE

- Attend training sessions and seminars to learn the latest information on materials and design techniques. Interior design professional associations have many free seminars on techniques, new products, and so on. Know the issues critical to your field.

- Get training in public speaking and self presentation. There are many workshops, classes, and private coaches or consultants available to help you.

- Learn from others. Observe closely. Find a mentor to learn from. Always ask questions.

- Form a peer group to pool knowledge and learn together. Practice being confident.

- Build your knowledge of good design through travel and study.

- Keep up with trade journals and professional associations.

- Use the power of synergy. Surround yourself with the excellence of other designers. Don't try to do it all alone. Get balance from others— share ideas and create together.

ed into a client's word-processing system. "This service is a great time-saver for clients. Once they have it in-house, they can pull it up and manipulate it — zoom in and out, add text, and then fax it directly out." This innovative idea creates a unique competitive marketing advantage. "Our approach has been to combine a deep investment in technological expertise with our design expertise. We feel we're on the leading edge with this and this is a benefit we can promote to our clients," says Deborah.

Ideas to Remember from This Chapter

- Marketing a design service is the process of building a relationship with the client. Marketing requires repeat encounters to build trust through *visibility* and *credibility.*
- Residential designers build visibility by participating in activities in which they will meet potential clients. Commercial designers build visibility by understanding their clients' businesses and by becoming an insider in clients' industries.
- Designing models and show houses and entering competitions are methods for demonstrating your design skills to the public. These methods are most effective when you take charge of reaching your target clients and establishing your reputation through publicity.
- Public speaking, publishing, teaching classes, and getting publicity are excellent methods for building visibility and credibility with prospective clients.
- Build your confidence as an expert in your design specialty by knowing the benefits of your services and by constantly learning and expanding your design knowledge.

CHAPTER 6

Building a Relationship with Prospective Clients

Marketing Methods That Get Results

The marketing methods described in this chapter build on your credibility and visibility as you move into the next stage of the marketing process — building a personal relationship with prospective clients. Your marketing packet, portfolio, and other materials will provide illustrations as you tell your marketing story to the client. Advertising gets your name and your message in front of the client. And your marketing promotions reach out to the client. The entire marketing process builds your relationship with the client to produce a meeting or presentation — your opportunity to sell your design services.

MARKETING IS A RELATIONSHIP-BUILDING PROCESS

Marketing design services is a multi-step process that takes place over time. Everything you do that is seen or heard by the client delivers a marketing message. All of your marketing methods should work together to build a consistent image and message.

125

፫፫፫

In This Chapter

This chapter explains the many marketing methods that can be used in building your relationship with prospective clients. In this phase of marketing, you have the chance to communicate directly with them. You will learn

- How to present a consistent professional image.

- How to create and use effective marketing packets, brochures, portfolios, and other marketing materials.

- The most effective advertising techniques for designers.

- How to use direct mail and telephone follow-up to build your relationship with clients.

"The more things you do, it just adds and adds," says Charles Gandy of Atlanta. "Plus you get into what you are doing. It becomes enthusiasm. I believe in the three E's in marketing—energy, excitement, and enthusiasm."

The array of marketing methods described in this book build a prospective client's knowledge and trust in your business. But remember to be selective—choose to use the methods that make the most sense for your business. Ask the following questions to assess how well each marketing method will work for you:

- How does this method contribute to your overall marketing strategy?
- What do you expect to gain by using this method?
- How will you use this method to your advantage?
- How will you know whether or not it works?

PRESENTING A CONSISTENT IMAGE

Your professional image sets the stage for the rest of your marketing communications. The marketing message conveyed through your office or studio and your personal image should be consistent with the rest of your marketing design.

Remember that your *image* is a reflection of your personal and professional *reality*. The phrase "creating an image" is misleading. No one can successfully conjure up and sustain a professional image not based in reality. Your image and style show your clients who you are.

How you dress is part of your marketing message. There is no uniform dress standard for designers. You'll find that dress varies according to your target clients—you want to look as if you fit in with them. The image you reflect through your dress should be appropriate to client expectations. It's fine to show your creativity and awareness of design through your clothing, but your image should promise reliability as well as designer ability. So strike a professional balance. If you're not sure how to dress, consider hiring an image consultant to check the image you convey and prescribe changes.

Think of your personal image and your printed materials as the "package" for your service. Since what you sell is essentially intangible, the client sees these tangible factors as the proxy for your service. Your office, your dress, how the phone is answered, how your studio looks—these are all clues for clients about your approach to design and how you will work on their project.

Make the package that introduces your business to the client as attractive and consistent with your service quality as you can.

1. Choose a business name that projects the character of your business. Many designers and other professionals use their names because their skill is the core of their service's benefits. Another approach is to choose a memorable name that describes a benefit or specialty of your service.

2. Your office should make a good first impression. Make sure your studio is an example of your best design work. Clients assume they are seeing an example of what you consider good design when they see your office or studio.

3. Your answering machine message markets for you—use the message to stress your uniqueness.

4. Use your studio to further your marketing—mount your design awards or reprints of publicity on a wall where clients will see them as they enter. Display boards from past projects in your studio.

TANGIBLE TOOLS OF THE MARKETING TRADE

Company Graphics

Company graphics are the "look" of the basic tangible items you use to conduct your business and communicate with your clients. Any item on which your business name appears is part of your company graphics. Your graphics should be consistent with both your market and your mission — the best graphics are always appropriate as well as stylish.

The basic components of company graphics are

- Logo
- Office or studio sign
- Business cards
- Stationery and envelopes
- Contracts
- Invoices
- Promotional and publicity material
- Advertisements

Lay out your marketing materials and evaluate them through your clients' eyes. What do the graphics and the quality of materials tell you about this company? Do you see the polished professional image you want to present?

Be sure you use your logo and elements of design to pull everything together. Your company graphics are your visual identity — make it easy for clients to recognize you and remember you (Figure 6-1).

Your company graphics stay with the client as reminders of what your business is — make them appropriate to the kind of client you hope to attract. "Our business card is very plain," says Rita Carson Guest. "It caters to the legal market. Law firms have very conservative cards and that's the way ours is. We want them to feel comfortable with us, so our cards are lawyer-like — not designer-like (Figure 6-2)."

Many designers are trained in graphic design and can confidently create their own logos and graphic images. But if you know graphic design isn't your strength — or you'd like help in focusing your graphic message — seek out a good graphic designer with experience in creating the right business image.

"One of the things people starting out should be aware of is to be sure to get a good advertising agency to help them with their cards," advises Sarah Boyer Jenkins. "The image they present through cards — the first thing the client sees — must be professional. Any ad or even a drawing in a brochure for a show house must be done professionally, not just scribbled off. That professional image we project really means business."

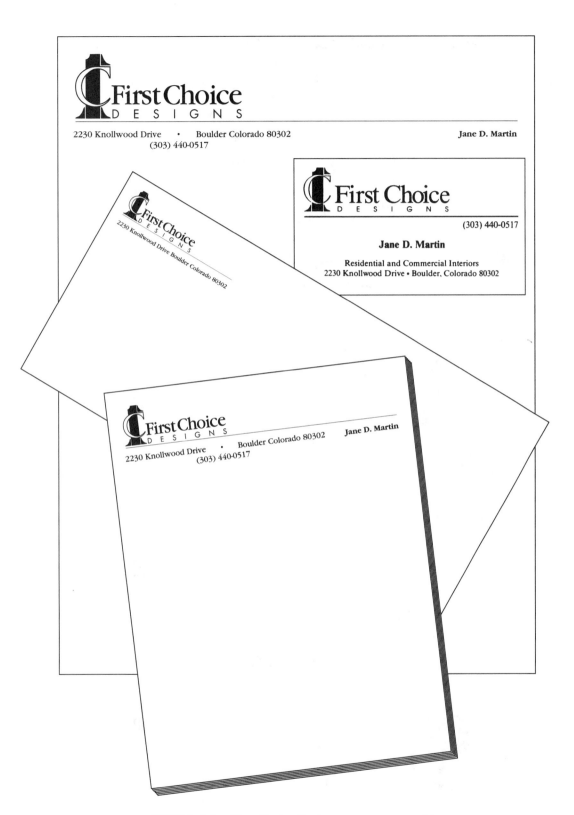

FIGURE 6-1 First Choice Designs company graphics.

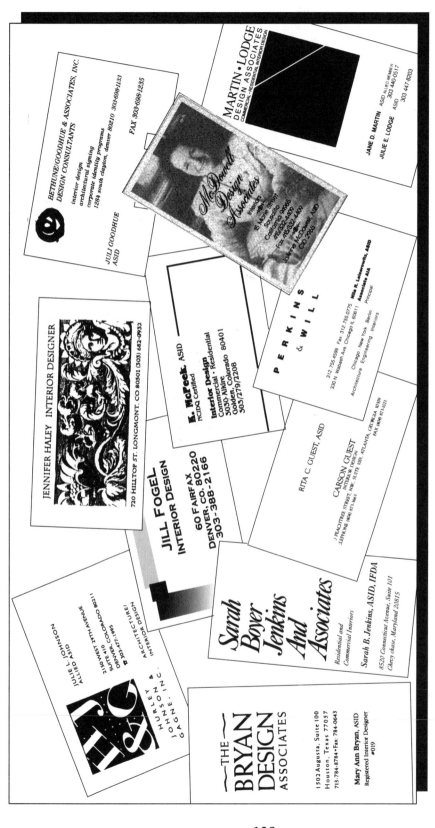

FIGURE 6-2 A sampling of designers' business cards. Clockwise from top left: Julie L. Johnson, Allied ASID, Hurley Johnson & Gagne, Inc. Card designed by David R. Baker; Jill Fogel, Interior Design; Jennifer Haley, Interior Designer. Artwork provided by Dover Publications; K. McPeek, ASID, Interior Design; Juli Goodhue, ASID, Bethune/Goodhue & Associates; Jo Anne McDowell, ASID, McDowell Design Associates; Jane D. Martin, ASID Allied Member, and Julie E. Lodge, ASID, Martin•Lodge Design Associates; Nila R. Leiserowitz, ASID, Perkins & Will; Rita C. Guest, ASID, Carson Guest; Sarah Boyer Jenkins, ASID, IFDA, Sarah Boyer Jenkins and Associates. Card designed by Greg DesRoches; Mary Ann Bryan, ASID, The Bryan Design Associates.

130

TIPS FOR EFFECTIVE BUSINESS CARDS AND GRAPHICS

- Use of graphics is a good way to set yourself apart from competitors. A good logo projects what your business means to you. It should convey the essence of your business in a crisp and memorable image.

- It is often helpful to be able to reproduce your logo in photocopy. It's also nice to be able to write on the back of it.

- Business cards must be functional, giving clients all the information necessary to reach you: business name and logo, your name and title, address, phone and fax numbers. Organize this information where a client would expect to find it—phone number at the bottom right and in larger type.

- If your office is difficult to find, consider putting directions to your office on the back of your card.

- For all company graphics use high quality design and materials.

Portfolios

A good portfolio is essential to show prospective clients the nature and quality of your work. Your portfolio can include photographs, drawings and floorplans.

Plan your portfolio with the client's perspective in mind. A collection of glossy pictures may not be enough to tell your full story and get the client's attention. Be creative and thoughtful in your text that accompanies the photos of your work. "Over my years in business the least effective marketing money I have spent has gone to our portfolio," says Mary Ann Bryan. "My thinking now is that a lot of the photos were worthless because we didn't do enough to stage them, to write a story about them. It pays to do more than just photograph.

"I know a young designer who has built her business in a very short time because she's really good at staging photos for her portfolio. A photograph is just romance—a good professional photographer knows how to do this. This designer had a friend who knew how to do it and it made all the difference in the world. Her first pictures were her own house, carefully staged views with details like more plants or a comforter added. Her portfolio always gets attention. It's amazing the business she has gotten from the pictures in the portfolio, basically out of thin air."

Residential designers may want to emphasize their ability to work in very different styles to express the clients' tastes. Or note the way new items and design work well with existing furnishings or collectibles. Clients of commercial designers may want to see examples of well-designed projects — that were accomplished smoothly on schedule and under budget. Make everything in your portfolio work to display all of your strengths.

When you are starting a design business, you usually have to scramble to fill a portfolio with photographed work. Have your own home photographed. Or do a special project just to get portfolio photographs. Arrange a discounted fee in exchange for the opportunity to get photographs. Or arrange to get photos of work you did while still a student or working for another design firm.

"I've developed an inexpensive way to create a portfolio that actually looks quite professional," says Ellen C. Jeffers. "It can be done using your own snapshots of jobs or pictures of your work published in magazines. I took my pictures to a copy shop and had them blown up on 8½ by 11-in. card stock. These pages are then spiralbound into a booklet. My business logo is enlarged on the front cover." As you collect more photos, you can create different portfolio versions to demonstrate different areas of client interest. As Ellen says, "You're only limited by your own creativity and that of your helper at the color copy machine." Especially if you're a new designer, this can be a good way to get started without spending a lot of money.

Marketing Information Packets

The marketing information packet is our favorite tool for getting your basic marketing message to a client. A marketing packet is more impressive than a single brochure, and it can answer specific client concerns more readily. The packet folder is a convenient size and format to keep for reference. Smaller brochures are far too easy to lose.

Use your company graphics to ensure an integrated image in your marketing packet. Invest in a high-quality folder for your packet with your logo and company name printed or embossed on the cover. Brochures and business cards can be included in the packet.

"I learned to do the packet I use at an old ASID seminar," says B. J. Peterson. "They had the idea of doing a flexible packet based on a nice folder with slots along the side and a place for your business card. I buy a high-quality folder and use a nice printed label with my logo, name, and address. Inside I can tuck all kinds of things appropriate to the client: current things I have published, an up-to-date bio, and so on."

PORTFOLIO BASICS

1. *Your portfolio should represent your best work.*
   "Take black and white photos before you begin work on show houses or your projects, then take great color photographs of your finished designs," says June Towill Brown. "Then you can show dramatic before and after photos in your portfolio—use the black and white for the before picture, with a fabulous color blow-up next to it for after. Clients love that."

2. *Good quality photos are a must.*
   Be willing to pay for the best photographer you can find.

3. *Keep your portfolio up to date.*
   Budget for this continuing investment in good photography. "When we interview we always show prospective clients our portfolio," says Sarah Boyer Jenkins. "We just updated ours—it's important to do that. We have photographs in the portfolio but we also carry copies of all the magazines we have been published in because seeing the magazines is important to them."

4. *Use the portfolio to show clients projects that relate to their needs.*
   Customize your portfolio before meeting with a client. Find out what sort of project they have in mind and take examples of similar projects.

5. *A mediocre portfolio is a waste of money.*
   You need high-quality visuals, an interesting narrative, and a strategy for using the portfolio in active marketing.

6. *Use an attractive and long-wearing binder for your portfolio.*
   Using a large portfolio allows you to display large pictures of jobs. These photos look like magazine covers.

JANE'S NOTE

I always go with the photographer to shoot photographs. We discuss the angle and the image I want. I tell the photographer the purpose of the photo—highlighting the window, showing special details, or capturing the outdoor feel of the room. We arrange the props together, moving a plant, hiding the phone, and adding fresh flowers. I always look through the camera when the photographer is ready to shoot so I can be sure I'm getting the photos I want.

SUGGESTED ENCLOSURES FOR MARKETING PACKETS

- *Bio:* Offer profile of you as a designer. Include your education, awards received, and your business/design philosophy.
- *Fact Sheet:* Include description and benefits of your service. Highlight your specialty and be sure to list all your services.
- *Client List:* Ask clients for permission to list their names with projects completed.
- *Testimonials:* Provide endorsements from satisfied clients.
- *Reprints:* Present copies of articles about your business or your published work.
- *Photographs and Descriptions of Projects.*
- *Blueprints:* Use for commercial projects.
- *Brochure.*
- *Reference List:* Include phone numbers for your references. Some designers keep references separate from the rest of the marketing material and tell the client a list is available if they are interested.

Clients find marketing packets more interesting than brochures. The packets are more involving and people are more inclined to browse through them. Organize your packet well, making things easy to find. It's nice to be able to see different items at the same time, so consider using a folder with staggered packets for inserts.

Think through how you will use your marketing packet and your portfolio to tell your story. Everything you need to demonstrate your skill and experience should be in them. But beware of including too much, drowning the client's attention in unimportant facts. Keep it simple so the most important things will be clear and memorable to the client.

The advantage of the marketing packet is its flexibility in tailoring your marketing message to each client. The packet is also easy to use and relatively inexpensive to produce. You can keep most of these items on file in your computer and print them out on regular size paper. It's convenient to copy small quantities as needed instead of the large print run required to make professional printing economical. Color copying makes photos and other visuals simple to produce for customized packets. Using a marketing packet makes it easier to keep your materials up to date.

FIGURE 6-3 *Jane's marketing packet. Simple and cost efficient—a shiny folder with the company label on the front. Contents include a client letter, designer profile, service offerings, current projects, testimonials, business card, and published project. Photographs by R. W. Springgate. Feature article reprinted with permission of Colorado Homes & Lifestyles magazine.*

First Choice
D E S I G N S

2230 Knollwood Drive   ·   Boulder Colorado 80302
(303) 440-0517

Jane D. Martin

Dear Client,

Thank you for the opportunity to meet with you. Your project sounds exciting and I would love to work with you. Updating and lightening your home are the kinds of projects I enjoy. I have enclosed a number of items for you to look at in my packet.

1. Profile
2. Services
3. Current Projects
4. Testimonials
5. Photographs of my work
6. Newspaper reprint
7. Business card

PS I will call yo

First Choice
D E S I G N S

2230 Knollwood Drive   ·   Boulder Colorado 80302
(303) 440-0517

Jane D. Martin

PROFILE

Jane D. Martin
Interior Designer

Mission Statement
My mission is to help clients create a beautiful home or office environment which reflects their personality, treasures and lifestyle. The design will be artistic, balanced and honest. Integrity is most important in all my relationships.

My specialties include space planning, design concepts, fabric and finish selections, furniture and lighting choices and working with contractors, craftsmen, and architects.

I have owned my own firm for 16 years in San Francisco, Nashville, and Boulder and handle both residential and commercial projects.

Education
A.A., Watkins C
B.S., Indiana U
A.A., Stephens,

Professional
Who's Who in
American Socie

Publications
Dining Room fe
Listed in Colora
Kitchen remodel

Community
Boulder Chambe
Leadership Bou
CEO Exchange G
Pizazz Decorati
Newcomers Boa
Student Leaders

First Choice
D E S I G N S

2230 Knollwood Drive   ·   Boulder Colorado 80302
(303) 440-0517

Jane D. Martin

SERVICES

DESIGN SERVICES

FURNITURE/DESIGN AND SELECTION

FLOOR COVERINGS

WINDOW TREATMENTS

PAINT AND COLOR CHOICES

FURNITURE ARRANGEMENT

LIGHTING

WALL COVERINGS

ACCESSORIES

ARTWORK

DRAWINGS

PURCHASING, INSTALLING AND EXPEDITING

FIGURE 6-3   *(continued)*

First Choice
D E S I G N S

2230 Knollwood Drive · Boulder Colorado 80302   Jane D. Martin
(303) 440-0517

RECENT PROJECTS IN BOULDER AND VAIL AREAS

<u>CLIENT</u>	<u>PROJECT</u>
Andrews residence	Complete face lift of 1970 home. Job included space planning, wall coverings, use of owners' furniture, upholstery, window treatments, rugs, fabric headboard, duvet, pillows, slipcovers, as well as art and other accessories.
Dr. Brenton office	Total remodel of 1960 office. Project included space planning, design concept, lighting, furniture selection, wall covering, window treatments, drawings, cabinetry, paint, art and accessories.
Greenhouse residence	Living room area update. Project included space planning and purchase of furniture, rug and artwork.
Hinchman residence	Pro... furn... the...
Jensen residence	Rer... livir... Pro... uph...
Johnson condominium	Rer... the... and...
Kohnen residence	Nev... uph...
Matheson residence	Rer... roo... furr... is...

First Choice
D E S I G N S

2230 Knollwood Drive · Boulder Colorado 80302   Jane D. Martin
(303) 440-0517

TESTIMONIALS

Jane Martin of First Choice Designs, through tremendous talent and true concern for her clients, has created in our home an elegant, classic look which is a delight for the eyes as well as being warm and cozy for relaxed living.

Her ideas and hard work are much appreciated.
Marcia Wyatt

My experiences with interior designers has been limited, mainly because I had the attitude that I knew what I liked, and I was afraid a designer would come in and push their "style" on me. A family's personality is reflected in the style and decor of their home and it takes a true professional to sense what will be appealing, as well as functional, for each family.

Jane Martin has that professional ability. With cheerfulness and sensitivity, she took the time to listen. Jane was open to my suggestions and ideas and then used her knowledge to "stretch" my imagination. We now have the look and feel I wanted in our home-but with Jane's help it is even more beautiful than I imagined it could be! Jane took the fear out of designing our home.
Janet Andrews

I have lots of ideas, but very little ability to picture them in my home, nor do I know where or how to execute them, and then some of the ideas aren't so great, and I need more creative ones. That is why I need an interior designer.

Jane Martin has been wonderful as an interior designer for me. She has guided, helping me to refine and develop my ideas, made suggestions, offered solutions for problem areas, and has helped me execute the whole into a reality.

Her greatest attribute has been her ability to make my house reflect my taste. Using most of my old furniture and treasures, she jelled them into a coordinated, artistic whole. I want to thank her and certainly sing her praises and highly recommend her talents.
Libby Kohnen

FIGURE 6-3   *(continued)*

137

Inside:
FLOORPLANS........2
FINANCE............2
MORTGAGE RATES....3
BUILDING TOUR
DREAM HOME 4
(303) 440-0517

Classified

Homes

BY DESIGN

Changing Seasons - and Styles

**by Jane D. Martin,
ASID Allied member**

Just as we change our clothes from season to season, it is fun to change our homes from season to season. It is important in Colorado, because the light in our rooms changes and many of our homes are open and have views that allow the outdoors to be a part of our living environment.

In winter we enjoy heavy fabrics, cuddling up with velour throws in deep rich colors. while in spring and summer we like a lighter, more playful feel. Bouquets of tulips, daffodils and daisies brighten our spirits.

Changing your home can be subtle or extensive, depending on desire and budget. The easiest way to make the change is with fabric choices, We can choose between heavy vs. thin and smooth textures; deep and rich winter colors vs. light and reflective summer hues, Toss pillows. duvet covers. chair cushions and placemats can all be made reversible for a winter/ summer look. Other places to change the look is with slip covers, area rugs, and family quilts that can be rotated. Candles. plants. flowers and pictures can accent different seasons.

The chart at right shows how a Dresden blue bedroom with an off white chair rail and off white subtle tone-on-tone wallcovering can be dramatically changed from a winter feel to a summer one.

THE BASICS

WINTER LOOK

1. Display the darker side of duvet cover—navy side up.
2. Highlight the original upholstery on a chair—a rich tapestry.
3. Use luxurious textures for toss pillows—burgundy and silk damask with fringe.
4. Finish the bed with a navy or burgundy stripe bed skirt.
5. Buy flannel dark sheets.
6. Add depth and color with oriental carpet runners.
7. Enclose the windows with burgundy Damask swags with tassels.

SUMMER LOOK

1. Reverse the duvet cover to a lighter look.
2. Slipcover the chair with blue and white ticking.
3. Use toss pillows with botanica prints, ticking and pastel cottons - yellow and pink are good summer colors.
4. Sew a bed skirt of blue and white ticking.
5. Buy crisp, floral cotton sheets.
6. Lighten the floors with pastel Dhurrie carpets,
7. Drape gauze fabrics around your four poster bed and windows.

ACCESSORIES

WINTER LOOK

1. Accent room with brass planter and green plant with up lights.
2. Place vanilla or cinnamon potpourri in a silver bowl.
3. Hang an oil portrait painted in rich colors.
4. Burn navy and burgundy candles
5. Build a winter-warming fire in the fireplace.
6. Add winter favorites to kitchen display with tea pots, pottery casseroles.

SUMMER LOOK

1. Accent room with crystal vase with fresh flowers.
2. Place jasmine potpourri in a basket
3. Hang a floral watercolor done in pastels.
4. Place a wind chime outside your window or install a small water fountain.
5. Put a plant, sculpture or picnic basket with flowers in front of the fireplace.
6. Add summer favorites to kitchen displays—baskets, an ice cream churn, ice tea pitcher or ice bucket.

Jane D. Marlin is owner of First Choice Designs in Boulder.

(303) 440-0517

FIGURE 6-3 (continued)

FIGURE 6-3   (continued)

139

"We customize," says Nila R. Leiserowitz. "We have brochure pages that have photographs of our projects with a tissue overlay that describes what the project is about and the square footage cost. We can customize this to fit the client; for example, if they are a small client with 300 sq ft, we share with them projects that are relevant to them."

You can easily create special information pieces to include for individual clients. "We use a brochure that is a folder so we can be flexible in the things we show to a client," says Mary Ann Bryan. "We have an insert for the folder that has three rectangular shapes for photographs. We keep photos of projects in files—we can get them reproduced reasonably 100 at a time. So we can customize the brochure by choosing which three photos to include: If we are seeing a client for a commercial job, we can have three commercial project photos in their brochure"(Figure 6-4).

Brochures

A brochure is a pamphlet that introduces and describes your design services to a prospective client. A brochure can play a strong support role in your marketing, but don't fall into the trap of viewing it as a complete marketing program.

Before you invest in developing a brochure, think through whether you actually need one. Be sure that you have sound marketing reasons for producing one. A more flexible marketing packet may be a better investment to meet your needs. It's easy to waste money on a brochure that doesn't really help you. Plan ahead and know how you intend to use your brochure.

Ask yourself the following questions before investing in a brochure:

1. Who is my audience: Who am I trying to reach and what do they need to know about my business?

2. What do I want to accomplish through this brochure: Get a request for more information? Get clients to call for an appointment? Create receptivity to future contact?

3. Would another marketing tool be more appropriate to accomplish my purpose?

4. How do I plan to use this brochure: How will it fit into my overall marketing program?

5. How will I distribute the brochure to prospective clients: Hand out at interviews? Send in the mail? Leave behind after a meeting?

"We have a simple brochure for mass giveaways at events like trade shows or to mail in response to a first inquiry," says Deborah Steinmetz.

"This simple brochure is trifold black and white that is easy to mass-produce. It has our name, address and phone, a couple of black and white photos, a bit about the firm, and our philosophy. I don't think it has directly brought me any business but people expect you to give them something when you are at a show or ask for more information. Often they don't care what you send as long as you have responded. I don't see what I would gain by having a wonderful, pristine $20,000 brochure. Particularly in my business you have to be very flexible and tailor materials to the needs of the client."

TIPS FOR CREATING EFFECTIVE BROCHURES

- Your purpose and strategy for using your brochure will govern what kind you need. The most common are the full-size bound pamphlet, the single front and back fact sheet, or a trifold single-sheet brochure. The full-size brochure is more expensive to produce, but it has space for photos and is less likely to get lost or thrown away.

- Be sure to focus the brochure copy on the information the *client wants* to know. Tell clients how you will solve their problems—focus on your benefits, not the features of your business. Use your clients' language rather than designer language.

- Have clients tell your story in the brochure. Use photos of projects and quote satisfied clients—use their words to tell the benefits of your service.

- Brochures have a lot of competition for client attention. Make yours memorable and don't waste the client's time. A good brochure uses concise language, gives a clear and sincere message, and demonstrates that you understand client concerns. It should use excellent graphics—appropriate to and representative of your design skill.

- Get a copy writer to work with you on the text. You want a clear message of your uniqueness and your benefits.

- Quality is important but an overly extravagant brochure doesn't make a good impression.

- Update the brochure regularly to keep it sounding fresh and to be sure it doesn't get dated.

The Bryan Design Associates' strength and depth of experience benefit not only our design staff but ultimately each of our clients.

Mutual respect, support, the freedom to explore and develop an individual style — all combine to allow a wide variety of design philosophies to thrive under the same roof.

And our project types are varied. We design homes for those who desire something unique and personal. We apply our considerable experience in the banking, legal and corporate communities as well as with restaurants, retail shops and the hospitality industry.

Established in 1961, we bring three decades of seasoned design experience to every assignment.

Along with that experience, a commitment to the future, yours and ours, is our pledge of excellence.

We believe beauty and order are essential to a life well-lived. Knowing something about how these bring harmony takes many years of training. However, the translation to an environment which makes you feel at home, productive and fulfilled takes more than just years.

It also takes a certain dedication to knowing and understanding the act of creating.

At Bryan Design we are committed to excellence, to our impeccable reputation and to creating in partnership with all our clients.

•••

We co-create special environments in partnership with clients who desire high level interior design and who appreciate the experience, talent and wisdom we deliver.

1502 AUGUSTA, SUITE 100
HOUSTON, TEXAS 77057
FAX (713) 784-0643
(713) 784-8784

FIGURE 6-4 *Customized marketing packet insert used by The Bryan Design Associates includes three windows for photographs chosen to fit client needs. Library photograph by Hickey-Robertson. Living room photograph by Rex Spencer. Master bedroom photograph by Hickey-Robertson.*

Brochures are useful because they are a simple tangible item to hand out, something for the client to take away with them. And a brochure offers more information than a business card. But we're all blasé about brochures — if they don't get read, they won't make a sale for you. So if you use one, make it good.

Desktop publishing makes it possible to produce your own brochures. Both brochures and enclosures for marketing packets can be created easily on your computer. But get coaching if you are new to desktop publishing. When you produce marketing materials you want to ensure a crisp professional look.

If you're designing your own brochure, check out your ideas by looking at resources on good typographical design. You can avoid many mistakes by taking a few hours to read the research on how readers respond to printed text, pictures, and colors. It's worth a bit of extra time — the reason you're doing this brochure is to get clients to read it, to become interested in your business, and be motivated to respond.

This sample brochure demonstrates how much information can be presented on one sheet of paper using the simple trifold brochure format (Figure 6-5).

Testimonials and Client References

A testimonial is a statement of commendation or gratitude from a satisfied client. Testimonials from clients are more convincing than your prepared marketing messages. The best testimonials are specific in describing the project's success.

"I do like to have letters of recommendation from clients," says Deborah Steinmetz. "For example, we had a doctor who wrote a very nice letter to us saying what a nice job we did on his office. And of course, I used that for the next doctor. It lends a lot of credibility. I do ask for them but probably not consistently enough."

Use your testimonials judiciously. Including several great ones in the right context is better than including everything you have. Testimonials support your marketing material. They show that clients agree with the claims you make for your services.

How to Request Testimonials

- When you get a letter from a client you'd like to use or quote, send back a letter saying *thanks* and asking for permission to use their comments. Ask the client to sign the agreement at the bottom of the page and send it back to you. Send along a copy for them to keep and include return envelope and postage.

COMMERCIAL PROJECTS

AMERITECH

STATE OF OHIO

SOCIETY BANK

CHECKFREE CORPORATION

ATTORNEY GENERAL OFFICES

NBD BANK

EASTLAND MANOR

THE OHIO STATE UNIVERSITY HOSPITAL

CENTRAL OHIO TRANSIT AUTHORITY

NATIONWIDE INSURANCE

EPHESUS SEVENTH DAY ADVENTIST CHURCH

BORDEN FOUNDATION

THE OHIO STATE UNIVERSITY

NATIONAL CITY BANK

AREAS OF EXPERTISE

OFFICE FURNITURE DEALER

◆ ◆ ◆

SPACE PLANNING & UTILIZATION

◆ ◆ ◆

COMPUTER-AIDED DESIGN (CAD)

◆ ◆ ◆

ADA COMPLIANCE EVALUATION & SECTION 504

WINDOW TREATMENT

FLOOR COVERING

◆ ◆ ◆

WALL COVERING

◆ ◆ ◆

SIGNAGE

◆ ◆ ◆

ART WORK

WILLIAMS DESIGNS

Williams Designs emerged in the design arena in 1985 with the goal to provide high quality interior design and consultation services provided by a team of professionals with experience in space and facility planning, Computer Aided Design (CAD), and American Disabilities Act (ADA) compliance evaluation.

Williams Designs is known for its personalized service, innovative designs and quality of work. As design professionals, **Williams Designs** takes pride in maintaining a high level of professionalism and customer satisfaction.

Interior design consultation for institutional, commercial, and residential clients.

CERTIFIED, QUALIFIED, AND HIGHLY RECOMMENDED!

WILLIAMS DESIGNS

CAROLYN WILLIAMS FRANCIS
PRESIDENT & CEO

Figure 6-5 Trifold marketing brochure of Carolyn Williams Francis, Williams Design.

- Add a permission to quote their comments to a client follow-up questionnaire. If they agree, you can use any positive statements they make as a testimonial. This process is quick and easy for them.
- When a client thanks you for doing a good job or compliments your work, ask for their help by putting their thoughts in writing for you.
- Make it easy for clients to give a testimonial in a telephone conversation. Ask them to dictate their comments to you. You quickly edit for grammar and style and check the final text by reading it back to them. Then you have everything you need to include a quote in your brochure or other material. If you want a full letter for a packet or a proposal, send their comments from the telephone conversation and ask that they send it back on their stationery.
- Always send clients a copy of the brochure or other material in which they are quoted — with a thank-you note.
- Set up a lunch meeting with several of your clients and use it as an informal focus group. Ask your clients to tell you what they like and dislike about your service. You'll find that there are testimonials that you can pull from this discussion to use as quotes. Ask these clients for permission to use their comments in your marketing material.

Reprints of Your Publications

Always get reprints of articles you have written and stories featuring your design projects. Reprints obtained through the publisher look more professional and are higher quality than photocopies. The editor at the publication can tell you how to order reprints of your article.

Or you can have your own copies printed of your article. If you only need a few reprints, photocopy them. You can get good results copying even newsprint if you print on high-quality paper and use a good high-resolution copier. To make your own copies you must get permission from the publisher.

"We're fortunate enough to be published, so we get reprints of those articles and use them in a direct mailing to clients and potential clients at least twice a year," says Nila Leiserowitz. "Last year we were on the cover of *Interiors* magazine. We got reprints and sent them to clients with a letter."

Reprints of your articles are impressive and versatile marketing tools. Here are some of the ways designers use them effectively.

- Enclose a reprint with a direct-mail letter to prospective clients.
- Use a reprint as an occasion to keep in touch with clients by sending it out with a simple letter describing recent projects or new developments in your business.

WILLIAMS
DESIGNS

April 13, 1995

Dear :

Williams Designs is pleased to hear that you are satisfied with the quality of our work.

At **Williams Designs**, we try to make the client our number one priority. Without you, there would be no **Williams Designs**, and we would just like to take this opportunity to thank you for that.

We would also like to request a reference letter from you, so that others may know how pleased our clients are with our quality of work.

Please feel free to call us at any time if you have any questions or concerns.

Thank You,

Carolyn Williams Francis
President

3349 E. Broad St.   Columbus, Ohio 43213
Phone (614) 338-3690 Fax (614) 338-3691

FIGURE 6-6   *Example of letter from Williams Design requesting client testimonial.*

- Mail reprints to prospective clients as follow-up to other marketing contacts — this is an easy way to nourish the developing client relationship.

- Use a reprint as an invitation to a special event.

- Include a reprint as an enclosure in your marketing packet — this adds instant credibility. "We get reprints of publicity on our own logo and letterhead," says Charles Gandy. "That way our packet of information all has a visual sameness about it."

ADVERTISING

The jury is still out on what kind of advertising is truly helpful for interior designers. One reason is that advertising is still new for professional services. In the late 1970s, court challenges to restrictive codes of ethics in the legal field resulted in the ruling that such codes are an illegal restraint of trade. Since this decision, all professional services are proceeding slowly into this new world of marketing and advertising. But increasing competition makes effective marketing more and more a necessity for those providing services. If your competition advertises in media that reach your specialized audience, it is best to match them and advertise there as well.

Designers are experimenting more with different forms of advertising. Observe the advertising you see and hear. Ask clients what they respond to — and what they dislike. You'll need to build your own knowledge of what works for your business and what will reach your target clients. Whatever your advertising message, guard your professional image carefully. Make sure that your advertising is ethical and tasteful — as well as effective.

Advertising alone rarely brings in clients. But it can be a helpful support piece in your overall marketing design. It is one more way to get your name and message in front of the client. "I market a professional image and the concept of comfort," says Linda Blair. "I use the word ergonomic heavily. Through ads I try to help people realize that we have a lot of knowledge they don't that will make their lives more comfortable and functional."

Stay aware of the difference between advertising and publicity. Know how to use both to your advantage. Advertising has so long been part of our lives that it is hard to advertise in any way that creates real impact. Unsolicited publicity has more impact because it isn't seen as a self-serving message. But advertising lets you present exactly the message you want — control you can't have with publicity.

Many designers have found that traditional advertising just doesn't work for their businesses. "I don't believe in advertising," says B. J. Peterson. "I have tried it and not found any tangible results. It's hard to show service and talent in advertising. For me, it is not money well spent."

Above all, you need to have reasonable expectations for advertising. It is reasonable to expect advertising to do these things.

1. Inform the public about you and your business.
2. Create a good impression of and build a favorable attitude toward your business.
3. Set the stage for selling your services.
4. Announce or describe a specific service you're offering.

If these aren't your goals, save your marketing budget for methods more useful to your situation. "I don't advertise at all," says Charles Gandy. "It's better for me to spend my money on photography and publicity efforts instead of advertising. Then we have good photographs on hand when someone calls to do an article."

Types of Advertising

1. Yellow Pages   The yellow pages directory isn't great advertising for designers, but you do need a listing. Clients will turn to the yellow pages to find you when they need your telephone number. Because you will be listed along with your competitors, your ad needs to have an eye-catching layout, color, or headline. Your ad should be at least the same size as those of your competitors.

"My ad in the directory is the opposite color of the page — if in the white pages, it is yellow, and white in the yellow pages," says Linda Blair. "It says my name and lists some of what I do: residential, contract, and renovations. It jumps out like something highlighted. I also list my name under L for Linda Blair — people sometimes have a hard time finding you. I have also taken the inside front and back of the handy directories that come out through Kaiser publications or the Chamber of Commerce. Great position, big picture, big ad. And I use the same ad for a number of years to build recognition."

Sarah Boyer Jenkins found that her simple listing in the yellow pages under the ASID heading consistently brings calls from interested clients. Clients want to work with a designer close to their home, because travel can be such a headache in a big urban sprawl like the Washington-Baltimore area. So clients who live in the Chevy Chase area see Sarah's zip code and choose her because of the proximity.

2. Business and Trade Directories   List your design business in directories that reach your target clients. Most niche businesses whose clients are companies advertise effectively in these directories. Find out which directories your clients keep in their libraries. The industry and trade organizations that serve your niche will have a list of directories that cover the industry.

"We keep a list of directories that could list us as a firm," says Cheryl Duvall. "Some are free or just have a nominal charge; some have a higher fee. Some directories require advertising in them to be listed. Others don't require it but they give you a different price if you advertise."

3. Newspapers and Broadcast Media — Advertising works best for design businesses when it targets your specific clients. Mass-market media, such as the daily newspapers or television, are not a good choice. Look for news media that reach your clients directly.

Targeted advertising to the legal profession works for Rita Carson Guest's firm. "We advertised in the local legal daily paper, in an insert on Class A office buildings. It had a map that showed the major design firms in the city. We took out a half-page color ad on the back page of this map. We listed our clients and basically said 'thank you' to people who have supported us. This paper goes to our target market. They gave us extra copies we use with our marketing literature."

4. Magazines — For a magazine to be a good choice, the circulation should be the same as your service area — and the demographics should fit your target client profile. Magazines with a more general audience are expensive and ineffective for small businesses.

"The least effective marketing we've done has been advertising in magazines or publications," says Deborah Steinmetz. "I have never had anyone call because they saw my ad anywhere. But we try to advertise if we have a new product or are working in a new area. Or if there is a targeted issue, like one devoted to real estate in New Orleans — if you're not in there, people think you've gone out of business."

5. Special Publications and Events — Look for special occasions in which advertising will reach your target clients. "I don't advertise frequently, but occasionally I will advertise in a National Symphony Orchestra Women's Committee show house," says Sarah Boyer Jenkins. "I'll go ahead and run an ad even if I'm not participating. I always try to get the back page or the inside front page positioning because those are the ones that are most read."

TIPS FOR MORE EFFECTIVE ADVERTISING

- Place ads where clients will see them. Choose publications that target your clients.

- Advertise in trade show programs for your target industry.

- Use advertising to tell the public you're starting a new business or changing your specialty. Moving, opening a new studio, or hiring new staff are traditional opportunities to advertise.

- Advertise repeatedly to get the best results. Advertising is an investment in getting better known—getting a specific message to come to mind when people hear of your business.

- Team together with noncompeting designers for advertising. Co-op advertising is more affordable.

- Beware of claiming to be better than the competition — this type of marketing doesn't work for professional services. Instead, focus on describing your service enthusiastically, stressing your unique benefits.

- Build in a response to know if your advertising is effective. Get people to write or call for information or a special offer.

- In creating your ad, focus more on the client problem or need than your solution to it—you're creating motivation to respond. Ads should be both tasteful and informative.

- Hire a professional to develop your ad. You want to project the best image you can if you're investing in advertising.

PROMOTING YOUR SERVICE TO PROSPECTIVE CLIENTS

After you have built awareness with publicity and advertising, use promotion to make direct contact with prospective clients. Promotion includes the tangible things you do to communicate the benefits of your service: direct mail, telephone calls, informal groups and entertaining, fliers, and newsletters.

This phase of marketing depends on persistence, patience, and religiously following up on every promotion. You're building your relationship with the client through repeat encounters. Every communication with a prospective client should get progressively more targeted and personalized.

"I used to argue for the different ways to market," says Gary Whitney. "The first is the equivalent of a shotgun blast — you fire hoping one pellet will hit something. The other is to take dead aim on who you want and what you want to do with them, and you use a rifle. I have taken up the concept of rifle marketing."

The goal of your rifle marketing is an invitation to give a presentation or send a proposal. You will typically use more than one type of promotion as you build your relationship with the client. Keep the focus on learning from the client while you communicate who you are and what you can do. Use every conversation to learn more about the client and their design needs or problems.

Getting Leads for New Business Promotion

Use your knowledge about your target clients — and your creativity — to develop leads to prospective clients. "We sit down every week and discuss potential leads we have heard about in our market," says Nila Leiserowitz. "We also talk about who we are going to call that week. For instance, we'll call if we haven't had contact with a real estate broker — we'll say we need to call so and so to see what they are up to and if there are any projects going on. Or we need to call our health care clients. So we assign ourselves duties every week to make sure we contact these people. We read the newspapers and go out to lunch with past clients and with real estate brokers." She emphasizes that you have to think marketing all the time to pick up potential leads: meeting with clients, socializing, and having your staff look out for leads.

Newspapers and periodicals can be good sources of leads. Cover all relevant publications to find out about potential design projects and to stay current on issues in your market. Cheryl Duvall's firm assigns people in the office the responsibility of reading various publications: the daily newspaper, the *Wall Street Journal*, the local legal newspaper, the *Baltimore Business Journal*, the *Washington Business Journal*, and magazines. They spread their coverage by having everybody reading different things. "We look for articles about potential clients we are chasing, current clients, current trends in business and current trends in our industry. Many companies like ours might hire reading services where you pay a fee to have them look for these kinds of things for you."

Tap your networks for potential leads. "Our best marketing is by word of mouth," says Deborah Steinmetz. "And reading the real estate section of the newspaper so I can see what transactions are going on or buildings up for sale. If I find something, I track down who is involved in it — this is a good opportunity for me to get involved with a new ownership."

HOW TO WRITE AN EFFECTIVE MARKETING LETTER

1. **Create a good form letter that you can customize for periodic mailings to leads.**

   It should be simple and effective, aiming to generate a response from prospective clients. You want them to ask for more information or ask for an appointment. Demonstrate that you understand the client's problems and pose your solution. Next, summarize your background and business experience. Finally, state that you will follow the letter with a phone call.

2. **Your letter should have a dynamic opening statement.**

   Promise a benefit, include a quote, statistics, or pose an attention-getting question.

3. **State in the letter *when* you will call to follow up.**

4. **Focus on the client in the text of the letter.**

   Use more *you*s than *I*s.

5. **Test your form letter by sending it out to a sample of prospective clients.**

   Mark it *test* and call for feedback. Or send a batch of letters and see how the response is. If it's a bomb, call for feedback to find out why. Such calls are also a good, nonthreatening way to practice your follow-up calls — you'll know how a client is likely to respond.

Types of Promotion

1. Direct Mail Marketing — *Direct mail* is sending promotional material about your services to prospective customers to get new business. In marketing services, direct mail is valuable as the first step in creating the opportunity for personal selling. Have a clear strategy for using direct mail. It must play its part with your other marketing methods and be consistent with your marketing design.

The marketing letter and the mailing list are the key components of direct mail. The application of direct mail that works best for designers is a limited, customized approach — one that is targeted and personalized. A mass mailing to a general mailing list will waste your money. The more targeted

6. **Don't send brochures or other information with your letter.**

   Your letter should create the opportunity to call the prospective client to give more information and answer questions.

7. **Hints for getting your letter opened.**

   - Send your letters via first class mail.
   - Use personal or business stationery.
   - Don't use address labels — type or print directly on the envelope
   - Use names — never just titles — on the envelope and letter.
   - Use handwritten addresses.
   - Include something like a recipe or business information that will be useful to the recipient.

8. **Check the appearance of your final product.**

   You want to send an attractive, readable letter, not too dense with text, using a friendly choice of typeface, and lots of white space on the page.

9. **Send an enclosure with your letter if you have something that relates to the need you address.**

   Enclose an article from a publication within the industry or something else that demonstrates your insider position and your grasp of client problems.

and prequalified your mailing list, the more successful your direct mail marketing will be.

Your marketing letter should come across as a personal letter — individual to individual. Used well, direct mail can eliminate cold calls because it takes the first introductory step, preparing the prospective client to hear from you. A specific message — selling a particular service or the solution to a well-defined problem — makes the most effective direct mail campaign.

Have reasonable expectations for direct mail. Low response rates — four to eight percent — are the norm. Your chances of a higher response are better if your list is targeted and your marketing letter is problem-focused. Your results should also be better because you don't expect the client to purchase, you just want to set a meeting.

JANE'S NOTE

The first year I moved to Boulder, I sent thirty marketing letters a month. I bought a list compiled monthly of people who had bought a home for more than $250,000. My letter told about my philosophy as a designer, my past jobs, and my services. I also enclosed a client list and testimonials. While I did not get many clients, I got my biggest client this way, a California movie producer and his wife who moved to the mountains in Boulder. I helped them with their new home as well as a condo in Breckenridge. The only way marketing letters are successful is with a follow-up phone call, a good interview, and a great portfolio. I cemented this great job because of my follow-up.

Demonstrating the benefits of your service to the client is the goal of a good marketing letter. Because the goal of a mailed promotion is to get a meeting with the client, be sure your letter piques the client's interest and clearly states what you will do next. All mailings should be followed by phone calls. So be careful not to send more than you can follow up with calls — be sure you do what you say you will. In every step of your marketing you are establishing your reliability.

The strongest position for a marketing letter is based on an urgent need of the prospective client. Look for problems for which you can supply the solution. One example of an urgent problem is the need for facilities to comply with ADA regulations. Even if you can't pinpoint an urgent need, always try to base your promotion on a need-solution process. And know enough about the client's problem to talk knowledgeably about the issue.

Team your well-written marketing letter with the right mailing list. Your list should provide names of people who need your service, can afford your service, and have already heard of your business. Names and addresses must be accurate and current. You also want names, not just titles, for mailing letters to companies.

Research potential mailing lists, looking for lists that match your target clients. You can buy or rent lists — arrangements vary with the type of list. Here are some list ideas designers have found useful in their marketing.

- Mailing list of weekly house sales in a geographic area.
- Membership list of trade organizations.
- Membership list of local organizations like the Newcomers Club.
- Zip codes for magazines such as *Elle, Decor,* or *Architectural Digest* (available from list brokers for national magazines).

BE CREATIVE AND BUILD YOUR OWN MAILING LIST

One of the best marketing tools you can develop is your own mailing list of potential clients.

- Read the newspaper and note what is happening in your market. Track down names and addresses related to potential projects and add these to your mailing list.
- Collect names and addresses at a trade show.
- Run a contest with free design service as a prize. Do this through a community event or a radio station—your payment is getting the list of names of those who entered the contest.
- Offer helpful information to interested people at any promotional or publicity event—add these names to your mailing list.
- Add names from any replies to your ads or promotions.

---

2. Cold Calls, Warm Calls, and Telephone Follow-Up—Promotion is wasted if you don't commit to thorough and persistent follow-up. The most common sequence is mailing a marketing letter and following up with a phone call. In your call, qualify the prospective clients and answer their questions. Be sure they understand what your service offers and schedule a consultation to discuss their needs.

Here is a typical sequence for a follow-up phone call.

1. Introduce yourself.
2. State your purpose in calling. Check to see if they received the mailing. If not, check their address and say you'll send the letter again and call back—don't try to reproduce your marketing letter over the phone.
3. Discuss the prospective clients' problems and your design solutions. Show the clients that you understand their business.
4. Ask to schedule a consultation to talk further about their needs and to tell them about your services.
5. Answer their concerns or objections.
6. Confirm the next step—tell the clients what you will do to follow up.

Call a week or two after your mailing—you want to allow time for prospective clients to read your letter, but not enough time to forget it.

Remember that these calls are not telemarketing. You are not trying to sell your service over the phone. You're just starting a dialogue and checking to see if there is interest in arranging a consultation.

The follow-up call is the time to begin qualifying prospective clients. If the client is interested, you need to know if it's worth your time to continue. As you talk, have in mind the characteristics of a qualified prospect. You can't verify all of these characteristics after one phone call, but you should learn as much as you can. Plan your approach and have a checklist in front of you. You may hang up knowing only the person is a *maybe*, but learn to screen out the clients who are obviously not good prospects.

Qualifying is easier if your marketing letter has been sent to a targeted list. A qualified prospective client has the following characteristics:

- An immediate or future need for your service.
- Can afford your service.
- Authority to make the purchasing decision.
- Would benefit from your service.
- Is a person with whom you want to work.

JANE'S NOTE

When I started my business, I bought a list of new people to the community from Longmont/Boulder Greetings for $3 a name. These names were prequalified—the people had told the representative that they were interested in hearing from a designer. I would make ten phone calls a day, hoping to get one good lead. Mostly I reached answering machines, but when I got someone, I tried to establish rapport.

My best approach in making these calls was to have something besides design to talk about. It was a way to establish a relationship. I would say "Welcome to Boulder. Are you enjoying your new home? Where are you from? Have you met a lot of people? Let me tell you a little about Boulder." I would tell them about activities in Boulder or invite them to go to a meeting of the Newcomer's Club with me. I would ask about their interests.

Having something to talk about besides what a great designer I am helped me feel comfortable when I did tell them about my business and my background—and that I was available to meet with them. I felt that they would remember me even if I was unable to set up a consultation at the time. Often, I did set up consultations as a result of this phone relationship.

When you call, be prepared with a plan to move the relationship forward. Few prospective clients will take the initiative to ask to meet with you in this first call. In this context, "nonselling" words like consultation, appraisal, free estimate, evaluation of your needs, or initial planning meeting are helpful to get you to a face-to-face meeting. Explain how your business works and what the next step is to see if you can help with their problems. People who haven't worked with a designer may not know the process.

Keep these points in mind in making your follow-up calls.

1. Make an action commitment — say that you'll prepare an estimate or send a packet of information on similar projects.

2. Involve the prospective client: start a file on the potential project; ask questions and take down background information on the client; set a tentative date for a presentation; draw out what kind of material the prospective client would like to see.

3. Be polite and personable with secretaries and other support staff. You need their benign approval now just to get to the decision-maker, and, when you start actual work, you'll need their cooperation.

4. In asking for a consultation meeting, don't set it up so the client feels it is a sales meeting. Act as if the decision is already made, even if it has not been — move forward and begin to provide service by evaluating client needs.

5. Pose your request so it is easy for the prospect to give the answer you want. "Is next week or the week after better for you?" You want a *yes* response and don't want to give them a chance to say *no* easily. But don't be pushy or manipulative about this. Your request for an appointment should be heard as being helpful and flexible.

6. Immediately after the call, mail or fax a letter saying *thank you* and confirming the time and date of your appointment.

"We all hate to do cold calls," says Nila Leiserowitz. "But it is very much a part of marketing for commercial design. Every year our director of marketing conducts a cold call seminar and we all practice and rehearse. It's just a very difficult thing to do. In interior design I would say most of our calls are warm calls. We already know something might be happening before we call."

3. Informal Groups and Entertaining — Many designers use informal gatherings as a way to establish a relationship with potential clients. This form of promotion works best for residential design businesses, but commercial designers shouldn't overlook the potential of entertaining as another way to reach clients.

TELEPHONING TIPS

- Prepare a phone script but always be flexible. The most important thing is to show the client that you listen.
- Smile as you talk. The smile will add warmth to your voice.
- Have your body relaxed and your desk clear of distractions. Have in front of you everything you need to answer questions and make appointments.
- Use a comfortable speaking voice and speed. Be polite and sound confident and authoritative.
- Make sure that you won't be interrupted while making the call. Use a telephone line without call waiting.
- Respond enthusiastically to client interest.
- Have well thought out answers ready for questions.
- Visualize a friendly person on the other end of the phone.
- Don't knock the competition. If the topic comes up, always be complimentary.
- Come to the point and don't waste the client's time. Before you call, rank your points into a short list of the most important things to cover. Move to these if the client is in a hurry.
- Ask questions. Show prospective clients that you are interested in their problems. Show that you are interested in listening — focus on their needs, not yours.
- Take your cues from the client's response to you—how chatty to be, note any questions. Ask if this is a good time to talk. Be relaxed and helpful.
- Know the habits and preferences of your prospective clients — this will help in choosing the time of day to call. Talk informally with clients to find out.
- If rejection starts getting to you, remind yourself with each call that it's a new start. Remember that you will always have more *nos* than *yeses*.

Be creative and think of similar ways you could entertain prospective clients. The most effective entertaining for prospective clients focuses on design. Offer some useful information or show people something new. And be sure to promote your business by ensuring that all aspects of your event are beautifully designed.

Ellen C. Jeffers and Helen F. Crockett share some of their successful ideas for marketing through informal group events. "Occasionally when the road representative for a fabric company makes an appointment to show a new line, we invite some people to Helen's antique-filled home to view the collection with us. A white sheet is placed over one of the sofas so the salesperson can drape the fabrics over a neutral background. We serve refreshments and make it into a fun and informative affair. People can ask the rep questions about the various fabrics and actually learn about the different weaves, materials, and uses. We have landed several large jobs this way.

"Another time, an associate of ours who is a professional floral designer and judge created several arrangements to complement fabrics we had selected. We also used pieces of eighteenth-century porcelain as accents. This forum gathered people of different interests and showed them how the design world is interrelated."

4. Fliers — Fliers are a simple and inexpensive method for reaching a consumer market in a limited geographic area. They work only if they reach the person who needs your service and if the person can afford it.

JANE'S NOTE

When I was establishing my business in Boulder, I used informal entertaining to get to know prospective clients. I had a coffee in my home every two months for about fifteen people who had been prequalified for interest by a screening service.

I made a nice invitation with calligraphy printing, a profile of myself, and a foldout of a reprint of a magazine article — a before-and-after kitchen remodel — featuring my work. This flier invited people to the coffee to discuss design trends and principles of window and wall treatments, space planning, color, lighting, and so on (Figure 6-7).

These coffees were very successful, and I always got good clients from them. Once prospective clients came to my home, met me, and discussed basic interior design issues, they wanted to use me for their interior design needs: The trust was there.

Designers often use fliers as hand-outs at trade shows or community publicity events. Fliers can also be effective as leave-behinds after speeches or seminars.

5. Newsletters — A newsletter is a periodic publication that you send as a service to clients and prospective clients. To be noticed and read, a newsletter must provide useful, current information that is of real interest to readers.

First Choice
D E S I G N S

2230 Knollwood Drive • Boulder Colorado 80302
(303) 440-0517

Jane D. Martin
Interior Design

My objective is to help clients create a beautiful home or office environment which reflects their personality, treasures and lifestyle as cost effectively as possible.

My specialties include space planning, design concepts, fabric and finish selections, furniture and lighting choices and working with contractors, craftsmen, and architects.

I have owned my own firm for 15 years in San Francisco, Nashville, and Boulder and handle both residential and commercial projects.

Education
A.A., Nashville School of Interior Design, Nashville, Tennessee
B.A., Indiana University, Bloomington, Indiana
A.A., Stephens College, Columbia, Missouri

Professional Affiliations and Honors
Who's Who in Interior Design, 1988, 1989, 1990, 1991
American Society of Interior Design, Allied Member

Publications
Kitchen Makeover in *Colorado Homes & Lifestyles*, Sept./Oct. 1991
Courtyard Garden in *Colorado Homes & Lifestyles*, Jan./Feb. 1990
Dining Room in *Nashville*, April, 1987

A Few Recent Clients
Carolyn and Glen Strevey	Susie and Eric Evered
Magpie Inn	Gayle and John Hinchman
Debora and Marc Sotkin	Free Spirit Travel
Fran and Bill Gillison	Vicky and Bliss Jensen
Mimi and Preston Davis	Serena and Ken Dubach
Grette and Gunnar Jansen	Dr. Nancy Bruington, D.C.

Jane Martin
Interior Designer

You are invited for coffee and an informal program on wall coverings, window treatments and other interior design ideas.

Date:
Time:
R.S.V.P. 440-0517

First Choice Designs
2230 Knollwood Drive
Boulder, Colorado

FIGURE 6-7 *Bifold invitation to a coffee for prospective clients. Jane D. Martin, First Choice Designs. Reprinted with permission of Colorado Homes & Lifestyles magazine by Weisner, Inc. Photograph by Don Riley.*

PARADE OF HOMES AWARDS OF HONOR

COLORADO
HOMES & LIFESTYLES
SEPTEMBER 1991

KITCHEN MAKEOVERS:
BEFORE AND AFTER

Thoroughly Modern Martin: Three years ago Boulder designer Jane Martin's 18-year-old home underwent a complete renovation. The goal was "to turn a very dark home with a choppy floor plan into a warm, contemporary home," says Martin of First Choice Designs. And a full kitchen remodel was a necessity.

"We totally gutted the kitchen. The only thing I kept were the trash compactor and the dishwasher—but I moved them to other locations," she says. The old cabinets were replaced with Formica cabinets, custom made by Creative Cabinetry in Boulder.

Martin enjoys cooking for her family—and when she does it's usually in large quantities to ensure plenty of leftovers. "Sometimes I like to line up three lasagnas and work on all three at once," she says. "I needed a real small, compact triangle area—the distance between refrigerator, sink and cooktop—and a large amount of counter space."

Busy cooks also have to think about the view from the counter where they spend their time. "The key to my planning was having my work surfaces face outward toward the lovely views at the rear of our home," says Martin. "Before, I was looking back at the garage."

COLORADO HOMES & LIFESTYLES

FIGURE 6-7 *(continued)*

161

HINTS FOR GOOD NEWSLETTERS

- Send your newsletter to the right list—you want to reach potential repeat clients and prospective clients.
- Number the issues but don't date them. Then they aren't perceived as out of date and thrown away and you can reuse them in other mailings.
- Don't think you have to send a long newsletter. It can be two or four pages, sent out quarterly or bimonthly.
- Keep your newsletter content relevant and current. Provide tips on effective design or information and advice on topics relating to your service. Include book reviews. Get an outside expert to write a feature article or do interviews.
- Provide information about new materials and industry trends. Keep your information impartial and objective about products.
- Make sure your newsletter looks interesting—don't let it be too wordy or dull-looking. Demonstrate your design sense with great layout and graphics.
- Share information about all of your services. Newsletters can help you illustrate the range of services you provide.
- Show prospective clients the personality of your business. Use the newsletter to tell about yourself and how you do business.
- Talk to clients about your newsletter. Find out what information they would like to read about design.

Newsletters can be a great forum for sharing your competence in defining and solving client problems. But most newsletters used as marketing fail to deliver any real news. They end up being a waste of time for recipients and a waste of money for marketers. Your newsletter must contain useful information. Your goal is to educate and be helpful, not to advertise.

If you publish a newsletter, have a well-thought-out marketing strategy for its use and have a way to evaluate whether or not it is working for you. Publishing a newsletter can be a way to establish a competitive advantage—if competitors don't do a newsletter, this is an opportunity to do something special for clients. The marketing advantage of a newsletter is that it builds recognition of the quality and scope of your business through regular arrivals of new information.

Desktop publishing software and computers make it possible for small businesses to create their own newsletters. You can create your newsletter—

graphics and all—on your computer and mail it to targeted clients at regular intervals. Send the first issue with a cover letter explaining that you're furnishing this information service to help clients.

Consider sharing the work involved to produce a newsletter with others. Create a joint venture with another professional who targets the same clients to publish a newsletter together. Or team with a designer from another area to create a newsletter together that each can mail to your own client list.

6. Using Your Prospective Client Data Base to Stay in Contact—Be prepared to maintain communication with prospective clients while giving them time to be ready to hire you. Remember that marketing a service takes five to ten contacts to make a sale. So have patience and be creative in finding ways to keep your business current in the prospective client's mind. In the next section, we share ideas and tips on continuing this connection from other designers.

Schedule regular follow-up mailings and calls to prospective clients. Vary your messages to maintain interest in hearing from you. You want to be seen as friendly and helpful—but not be perceived as "bugging" people. Your messages should come across as "thinking about you" instead of "why haven't you hired me yet?"

Make this process easy for yourself by setting up a data base of client leads. As you get names of prospective clients, capture names, addresses, phone numbers, and other important information. Then you have the information you need to stay in touch.

The most efficient way to keep prospective client files is with a computer data base program. But if you don't use a computer in your business, you can set up a hard-copy file of index cards or a binder for your prospective client list. For more information on creating a data base, see the *Client List* section in Chapter 8: *Keeping Clients for Future Business and Referrals.*

Keep a record of your contacts with each prospective client. Create a system to track all requests from prospective clients and your calls and mailings. Make notes for yourself to remind you of what has been discussed. Keep track of your marketing process with each potential client (Figure 6-8).

IDEAS FOR STAYING IN TOUCH WITH PROSPECTIVE CLIENTS

1. Call periodically to say hello. —Say you're thinking about them—wondering if they have something you can help with or a question you could answer.

2. Send a keep-in-touch letter. —Tell about your business activities or simply remind them you are available to help and that you would like to work with them.

PROSPECTIVE PROJECT DATA FORM

Name   Date

Address   Referral/Source

Phone   Directions

Fax
                                        Best Time to Call

Project Information:

                                        Record of Contacts:

Sq. Ft.
                                        Information Sent

Budget Range
                                        Telephone Followup

Client Needs/Objectives
                                        Client Interview

                                        Presentation/Proposal
Likes and Dislikes

FIGURE 6-8   *Prospective client data form.*

3. Think of ways to research and package information that will be of interest to your clients. — Information is valuable in any industry. "We stay up to date on the latest in law office design," says Rita Carson Guest. "We have put together a lot of statistical information that is really interesting to law firms. We break them into different sizes of law firms, and we can say, 'These firms have this many square feet per lawyer or this many paralegals per lawyer or this many secretaries per lawyer.' These survey results are helpful to law firms when looking for space or looking for a range of square feet to allocate per partner."

4. Send reprints of articles you've written or publications of your work.

5. Notify people on your list of a change of address. — You could send a rolodex card preprinted with the new information. "We recently moved into our new office," says Nila Leiserowitz. "We printed postcards with a photograph of the interior of our office."

6. Send a copy of an article that would interest the prospective client.

7. Send a letter and material about a recent successful job. — Stress the positive results of your work. Include client endorsements. "What I've found to be most effective is sending a good case study of work we've done for a particular client," says Peter Miscovich of Los Angeles. "I sent out a case study of a recent project with Eastman Kodak — the design of their new sales and marketing research center — along with an article I'd written about it for the *Los Angeles Business Journal*. The combination was a very effective sales tool. We had incredible response from other companies who received that mailer — because it was a relevant topic. Companies called to ask, 'How did you help Eastman Kodak reduce occupancy costs and develop these alternative work strategies?' "

8. Send cards for holidays or birthdays.

9. Send a copy of recent publicity about you or your business.

Ideas to Remember from This Chapter

- Your company graphics, your office or studio, and your personal image are the "package" on which prospective clients judge your service.
- The tangible tools of marketing — marketing packets, portfolios, and brochures — are most useful when they are guided by a marketing strategy and customized to fit client needs and interests.
- Advertising alone rarely brings in clients, but it can be effective if the advertising vehicle reaches your target clients.
- Direct mail works well for designers used as a first step in creating the opportunity for personal selling. Use direct mail to send a highly individualized letter to a targeted mailing list.
- Telephone follow-up is essential to getting clients through your direct mail promotions.
- Newsletters serve to keep your name in front of your clients while showcasing your design expertise.

CHAPTER
7

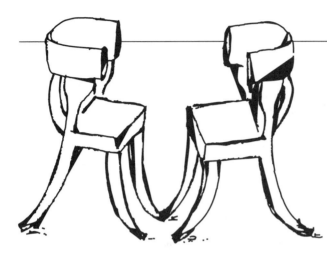

Selling Design Services

Client Interviews and Sales Presentations

Selling is the stage of marketing that brings you face to face with clients. It is the personal communication of your solution to the client's problems and your request for this job. Your goal is to make the marketing process flow naturally into the selling stage. By the time you reach the sales stage, clients should have the information and confidence in your business they need to make a decision.

WHAT IS DIFFERENT ABOUT SELLING DESIGN SERVICES?

The process of selling a design service is different from selling a product. It's also different from selling standardized services such as banking or dry cleaning. The critical difference is that the designer is creating and supplying the service as well as selling it. The service can't exist without the professional. So each design project is unique — the product of the context, the client's needs, and the designer's talent.

This difference means that selling a design service is very personal. The client is buying both the designer's skill and a working relationship with the

166

In This Chapter

This chapter takes you through the steps of selling design services. Effective selling focuses on relationship-building and good listening.

In this chapter you will learn how to

- Build effective relationships with clients.
- Improve your listening skills.
- Qualify clients.
- Conduct client interviews and needs assessments.
- Develop effective presentations and proposals.
- Close the sale.

designer. If this relationship isn't established, there is no sale. Both the sale of design services and the success of the project depend on mutual trust built into the relationship between buyer and seller.

Because of this critical difference, many traditional sales techniques don't apply to selling professional services. Much of traditional selling assumes an adversarial relationship between seller and buyer. The salesperson must overcome the buyer's resistance and objections.

In the design business, however, selling doesn't mean manipulating people to buy against their inclinations. High pressure tactics don't work well in selling design. Adversarial selling creates the wrong environment for nourishing a long-term relationship between designer and client. Adversarial sales techniques subtly poison the relationship with mistrust and disrespect.

OUR DEFINITION OF SELLING

In our definition of selling, we focus on the client as a reasonable person, with needs and expectations, who is motivated to enter into a fair mutual commitment with you for help with those needs. The key to sales is superb *two-way communication*, in which listening is just as important as the sales presentation. The sale and the relationship are of equal importance.

Trust the marketing process to prepare your clients, bringing your service and their needs together in the sale of the project. By the time you make your sales presentation, your relationship with the client has already been developed. The actual sales discussion just makes this relationship more immediate and specific.

Selling Is Relationship-Building

Selling design services isn't accomplished in one encounter. Typically you will have several conversations or meetings with a prospective client before you present your proposal or presentation. This process allows the designer-client relationship to develop over time, building the trust necessary for commitment. The relationship you create throughout your marketing and selling process will be one of the things that makes you unique in the client's eyes.

The face-to-face phase of selling personalizes the relationship you have been building. Know what you want to achieve in developing the relationship through each meeting or conversation with the client. Find points of common interest with your client.

Get clear on what your client wants from this professional relationship. What values is the client seeking? The following are some of the values clients may seek in choosing a designer:

- Caring about the client's problems.
- Honesty and sincerity.
- Belief in yourself and your ability to solve design problems.
- Reliability and trustworthiness.
- Flexibility and reasonableness.
- Getting to the heart of issues — being a straight-shooter.
- Respect for the client and the value of their time and money.

In selling, *showing* is always more powerful than *telling*. You can tell the client that these values are important to you, but the success of the relationship depends on your ability to show the client by living these values.

In a good designer-client relationship, the client enjoys sharing your enthusiasm about design and your confidence in your abilities. Be willing to let clients see who you are and what matters to you. "The important thing in effective selling is loving what you sell and believing in what you do," says Los Angeles designer Sally Sirkin Lewis. "I love interior design. I can do an art collection for someone because I also love art. Or I can sell furniture or fabric because I love visually beautiful, wonderful quality things. My caring and my enthusiasm for what I'm doing is what sells. It makes people believe in me. People want to believe. Clients want the people who sell to them to believe in what they are selling, to be honest. People do know the difference. You must have credibility."

And you reciprocate by sharing the client's enthusiasm for their business or home. Show your sincere interest and desire to help. "If we were really partnering with our clients—so married and committed—we would never have to market," says Gary Whitney. "It's easy to sell when you believe in something. If you don't like the product, you can never pull it off. When I believe in what my client is doing it is a complementary marriage. I'm passionately committed to a particular client—Disney. I like what they stand for and what they do for the American family, the way they celebrate man's differences and cultures. I think there is a higher purpose in what Disney does."

Respect the client's need to get to know you. Let the client's needs and comfort set the pace for your developing professional relationship. Use this time to get information about the client's situation, needs, and problems. If you take this approach, your sales presentation for the job should be easy to prepare. You'll be ready to present your design solution to the client's specific problems.

In teaching ASIDs Marketing by Design workshop, Mary Ann Bryan is finding that designers—particularly residential designers—keep saying that "marketing is about building and maintaining relationships. The key to marketing and selling your service is doing excellent work and the moment-to-moment, day-to-day process of building good relationships."

Commercial designers are also aware of the importance of relationship building in selling their services. "It seems like chemistry is becoming even more critical in getting projects—in terms of how well clients feel you could work with them," says Nila Leiserowitz. "It has always been important, but I'm a firm believer that, with today's instability with jobs, people are looking for relationships in work because that is the only thing they can grasp on to."

Selling Is Listening

Building relationships depends on showing that you're interested in clients and that you care about their concerns. Demonstrate this by *listening* to them. Avoid the common mistake of viewing selling as talking—convincing someone. Remember that listening is far more important than talking in making a sale.

What is important to listen for in talking to prospective clients? Listen for the answers to the following questions:

1. What are your clients' problems?
2. What do they need?

3. What do they want?

4. How do these needs translate into design services?

5. What problems do clients foresee?

6. What are their style preferences?

FOCUS ON CLIENT PROBLEMS AND DESIGN SOLUTIONS

The focus in selling should be on mutual exploration of client needs and creative design solutions to the client's problems. This focus simplifies selling because your design solution stays rooted in the client's needs. Selling problem solutions is much easier than selling "generic" interior design.

Sell the benefits of your service to the client, not just its features. When you are deep into what you do it can be hard to stop seeing features and make the leap to benefit thinking. An exercise to learn to do this is to write down the features of your design business — your particular expertise and things at which you excel. Then switch to the client perspective and translate each feature to a benefit statement.

The following example illustrates this process by listing five benefits of a design service and translating the features into benefits the client will receive. Study this example and try converting your design service features into benefit statements.

STEPS IN SELLING YOUR DESIGN SERVICES

1. Selling begins at the point you have personal contact with the prospective client: a call or visit in follow-up to marketing or in response to a client request. This contact is your opportunity to tell what you have to offer — in general. Specifics will come later. Tell your story briefly, then listen.

2. The next step is interviewing the client, getting information on client needs that will form the basis of the project. If the client is a company, be sure that you don't take up the client's time asking for basic information about the company that is public knowledge. If you have researched the company, the client will be impressed and pleased to see your interest and initiative.

3. Qualify clients at the same time you are assessing their needs. Make sure that there is mutual benefit to pursuing this project.

Features	Benefits
1. I use high-quality resource people and installers.	1. You can count on the *reliability* of our workmanship and service.
2. My work and installation is efficient and coordinated.	2. Your project will stay *on time* and *on budget*, and *will be completed without interrupting your medical practice.*
3. I have creative design sense.	3. I will translate *your concepts of good health and safety* into a functional design that projects the *prosperous and professional image* of your practice.
4. I have thorough technical knowledge of standards and codes.	4. Your project will be a *turnkey product with no legal problems*—and no bad surprises after the job.
5. I am a good communicator.	5. My emphasis on communication will *prevent personnel problems* by ensuring that staff participate in space and design decisions.

FIGURE 7-1   *Example illustrating the translation of features to benefits.*

JANE'S NOTE

Look for opportunities to be creative. Clients are excited when you suggest an unusual solution. I had a client who didn't like the Palladian columns between her living room and dining room. I replaced them with cherry wood and glass showcase cabinets for displaying her porcelain, crystal, and antique silver collection. One creative architectural solution eliminated a problem and satisfied the client's desire to display her collections. The client was delighted.

4. Take the lead in presenting your solution to the client. This step may be an informal discussion culminating in a proposal, a formal proposal, or a formal presentation. The vehicle for your sales presentation will be dictated by the client's needs and context. Choose the method that puts the client at ease and gives you the best chance of a positive reception. If possible, you want to present your ideas in person. This presentation is your chance to showcase your unique capabilities.

5. Ask for the job and close the sale.

The actual steps of the sales process vary, of course, with each sales situation. The key is to be prepared for the steps required and to create a series of smaller agreements that keep moving you and the client toward the eventual close of the sale.

Think of these steps as a continuum. Selling can involve the whole process or it can start and finish at any point on the continuum. Be aware of this continuum in assessing where you are in a particular selling situation. If your sales situation compresses the process into one or two contacts, you must be prepared to cover the content of all the steps — to be sure the client is ready to buy and you have the information you need to qualify the client and do the job.

There will be fewer steps and fewer meetings involved in selling smaller jobs. For very simple jobs, be prepared to outline a basic proposal at the end of your first meeting with the client. Other projects will take more time and more meetings to complete the process. It doesn't pay to rush your own preparation of a design solution to present to a client. Design is a complex service and people expect you to take the time needed to assess their situation and make recommendations.

Because the selling process is often extended over a period of time, you need a good system for capturing client information as you go through these steps. Start project files for prospective clients and carefully keep records of conversations and all your notes. Once the contract is signed, you don't want to have to ask the client to repeat what's already been told to you. A simple form can help you remember to write down the basic client and project information you will need (Figure 7-2).

Problem Finding: Interviews and Needs Assessments

In interviewing you are gathering the information you need *and* building rapport with the client. Before you meet with a prospective client, pull together everything you already know about the client and his or her needs. Have your questions ready to get the rest of the information you need. Know what you

---

PROSPECTIVE PROJECT DATA FORM

Name   Date

Address   Referral/Source

Phone   Directions

Fax
                                                  Best Time to Call

Project Information:

                                                  Record of Contacts:
Sq. Ft.

                                                  Information Sent
Budget Range

                                                  Telephone Followup

Client Needs/Objectives
                                                  Client Interview

                                                  Presentation/Proposal
Likes and Dislikes

FIGURE 7-2   *Prospective client data form.*

think the problem is in general and be ready to find out the specifics about this situation.

Set outcome objectives for this first meeting, but also be prepared with alternative objectives if the meeting takes an unexpected direction. It could be that you haven't reached the decision-maker yet and you realize you'll need to set another meeting. Or that you'll need to prepare a presentation and come back.

Modify this basic interview format to fit your interview situation.

- State the benefits of your service briefly.
- Verify the information you already have on this client's situation.
- Gather additional information on the client's needs and the potential project.
- Take action and move to the next step in the sales process.

RESIDENTIAL CLIENT INTERVIEW FORMAT

Use these questions to understand the residential client.

1. Age.

2. Spouse's Name and Age.

3. Names and Ages of Children.

4. Pets.

5. Grandchildren.

6. Hobbies—Are you active, sports oriented, or quiet and enjoy reading?

7. Do you have lots of company?

8. How do you entertain? Small or large, casual or formal.

9. Do you have special collections?

10. Are people in your family allergic or handicapped?

11. Are you neat and tidy? Do you like everything to have a place?

12. Describe the good and bad points of homes you have had.

13. Describe the good and bad points of your new home.

14. Find four pictures in magazines you like and tell me why you like them.

Be relaxed and open. Your role in this sales step is attentive listening. Be genuinely interested in learning about this client. Put the client at ease. Focus on building long-term rapport and trust. Make the client feel important. Get clear on what they want and what they really need—be aware if there is a difference.

Probe for the client's expectations about the project budget and the amount of time it will require. Also find out how much disruption they can tolerate if the project is a redesign or remodel of existing space. You need to know in the beginning how realistic the client is and how knowledgeable about the design process.

In a client interview, asking the right questions is more important than giving the right answers. Clients will know that you understand their perspective from the questions you ask. If you ask clients enough questions,

15. Find four pictures in magazines you don't like and discuss why.

16. How do you feel about

> Fireplaces
> Sunny places
> Real plants
> Fake or silk plants
> Mini blinds or drapes
> Antiques or contemporary furniture
> Books
> Wallpaper or paint
> Laminates or Corian or tile or granite
> Wood floors or carpet
> Metal finishes
> Dark or light woods
> Curved lines or straight lines

17. What fabrics or prints do you like: floral, geometric, minis or large prints, stripes?

18. What are your color preferences: light, dark, quiet, lively, dramatic, or subdued? Any favorites or dislikes?

eventually they'll tell you what bothers them. If you keep listening, they will tell you what they value.

Some clients can be difficult to interview because they don't know — or can't verbalize — what their preferences and needs are.

Be observant in an interview. Seeing clients' present work or living space lets you know what they are comfortable with now — and gauge how much change is advisable. Also the quality of furnishing and art they have presently lets you interpret what their quality standards are and the amount they might expect to spend.

If you're hearing a tangle of problems, take time to clarify what help is wanted from you. Some problems will be out of your area of expertise, and some may be issues your clients aren't ready to resolve. Take the time now to get this clear. Let them tell you how much of your service they want, rather

JANE'S NOTE

One of my most difficult clients now is a couple with very different tastes. The wife is traditional; she likes hardwood floors with area rugs, likes light wood, plain patterned fabric, and bland colors. He likes carpet, carved mahogany furniture and some color for interest. Their living room setting needs to work for sitting, reading and map study, and entertaining.

This required a lot of interview time to make sure I didn't waste our collective time and money. I gave them some reading to help them be specific and start verbalizing about the space. I gave them design magazines and asked them which rooms they liked and which they didn't.

than taking over too much by assuming. Clients should set the boundaries and priorities for the project.

In this interview, you're building your relationship with the client, finding points of common ground that will help you manage the project successfully. You can prepare for the next step of the sales presentation by getting the client's agreement on small things, starting to move together toward the solution for the whole project. A good interviewer can involve the client in the discussion to make a series of small but linked commitments that make the larger commitment of purchasing easier to reach.

Pay attention to the roles and relationships in a client organization. In the interview stage, you need to talk to *all* the people who should participate in design decisions.

JANE'S NOTE

I recently designed a doctor's office. Once into the project, I realized you must talk with everyone who is going to use the space, not just the people who are paying the bills. I needed to understand how the secretaries, nurses, doctors, and patients used the space. If you don't ask at the beginning, they will tell you midway in the project and it will cost you much mental stress as well as financial problems with the project. Or worse, they'll complain at the end—and there go your happy clients and your referrals.

Listening Is a Critical Skill

Take the time to find out how well you listen. It doesn't matter how good a listener *you* think you are—what matters is how you are perceived by your clients. Get some feedback on how well others think you listen. The best feedback is from a former client. If you can't get that, ask a friend or someone

---

HOW TO IMPROVE YOUR LISTENING

- Create the right setting for good listening when you talk to clients. Arrange for no interruptions and hold phone calls.
- Be aware of the amount of time you and your client each talk in a client consultation—aim for getting the client to talk while you listen for at least 80 percent of your conversation.
- Show that you are listening—take notes and make eye contact. Use nodding and other nonverbal responses.
- Never interrupt.
- Ask for clarification by asking more questions or making a reflective statement of what the client has said.
- Listen for ideas, not just words.
- Hold off the impulse to fill silences—let the client speak first.
- Have your questions ready so you can focus on what the client is saying—not on forming your next question.
- Rather than interrupt to ask a question, wait for a pause and ask, "May I ask a question to clarify what I'm hearing?" In this way you ask for clarification without taking control of the conversation from the client.
- Reflect your listening and receptivity to the client's comments through your body language—don't lean back and cross your arms, making a barrier between you and the client. Keep an open stance and lean forward slightly.
- Don't jump to conclusions or make assumptions about what the client really means without verifying. Check your understanding by repeating what you hear the client saying.
- Answer the client's questions briefly and to the point—don't get off on a tangent—and bring your focus back to hearing the client.

who's worked with you to rate your listening skills. Ask someone who will give you honest, accurate feedback. Don't ask someone who is too nice to tell you what they feel.

Aim high when you listen. Make it your goal to hear the whole meaning of what your client is saying. Good listening goes beyond words to understanding the underlying meaning of the words. You need to "hear" clients' fears, anxieties, hopes, and expectations by attending to how their words are spoken and watching body language. Your goal is active, engaged listening — show the client that you're listening.

Free Consultation or Not?

Professional service providers often offer free service time as part of their selling process. Free consultation gives potential clients a chance to sample your service. It's one of the best ways to demonstrate to the client what your service is worth and to demonstrate your problem-solving skills.

Consulting shows the client that your agenda is helping, not just selling. But you need to have a strategy for how much help to give without giving away the client's need for your service. Don't jump in with all the information you have to solve the problem, just enough to convince the client to hire you.

Qualifying Your Client

Qualifying prospective clients is important. Because selling a service takes a lot of time, you need to know early in the process that this relationship can lead to a potential sale.

"What I learned was to begin to qualify referrals," says Mary Ann Bryan, talking about her experience in expanding her business scope with leads from new referral sources. "That is the key piece for most young designers. They just take anything that walks in. Until you learn to qualify a person who is really interested in design and has enough money to pay for it, you're never going to do design. You're just going to shop for someone."

Qualifying means being clear that this is a potential sale for you and a potential profitable job. As you get to know a prospective client, begin gathering the information you need. To qualify a client you need to know that

1. You are dealing with the right person — the person who has the information and will make the buying decision.

2. The client can afford your service.

3. There is a need for your service.

4. This is a job that you want—will it be profitable and does it fit into your marketing plan?

5. You have the skills and expertise to service this client well.

6. This is a client you can work with.

"Qualifying clients is part of setting the parameters of who you are and what you want to be," says Michael Temple. "There are so many designers who are afraid to say *no*. Or they realize it's not working after they signed the contract. Because you can spend so much of your energy and time losing money by taking on every Tom, Dick, and Harry—I think we only learn that by experience.

"When the client calls, you have to be able to have them explain what they are really looking for. And you can tell if someone has worked with a designer before. Those who have not I usually pass on. I give these names to other designers or give them a list of five or ten designers I recommend they work with. This, in turn, gets me business in referrals from these designers."

But remember that qualifying clients means finding the clients that fit into *your* unique marketing design. Not all designers have chosen to limit their practice to larger jobs. Mary Ann explains her marketing strategy in accepting small jobs. "I want small jobs because they keep people thinking of me and can lead to big jobs for me. Some of my very best clients now were young ones who had very small projects 20 years ago. And they grew up and made more money. It's important to do small jobs for several reasons. One is not to lose someone from your fold. The other is to get someone when they are just getting started and help educate them. They never become a good design client if the right designer doesn't reach them early on."

Sarah Boyer Jenkins explains her process of qualifying clients. "When doing show house rooms, I leave cards offering a free in-house consultation. After a phone interview, if I feel it is going to materialize into something, I would go to their home. But if they just have a question or a problem they want to solve, I have them come to the office and I give them that free time. It may not lead to work for them, if their problem really can be solved in an hour. But it can lead to their giving your name to another person."

How do you research potential clients to know whether or not they qualify? Check them out through your network of professional friends—see who may have worked with this client before. If the client is a business, ask the company to send you its annual reports and company literature. Ask a reference librarian to help you locate recent news articles about the company.

Presentations

A presentation can be a simple face-to-face meeting to discuss the project with the prospective client. Or it can be a formal, carefully staged audiovisual show involving your entire staff, presented to the interview committee of a large company, or any other dialogue situation that falls between these two extremes. Always fit your presentation to the context of the client's needs.

Many sales situations will specify for you the kind of presentation required. In less formal situations, though, ask questions and investigate the client's situation to know the kind of presentation that will be most effective. Designers eventually learn the expectations of their target clients regarding presentations. But when you're presenting to different clients, ask around to learn the norms and expectations in this context.

Keep the presentation focused on the clients' interests and what they need out of this project. Use phrases the client has used in your previous discussions and refer to the project the way the client does. Pose your design solutions in terms of the client's point of view. Keep your benefit statement part of the discussion all the time — stress your unique benefits. Your presentation should build the client's excitement and confidence in you as well as answer their questions.

A good presentation should cover the following points:

- Client problems and needs — use these to establish a theme for the presentation.
- Your design solution.
- Your qualifications and experience.
- Project schedule and management.
- Project budget.

Commercial Design: How to Prepare Presentations

1. Research the client and the project thoroughly.   If the client is a company, ask for copies of annual reports and other published materials. Look at similar projects done for this client or their competitors. Read trade publications. Talk to the client and ask questions. Know as much as you can about the client's decision criteria — if the bottom line is staying on schedule and under budget, don't base a presentation totally on creativity and innovation. And know who will make the selection decision. Know who your competitors are for this project — know their strengths and weaknesses.

2. Customize your presentation to focus on the client.   "We can do customized slide shows for presentations," says Deborah Steinmetz. "I may have three or four basic shows—for retail, for office, for industrial. I'll actually put slides together that explain why my company is of benefit to this other company and use this other company's name in the slides. It personalizes the presentation for them. We try to personalize the presentation, using our background of knowing what the people are looking for. For instance, we might put slides together that show how our computer system is going to help them."

3. Plan your presentation and have a rehearsal with all the people who will participate.   Always have a practice run with the audiovisual equipment you plan to use.

4. Use well-prepared presentation visuals and audio, but be sure that you've chosen the right visual and audio devices and that you use them effectively.   Know how and why to use slide shows, boards and photographs, overhead projectors, handouts, or a proposal. In a design presentation, be as richly descriptive as possible—use touch, sound, and visuals to reach out to those listening. Use vivid illustrations. But don't fall into the trap of seeing the visuals as the center of your presentation. Remember that visuals are only aids to presenting ideas. The presentation isn't show and tell—it's people relating to other people and communicating.

5. Anticipate concerns or questions the client will raise.   Prepare answers to possible questions but also be ready to think on your feet. If you don't know the answer to a question, never try to bluff. Without dropping your relaxed, confident manner, say you don't know the answer now but will find out and get the answer to them right away. Then go on with your presentation.

6. Engage the clients in your presentation.   Ask them questions to draw out discussion and participation. Test for agreement using phrases such as— Does this make sense? Have we covered your questions?

"We rarely use slides in presentations," says Nila Leiserowitz. "We use a black box which has matted photographs of our work. This way we can hand the photographs to them and they can touch them, instead of turning the lights down to watch slides. We also physically move across the table to sit beside them and show them the photos. That seems to be very successful. After the presentation we leave a "leave-behind," which will be everything we discussed in the presentation in a binder."

7. Demonstrate to the clients that you will manage this project as well as you are managing this presentation.   Be able to visualize the future project for the clients. Plan and manage your presentation to demonstrate your skill at managing details and getting results.

Nila Leiserowitz's firm recently got a hospital project by doing a creative presentation using computers. "Part of this client's question about us was how well we work with technology. So we brought a computer in and did part of the presentation on the computer. We showed them floor plans and project management — how we track a project. We were successful."

Residential Design: Tips for Successful Presentations

1. Plan the presentation at a time that is convenient for your clients. Minimize external distractions; suggest a time when young children are napping and clients aren't hungry or rushed at the end of the work day.

2. Suggest a meeting time during the day when you are presenting colors and fabrics. For working people, a daytime presentation on a Saturday is a better time than evenings because colors can be seen better in the daylight.

3. Dress appropriately. If your clients are blue jeans people, you can be more casual, but you should still take care to maintain a professional image.

4. Know your clients. Be sure you know what their objectives are in this project. Make sure you are meeting with the decision maker — the husband, the wife, or the mother. Arrange to meet with all who are involved in the project so you can resolve questions and conflict as soon as they come up.

5. If you have limited time for your presentation — for example, a meeting with out-of-town clients — prepare and distribute an agenda. Your agenda should list what you want to accomplish. It keeps everyone on track and focuses time available on the necessary decisions.

6. Make clients feel comfortable. Picture where you will discuss the project. Plan comfortable seating and adequate space to lay out fabric samples, drawings, and make notes. Take an associate with you to write down notes, measurements, and comments. Having someone take notes frees you to concentrate on the clients and be creative.

7. Begin your presentation by sharing your design concept for the project. The concept could be blending some newly acquired 19th- century antiques and art with the owners' contemporary furniture and home. Practice and organize your thoughts before your meeting, to be prepared to demonstrate your solution to the clients' needs.

MANAGING YOUR PRESENTATION PERFORMANCE

- Try to see the room before your presentation. Check that the facilities will be compatible with your equipment.

- Get into the room early to set up and do a quick test of your equipment. You may want to rearrange seating to create the atmosphere you want or promote discussion.

- Create an informal setting for yourself—maybe sit on a stool or table. Appear relaxed and conversational.

- Clue your audience into the presentation so it will make sense—tell them what you will tell them and show them. Don't make them guess what is coming—avoid surprises.

- Dress appropriately, slightly more formally than your clients.

- Prepare a good introduction and give it to the chairperson or introduce yourself.

- Hand out an agenda to guide the audience through your presentation.

- Be sincere.

- Stay within your allotted time.

- Stay calm, confident, and flexible.

- Don't overwhelm the client with too many choices.

- If possible, keep from dimming the lights and losing the audience's attention.

- Don't turn your back on the audience when presenting any visuals.

- Watch the body language of your audience and use it as a cue to your delivery. Pick up your pace or stop to ask questions if you see the audience getting restless.

- Avoid techno-speak and jargon. Define your terms clearly.

- Distribute leave-behinds personally.

- Thank the clients for this opportunity, shake hands, and make your goodbyes personal and confident.

- To make good formal presentations, you need to be comfortable with public speaking. Refer to the section on giving speeches in *Chapter 5: Breaking the Ice with Prospective Clients* for more suggestions.

8. Presentation materials should be clean and orderly. Arrange the materials in the order of your presentation. It's helpful to have materials in zip-loc bags, folders, or notebooks. Clients like to see several choices but not too many to be confusing. The worst presentation outcome is to end up with heaps of stuff on the table and everyone in confusion. Small boards are useful for residential designers.

9. Be sure to check availability on all materials you show clients. There is nothing worse than to have clients fall in love with a fabric, build a room around it, only to find that the fabric is discontinued.

10. Be candid with clients about the value and problems of materials. Be honest — be willing to say that this silk fabric is the most beautiful choice, but it may not last more than two years because the sun could cause it to rot. Discuss guarantees and service warranties when appropriate.

11. Help the clients visualize how the project design will look. If you are using a fabric for draperies, you can fold it to give it dimension and take it to the room where it will be used. Use masking tape to tape wallcovering samples to the wall. Leave samples with the clients so they can see them in all lights.

12. Get clients involved and excited about their projects. Encourage questions. Help them visualize by painting a picture with your words and showing them how they will use the new design. For example, say "This will be a perfect intimate corner for you and your husband to read, listen to music, or have a glass of wine away from the main flow of the house."

13. Listening is an important part of a good presentation. Reflect what you are hearing back to the clients to be sure you have heard them correctly.

14. Tell clients you are excited about working with them and confident about the success of the project.

Using Boards in Presentations

Boards are an indispensable support to good presentations. But always have a plan for using boards as effectively as you can. Each client's situation is different. Think about how the client will see the boards and how you can use boards most effectively to make your points. Strong boards are primarily visual, so keep the text to a minimum. Where text is needed, use large lettering that will be visible to your audience.

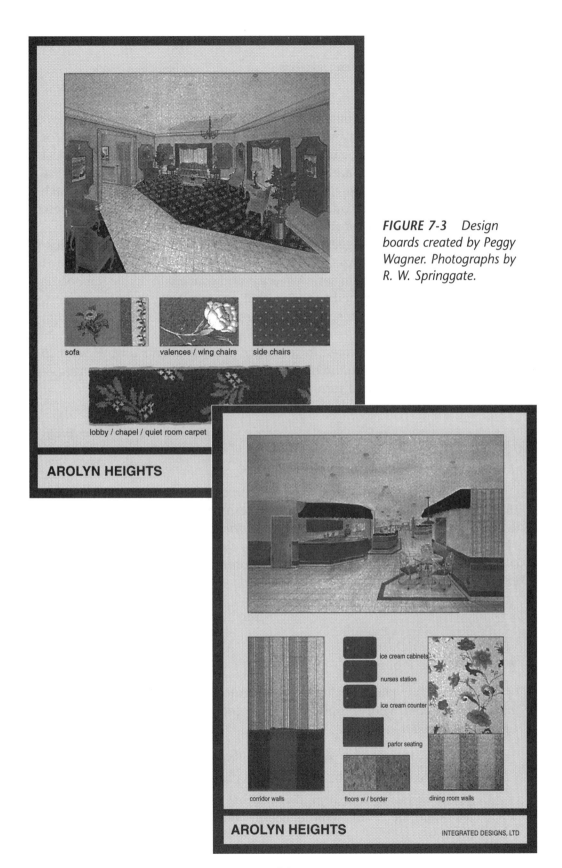

FIGURE 7-3 Design boards created by Peggy Wagner. Photographs by R. W. Springgate.

sofa

valences / wing chairs

side chairs

lobby / chapel / quiet room carpet

AROLYN HEIGHTS

ice cream cabinets

nurses station

ice cream counter

parlor seating

corridor walls

floors w / border

dining room walls

AROLYN HEIGHTS

INTEGRATED DESIGNS, LTD

185

"We often use boards, but we always sit down and strategize — to know what would be truly relevant to this client," says Nila Leiserowitz. "For instance, we may make a board for identifying and talking about the project issues. We may say these are the issues we see your project has and these are the ways we would solve these issues. We do a customized board for each client with the client's logo on the board. We make sure they know that these boards were created just for them."

Cheryl Duvall's firm suggests a useful system for preparing boards quickly. "We're using a standardized board format for all of our boards. Our boards are all 24 x 32, made of foam core. We use a grid concept to divide the boards into six rectangles. Everybody follows that concept for each presentation. Floor plans, photos, sketches, whatever we need to show in a presentation, all fit the grid.

"We keep the boards stored in the office because clients always want to see past work. We can grab the boards and go and it all looks customized — because it's in the standard format."

JANE'S NOTE

I find it helpful to use boards even for a small jobs. I use a small board to show the client how the project will look. For example, a board would show tile, wallcovering, wood tones, fixture colors, and the cabinet style for a bathroom. These boards are helpful in selling the job. And then it becomes a nice gift to the client. It's something the client can keep and use to select towels and accessories in the future.

Writing Effective Proposals

A proposal provides the client with technical, management, and pricing information about your proposed design project. Your proposal should accomplish three things.

1. Present your analysis of the clients' needs.
2. Convince the client you are able and eager to deliver results.
3. Justify choosing your firm in terms that make sense to decision makers. Build the client's confidence in your firm and your ability to do the work.

When you receive a Request for Proposal (RFP), your first decision should be whether or not to respond. Investigate the project and find out if it is something you can do. Many firms feel compelled to respond to an RFP "just in case." But this is a poor strategy. A half-hearted proposal wastes your time and tarnishes your reputation for quality.

Don't do a proposal unless you're going to show your professionalism at its best. Be sure the project is one you really want should you win the bid: Is this a client you want? Will the job be profitable for you? Will it move you in the direction of the work you want? Do you have the resources you need to do this job?

If you decide to respond, study the RFP and be sure you understand what the client wants. Research the client and project as thoroughly as you can. The research process for presentations described earlier in this chapter will help you prepare proposals as well. Commit your time to write an outstanding proposal.

A winning proposal should

- Demonstrate your understanding of the clients' business and industry.

- Demonstrate your understanding of the project—and of the client's problems, needs, and situation.

- Outline a good project plan, backed by a sound, persuasive rationale —linking what the client needs and wants with your solution based on your unique services. Offer creative ideas and innovative solutions.

- Provide evidence that you can pull it off—demonstrate your ability to meet the client's needs.

- List adequate staff and their qualifications for this project.

- Provide a reasonable cost estimate, well supported with cost explanations.

- Be well organized and clearly written.

- Use well-designed graphics and visuals effectively.

- Be responsive to the RFP.

After drafting your proposal, take a break and then reread it. Does it sound like a real person wrote it? Does it have some warmth and personality? Does it sound as if a real person will want to read it and will understand it? If not, go back and deinstitutionalize it a little. Remember that even a proposal is communication—a step in the process of relationship building.

Preparing a proposal has become much easier with computer technology. You can use graphics programs and desktop publishing to create a product that would have been prohibitively expensive for a small firm in the pre-

OUTLINE OF A DESIGN PROJECT PROPOSAL

1. Introduction

2. Problem Analysis
   Demonstrate your understanding of the client's situation and needs.

3. Problem Solution and Scope of Work
   Describe the project. List the tasks required and what will be done at each step—what, how, and why. State the benefits to the client of this solution.

4. Estimate of Time and Charges
   Explain the project schedule and budget.

5. Starting Date

6. Related Past Projects

7. Qualifications Statement and Staff Resumes

8. References

computer era. Using computers also streamlines the amount of work required for each proposal. You can store standard items like resumes and project histories in files and customize them to fit the RFP before printing out your copies.

"We use Ventura Desktop publishing to prepare proposals and presentations," says Deborah Steinmetz. "We have standard proposals and presentations that we tailor to fit the client. For instance, if we're going after a retail client, we highlight our retail work; if we're going after a corporate office or a high-rise development, then we highlight that. We can change the verbiage within these set formats.

"Then we can come back in and change the photographs by using color Xeroxes. You can actually produce those on color glossy paper. It's not quite as nice as your basic offset glossy full-blown color brochures, but it comes off as something well thought out and more oriented to the person who gets it. And it's a lot less of an investment."

Cheryl Duvall's design firm uses a list of questions to compile the basic information they need to develop a proposal. They reduce the time required to respond to an RFP by having key items ready. "We have resumes for each designer according to their particular focus. So I would have a health care resume, a CAD resume, one for facility management, tenant planning, or whatever. All of these are on file so I can easily pick the one that is most similar to the next project I would be chasing. We do the same for project descriptions and case studies."

THE ART OF CLOSING: ASK FOR THE CHANCE TO GIVE YOUR BEST

Closing the sale is the mystique in selling, viewed as a complex ritual known only to the initiated. We hope to demystify closing by taking a common sense approach. If you have been careful to qualify the client and to clarify the client's needs, the step to closing should be a small one—not the giant step it seems.

A purchase decision is both emotional and intellectual. In closing your sale, attend to both aspects of the client's decision. Make it easy for clients by anticipating and answering their questions. Remember that the larger and more complex the project, the more difficult the decision will be for the client.

Presenting solutions to client problems takes care of the emotional side of the decision for the client. Your focus on problem solutions should relieve client anxiety. You hope to show the client that saying *yes* is less risky than saying *no*—because you can solve the problem. Your enthusiasm and ability to share the visual excitement of the project also build an emotional commitment.

Your proposal, or presentation, takes care of the intellectual side of the decision. Present all the facts and details and showcase your own expertise to assure the client that this will be a wise decision. List the reasons why this project is the logical solution to the client's needs.

Your *facts* should be persuasive, so *you* don't have to persuade. Let your facts speak for you. As you close the sale, you're *pulling* the willing client with you—because your benefits match their needs. You don't have to switch gears at the close and start *pushing* a reluctant client into saying *yes*.

Closing the sale for designers is

- Answering questions and providing additional information.
- Clarifying concerns and issues.
- Cementing a mutually beneficial partnership.
- Asking for the job.

If you've built your case carefully and based it on client perspective and needs, your client should be ready to say *yes*. But remember that you still need to ask. And *how* you do the asking is important. Be aware of the context of each selling situation and attend to what your client is saying and feeling.

Communicate to the client that closing is a small step that leads naturally out of the relationship that has already been established. Be sure to stay relaxed and confident—it's easy for your client to get anxious in response to a higher tension level from you. Strive for a comfortable balance between being matter-of-fact and making it clear that this is the point of commitment.

You might structure in a series of "trial closes." This simply means checking with the client that you are moving in the right direction and getting an affirmative answer. This practice sets a positive direction for the conversation and gives you feedback on how the client is reacting before you ask for the job. Ask the client to begin stating preferences and making choices. But don't overwhelm the client with too much to think about.

Closing requires getting clear on mutual expectations for the project. Neither you nor the client should rush through this process. Explain how you have managed similar projects. To check whether the project is clear, ask the client to state his or her expectations. Ask something like: How will you and I both know that I'm doing a good job?

Suggestions for a Smooth Closing

1. Offer a guarantee to reduce the risk of the purchase decision—standing behind your service can prevent many objections.

2. Since buying design services is a complex decision, offer to provide a proposal or estimate based on the discussion so far. After you submit your proposal, follow up and ask how they feel about the proposal. If their response is positive, ask: "When shall I start?"

3. Summarize the main points of the discussion, revisiting the problem, the benefits and the solution, focusing on the client; then ask for the job. "In terms of closing, what we typically do is repeat why we are unique, why we are not a commodity, and that we are qualified and competent," says Nila Leiserowitz. "And we ask for the job. We'll say to them that we would like to work with them and when will they be making a decision. I think you need to ask the question and show you are really aggressive in wanting their business. But I would not say: We want to know right now if we are a candidate. We ask when the

decision will be made and then ask what additional information we can provide to actually receive this job."

4. Talk the client through a simple step-by-step explanation of what is involved in purchasing your service. Make it simple for them to imagine doing it — clarity helps resolve anxiety.

5. Learn to spot the signs that the client is ready to close the selling discussion — a change in body language to be more relaxed and open, maybe leaning forward; taking notes; agreeing with your ideas. Or when the client starts asking questions about how the project will be done and who will do the work. Ask for the job when the client has no more questions and you have no more information to give.

6. One way to move into closing is with a question that assumes the sale is made and moves ahead into the body of the project. Or you can sidestep the actual purchase decision and ask the client to choose between two secondary service alternatives: Shall we start Friday or Monday?

7. Ask for the job. After you ask for a purchase decision, be quiet until the client responds. If you start talking again, it gets them off the hook in responding to your request for a decision.

8. Remember that the client is saying *yes* to a working relationship with you. Let the personal context help you. Express your enthusiasm and interest in the project and in working with this client. One positive response is often mirrored by another. If you seem diffident and non-committal, the client will probably be, too.

    "I think sales close themselves," says Michael Temple. "If you're good at what you are doing and listening to what the client wants, your enthusiasm in the presentation does it. Watch to overcome objections when they come up or redirect them into the real issue. I think when you get done with the entire concept, there is no selling to it. You are understood from the beginning. When you get to the end of the process of explaining the design you will do, the client says, 'Yes, I love all those things.' What close is left except: OK, let's get at it, give me a check."

9. Be ready with a contract or purchase order, whatever you use to complete the sale. You don't have a sale until you have the money. Spell out the terms as clearly as you can.

TIPS ON MANAGING THE FINANCIAL DISCUSSION

Closing the sale means reaching a clear agreement with clients on the project budget. Be ready to manage this discussion and give clients the information they need to make a decision.

- Discuss the question of budget on your own terms, after you've built a solid design solution. Explain the costs in terms of the benefits to the client.

- Don't talk about costs or fees. Instead use the terms *budget* or *investment.*

- Let the client be the one to bring up fees. When they do, let it be a neutral part of the discussion, not tense and loaded. Don't make the client feel in the wrong for asking about the cost.

- If the client needs to spend less, focus on satisfying mutual needs and get to the underlying issues as the basis for negotiating. But know your true bottom line— don't compromise quality or cut into your profit margin.

- Remember that you are building a long-term relationship with this client. You hope to do future jobs with him/her and hope for referrals. So be sure that your client walks away from any negotiation over the budget feeling that you are fair, honest, and reasonable.

HANDLING OBJECTIONS

Welcome objections and questions from the client. Objections give you a chance to discuss legitimate doubts and concerns and to clarify points for the client. Some objections may give you good information about the client's attitude and motives. Remember that you're still qualifying this client in terms of whether this is a job *you* want to do— is this a person you can work with effectively? Some objections may be a tip-off that nothing you can do will please this person, and it would be best to decline the project.

Remember that you're still aiming for a good match between client needs and your benefits. Don't dismiss objections that point to a real gap. This won't be a good job for you if you aren't going to meet the client's real needs.

If the client seems to be stalling by bringing up objections, probe for the reasons beneath the surface objections: "What will it take to get your business?" or "Can I give you any more information?" Learn how to ask probing questions in a relaxed, nondefensive manner to get to the underlying issues of objections. Then have a discussion about the real issue instead of the surface objection.

Effective management of objections requires the following:

1. Always be candid—it reinforces your credibility.
2. Anticipate objections and be ready to deal with them.
3. Acknowledge that you have heard and respect the objection—repeat it back to the client as a question. Then answer the concern with as much factual evidence as you can; offer to have the client talk to references.
4. If the objection is a real drawback to your solution or your service, counter it with one of your strengths, couched as a client benefit.
5. When someone brings up an objection, allow a slight pause before you respond; often the client will continue talking and will give you more information about what he/she is thinking.
6. Explain how you have overcome that particular problem in work for other clients.
7. Remember that dealing with objections is not a contest you are having with the client. Always work toward a mutual-gain resolution to objections instead of having to prove you are right.

WHEN YOU DON'T GET THE JOB

If you don't get the job, ask why. Asking why you lose jobs helps you to understand your weaknesses. And it's another contact with the client that makes a good impression for future jobs. It also gives you valuable information on what competitors are charging and whether they are marketing more effectively.

In addition, asking for feedback leaves the client with a positive impression of you. People often feel guilty about turning you down and they may react by avoiding you. If you take the initiative to show you have no hard feelings and leave a positive last impression, it's more likely that this prospective client may respond positively to you in the future.

Accepting an occasional loss of a sale without taking it personally is a helpful skill. Learn what you can from the ones that get away, but don't let yourself worry about it. Learn what you can from it and move on to be ready to close the next opportunity.

"Designers, by temperament, have a very hard time selling because we have a hard time dealing with rejection to begin with," says Gary Whitney. "It's very hard on most designers psychologically to put themselves in that marketing mode. A *marketer* has to say that every rejection is that much closer to a job."

ABOUT COLD FEET AND SECOND THOUGHTS

Postpurchase anxiety is a natural hazard of any large expenditure. The larger the purchase, the chillier the feet. The client signs your contract in the glow of the presentation and then wakes at 4:00 AM with doubts and anxiety. "Did I make the right decision?" "Is my husband going to hate it?" "Is the CEO going to say the new office is too extravagant?"

So anticipate this response and be prepared to reassure the client before the feet get any colder.

- Call right away or write a personal note to say how pleased you are to be doing this project with this client—be warm and enthusiastic.

- Call immediately with some positive news about the project—a new material that will be available, a key person who will have even more time to work on this, a craftsperson who is excited about participating.

- Take the client to lunch with another former client who had a similar project.

- Get going, be on site, and start making things happen—smoothly of course.

JANE'S NOTE

I once gave a very good presentation for a remodel of a home. I knew the rapport was good and my ideas were sound. I thought I would get the job. I didn't hear in two weeks, so I called the client and asked why I had not heard from her. She said her architect had convinced her to use an out-of-town designer he liked to work with. I said fine and thanked her for her candor. In six months, she was calling me back because she couldn't work with the architect's designer.

Ideas to Remember from This Chapter

- Selling is superb two-way communication between designer and client—the keys to the sale are relationship-building and listening.

- The early steps in the selling process are qualifying the client and assessing the client's needs and problems—both steps rely on good questions and active listening.

- Effective proposals and presentations describe the client's needs and present creative design solutions.

- The art of closing is resolving the emotional and intellectual concerns in the client's decision.

CHAPTER

8

Keeping Clients for Future Business and Referrals

Quality and Customer Service

Satisfied customers are your most powerful marketing communication, and one of the least expensive. But just one dissatisfied customer can be devastating in seeding doubts about your service or in discouraging others from considering you.

THE VALUE OF A GOOD REPUTATION

Generating and nurturing client loyalty through good service and products is very important. The only control you have over what gets passed on about your work in the word-of-mouth grapevine is to have strict standards for quality and put top priority on client satisfaction.

It is also important to contribute to a reputation for quality throughout the design profession by carefully upholding professional ethics, values, and standards. Accept responsibility for knowing your professional code of

In This Chapter

This chapter focuses on marketing *after* you've got the job. You will learn how to continue marketing effectively through the entire project and beyond.

This chapter suggests how to

- Maintain a reputation for quality.
- Deliver outstanding customer service.
- Get valuable feedback from clients.
- Use your client list to keep clients for future jobs and referrals.

---

ethics as well as all laws and regulations that apply to your business. If you're not sure you have copies of everything, ask your accountant and your attorney to check your list.

Take your professional code of ethics seriously. Keep it in a prominent place in your office, and let both clients and co-workers see your dedication to ethical business practices. But it is your behavior that counts, not the code of ethics by itself. Every designer contributes to the image the public holds of the profession. Once a profession's reputation is tarnished, it is very difficult to restore.

Concern with ethics leads to a long-term view of your relationship to clients and competitors. Each designer's integrity in the present protects the viability of the profession for the future. If the public stops believing the design profession is ethical, there will be fewer clients for all in the future. And the few clients who remain will surely be litigious.

WHAT IS QUALITY?

Quality is difficult to define and measure in a service. It exists in the client's perspective. Also quality will vary in definition from client to client. You can aim for quality by maintaining your standards, preventing mistakes, and never cutting corners. You can use only top quality products. But you can't control whether the client perceives the quality of the job in the same way you do.

This is the reason that finding out what the customer is thinking and feeling during the job and after is so critical. Perceived quality service comes out of a match between client expectations and experience. You have to stamp even the smallest details of the client experience with quality.

Ensure quality by doing well the things that clients consider important. "Success is a question of quality — not only of design, but of service," says Peter Miscovich of Los Angeles. "My definition of quality would be to give the highest level of service: to create solutions that support the business objectives of a corporation, maximize organizational flexibility, minimize occupancy cost, and serve the long-term needs of the facility or company."

Learn what is important to your clients at the beginning of the project. Ask them their expectations of you in managing the project and meeting their needs. Some simply want you to do the project for them, saving them time to devote to other things. Others want frequent progress reports and involvement in decisions. You can't know these expectations without asking. It's rarely safe to assume the client cares about exactly the same things that you do.

Once you sign a contract to do the project, schedule a meeting with the client to go over the way the project will be managed. This meeting is your opportunity to clarify what you will be doing and how, as well as drawing out the client's expectations. Also explain what you need from the client: access to information or people, timely decisions, or support. Talk over how you will work out any problems or differences of opinion. Let the client know how and when to reach you. For clearest communication, ask clients to tell you in their own words what they have heard you say about the project.

Clients know that there are a number of design firms that can deliver a high-quality design. It is much more difficult to pick a firm that can deliver service to their expectations and that has professionals with whom the client feels comfortable working. These more nebulous qualities are often the most critical in a client's decision between alternatives.

So make it your business to find out how your clients would define quality design service. Some of the characteristics that clients typically look for in a design service are

- Reliability
- Responsiveness
- Mutual confidence and trust
- Empathy
- Integrity
- Easy-to-work-with manner
- Personal involvement and caring
- Competence — in project management as well as design

But beware of delivering a standard of quality that isn't important to the client. For the client, quality is a bundle of attributes — quality and durability of materials, aesthetic appeal, function, appropriate cost, and timely project completion. Each client will care more about some attributes than others. So be aware of the difference between your definition of a quality and your client's. The *value to the client* is what matters.

"Clients are much more sophisticated today and their expectations are greater," says Peter Miscovich. "The design product I sold in 1986 was one of high concept — typically with more expensive finishes and more embellishment of space. I was much more focused on design. The design product I sell today is about efficiency and technology. It is about operational issues relating to the performance of a business. It is about ergonomics, environmental criteria, and ADA issues as well. Today, as a professional, I have developed a much more comprehensive awareness of what quality and client needs mean."

Quality has to be a continuing effort. It can't be a slogan but must be a commitment. Demonstrate to clients that you take the responsibility for delivering quality. Show clients that quality comes out of integrity and keeping promises.

DELIVERING CUSTOMER SERVICE

Quality is your client's judgment of your business and its results. Customer service is what you can do to influence the client's judgment of you. Good customer service requires putting the needs and interests of clients first, remembering every day that the only reason your business exists is to satisfy client needs and expectations. "Customer service and quality are very important to success," says Sally Sirkin Lewis. "I believe strongly that back-up in customer service is as important as sales. Even if you have the greatest product, without a strong customer service base you could be finished."

Your talent and skill are important to the success of your business, but always remember that customer service is the true foundation of a thriving design business. Most people don't need a creative artist. They want to hire a designer who is good, personable, and reliable: someone who will make them look good — and smart for choosing you.

Customer service is marketing. In a service like design, you have to keep marketing all the way through the project. "What people do not realize is that marketing does not just happen at the beginning of a job," says Gary Whitney. "It happens through and after a job. Every call I get I think marketing. I'll go out to the marble yard, I'll get on a plane, I'll stay up all night — because I'm marketing, not just designing."

Guidelines for Superb Customer Service

1. Define expectations and clarify everything you do—all through the job.

- Explain all design terms and contract language. Give clients plenty of time to ask questions.

- Make sure you understand client expectations. Keep accurate notes on discussions. Know what you have agreed to do. Never let the project stall out over a question of whose memory is most accurate —get expectations on paper and give a copy to the client.

- Don't assume that you understand what the client's expectations are. Keep checking. Don't wait until the end of the project to find that either of you misinterpreted the other. In large projects, set up periodic checkpoints to review progress and be sure the client is content.

- Refine your skills in visual communication. Visualizing the final design is often the most difficult aspect for clients. Learn to sketch, show photos, or take clients to see similar past projects — you have to supply the visual reference for clients who don't have the trained visual imagination that you do.

2. Meet and exceed client expectations.

- Give your clients more than they expect.

- Make a habit of beating deadlines.

- Make sure you never miss deadlines by keeping your workload manageable. Don't take on that extra job if it could delay current work. Be willing to say *no* or negotiate a longer time frame for the new job, rather than accepting the new job and making your schedule too tight to do quality work.

- Present opportunities for the client to shape the direction of the project. People are less likely to be critical if they feel involved and can voice their opinions.

- Don't give less service to smaller jobs. If you accept them, be outstanding.

- Don't make promises you can't meet. And never inflate client expectations. If anything, be cautious with promises so you can deliver more than the client expects.

3. Be responsive to client concerns throughout the project.

- Don't wait until the end of the job to get feedback. Check in regularly to make sure clients are satisfied.

JANE'S NOTE

Sometimes this extra service is difficult to give. But the good will is worth the extra effort. The day before Thanksgiving last year I had a list of things to do a mile long. But instead of baking pies as I'd planned, there I was in my car late Wednesday, driving 70 miles to deliver pillows as promised to a good client. The workroom couldn't have them ready until 4 o'clock that afternoon. But the client was counting on having the pillows to show visiting relatives on Thanksgiving.

- Return phone calls and answer letters as soon as possible — show that you are responsive.

- Schedule phone calls to keep the client up to date on the project. Calling clients regularly reduces their anxiety and lets them feel a part of the job. Also, if you schedule and place the call, you can manage your time by avoiding constant interruptions from client calls.

- Make time to listen to client concerns or problems and to answer questions.

4. Fix all problems immediately.

- Anticipate and prevent potential problems. Try to imagine the worst things that could happen and have contingency plans ready.

- *Never* give excuses — no matter how badly a supplier or subcontractor has let you down.

- Be quick to correct any problem. Always tell the client exactly what you will do to make it right and follow through.

- Take responsibility for any problems caused by subcontractors. Never imply it's not really your problem by blaming others. Clients don't want to hear whose fault it is — they want solutions.

- Have solutions to propose when you call to tell a client about a problem.

- Create a contingency fund — for your own peace of mind. Set aside a fund you can use for the occasional unexpected expense to fix problems. You can more readily soothe an upset client and correct the problem with poise if you're not frantic over how to pay the extra cost.

- If there are problems or adjustments during the project that will increase the cost or cause delay, let the client know as soon as possible and work out the best possible solution for both of you. Be ingenious and work out solutions that have mutual benefit. "We believe in a lot of service," says Sarah Boyer Jenkins. "This service pays off for us in client referrals. If I have a problem, I go out the same day the call comes in and we solve it. Don't let anything fester."

5. Train staff to ensure customer service will be consistent.

- If you have staff or partners who will be working on a job, make sure they are knowledgeable about the project. Authorize them to act for you in solving problems immediately.

- Put your customer service policy in writing and spend an afternoon training staff. Go through potential scenarios with customer problems and plan together how to resolve them. You want everyone who works with you to give a consistent message of excellent customer service.

- Ask your staff for their ideas in improving customer service. Find out how you can support them in working with clients.

- Reward staff for caring about good service.

6. Make your service personal—show clients that you understand their concerns and that you care about them.

- Show an interest in your clients, both during the job and afterwards. Care about their businesses or other interests as well as how well the design is working for them. Show that you see them as real people and care about them.

- Know your clients and what will help them. If the client is a business, make an effort to help—share a referral or make helpful introductions to others.

- Look for the small things you can do to please clients. In each job, include one unexpected freebie.

- Supply helpful information—not associated with selling—as a service to clients.

- Participate in client activities. If you're invited to celebrations or social events, go.

- Take a consultant or facilitator role with your clients. Look ahead for them—help them anticipate issues or problems in which design can be part of the solution. Don't wait for them to come to you. Show that you have their interests in mind by making suggestions and contributing your ideas. Become part of the client's solution team.

7. Keep improving your service. Don't assume that what you're doing is enough.

- Ask clients for candid suggestions on how to improve your business. Ask how you could improve the project or provide better service the next time.

- Create a guarantee. A guarantee shows clients how much you care about customer satisfaction.

- Keep learning and changing to make your business better — and make sure your clients know about it. Share your plans through a newsletter or regular mailings. If you get some good publicity about your business, mail copies to clients.

- Ask clients what they think — call on them to test ideas or to see if new products would be useful. People like to feel that their opinions are respected.

8. Thank clients for choosing your business.

- Thank your clients for their business and for referrals. And keep thanking them long after the job is history.

- Send thank you notes after each job. Make sure that the client has a way to refer others to you easily — leave business cards with them or something with your logo and phone number (Figure 8-1).

- Send gifts to thank clients for their business. If you don't want to get into the regular Christmas gift routine, you can send "random" gifts just to say *thinking of you* or *thanks*. Or send gifts for birthdays instead of holidays, when your gift can get lost in the crush.

- Even with the worst, the crankiest clients, make the effort to part on good terms. Say thanks, sorry it didn't work out — and wish them the best. Always leave the door open for future opportunities.

9. Show consideration for your clients — respect their time and money.

- Wait a short time after project completion to bill the client. Use this time to check in and make sure everything is right and the client is happy.

- Be considerate of everyone in the client organization. Cultivate relationships with as many people as you can. Assume that *everyone* matters.

- Make it simple for clients to maintain and care for furniture and other new items. Create a maintenance manual to leave behind. Even for very small jobs, take the time to create a list of tips on proper care.

Thank you for choosing First Choice Designs. We enjoyed working with you and hope to help with your design needs again.

First Choice
D E S I G N S

(303) 440-0517

Jane D. Martin

Residential and Commercial Interiors
2230 Knollwood Drive • Boulder, Colorado 80302

FIGURE 8-1   *Example of a thank-you note to a client.*

10. Share your successes with clients — make them proud of their connection with you.

- Position your business as one of the leaders in your field. Clients are pleased to be associated with leadership and innovation.

- Share the praise and good feeling of accomplishments. If you win awards, credit your clients for their great ideas and vision. Make clients feel like partners. Praise the taste and values of your clients — see the project as *theirs,* not yours.

11. Be honest with your clients.

- Avoid any unexpected fees or charges. Talk clients through what the bill will look like before they receive it. Explain every charge.

- Be candid in sharing your opinions about products and materials with clients. Be honest and impartial in recommending products.

- Be straightforward about your fees. Don't feel you have to conceal from clients that you are making a profit on this project. People do understand that this service is a business. See *Chapter 3: Setting Your Fees* for more suggestions on talking to clients about money.

Always be yourself. We're convinced that most clients are reasonable when they are dealing with a professional who is positive, sincere, and honest. Being honest includes being a real person — let clients know who you are.

Good customer service isn't playing a role. It has to come out of what you believe. The old slogan — the customer is always right — is misleading because it implies saying *yes* to the impossible customer through clenched teeth. Being a doormat isn't honesty any more than being an arrogant snob is. Be yourself, be reasonable, and focus on your client. Use your energy to find solutions to problems that benefit everyone.

How to Stay Motivated for Great Customer Service

"A service is a continuing relationship you have to be geared for," says Mark Hampton. "Some people are not temperamentally prepared to deliver that service over and over and over again to clients who can frustrate you or make you feel that you are always on the job. You have to have the kind of disposition that does not despise being in a service business. It's an ongoing business. Everyone laughs about the plumber who won't come, but we can't be like that and be successful."

Do whatever it takes to keep your liking for people and sense of humor intact. Both are critical to succeeding in — and enjoying — a service business as personal as design. Most clients are great, and the chance to know and work with them can enrich your life. But some are not. Clients can be difficult and demanding, and problems rarely wait for reasonable business hours.

JANE'S NOTE

I find one of the best ways to deal with the frustrations of this business is to share them with a friend who is also a designer. We have a pact to call each other with our "horror stories." I'm often angry and frustrated when I call Pat. But, by the time I finish telling her what happened, we both can't stop laughing. Then I can get back to work with my perspective and sense of humor restored.

QUALITY SERVICE AS A COMPETITIVE ADVANTAGE

Superior service can differentiate your business from competitors. If you can truly deliver the extra and demonstrate your dedication to customer satisfaction, you can promote this benefit in your marketing.

"Our clients know that we are going to service them from now on. They are important to us," says Mary Ann Bryan. "We are reimbursed for all costs involved for servicing, and we don't try to make a profit off that. We're not making a profit helping people maintain things. We consider it a benefit because it allows us to evaluate our work at a later date. And it's a PR kind of thing."

Think through what *you* would like as a client: What would convince you that this designer took a personal interest in making you happy with the job? Then do it. Personal touches are effective. Do something extra beyond the expected that surprises the client.

"We are buddies by the end of a job," says Michael Temple. "That is the service I offer — I think it's important. Clients have to feel they have won in every situation. You cannot be just the glorified salesman. You must be the service-oriented designer. If you don't change to that paradigm in the next ten years, I think you are going to be left out in the cold."

WHAT DO YOUR CLIENTS REALLY THINK?

To learn your reputation with former clients, you have to ask. Set up a systematic follow-up program to find out what clients think of your service. A good follow-up program presents a professional image to the client. Ask for feed-back with a mailed questionnaire, telephone questions, or personal interviews.

"With a job I try to make sure we have communication during and after the job so the client has plenty of opportunity to tell me about things they may have concerns about or if they are not happy. So we can make sure we have a satisfied client," says B. J. Peterson. "I don't do a formal survey but I try to make sure clients are satisfied. Some people are willing to tell you prob-lems. But others, unless you give them an opportunity, might not. But then they hate you afterwards—they carry a grudge. It's important to make sure they have those opportunities to tell you and that they are happy."

Developing and Using a Mailed Questionnaire

You are creating this questionnaire for your own information. So concentrate on asking open-ended questions that draw out client comments. You won't learn much from a list of simple questions that can be answered with *yes* or *no*.

Ask about client satisfaction with both the completed design project and your management of the job. "We can see if we have been effective in what we designed," says Cheryl Duvall of her firm's postoccupancy evaluations. "We try to incorporate that information into business development activities by summarizing the information in case studies, making it into a reason for people to use us in the future."

One excellent way to develop the questions for your questionnaire is to ask a former client to help. Choose a client whose project had some problems —you want to think of the questions an unhappy client wishes you would ask. Ask your client: "What did you want to tell me about your experience at the end of the project? Do these questions ask the right things to draw out a negative experience and suggestions for improvement?"

After you have developed your questionnaire, follow these steps for get-ting feedback from your clients.

1. Mail the questionnaire 10–14 days after the project is complete. You want the clients to have long enough to evaluate the design but not long enough to forget how they felt about the process and your ser-vice. Mail the questionnaire with a return envelope and postage to make it easy for the clients to respond.

2. If you don't get the questionnaire back, call the clients and ask if they would be willing to answer the questions over the phone.

3. Send a thank-you note when you receive a completed questionnaire. Thank clients for the feedback and for their business. If they express some good ideas for improvement or substantial critical comments, take them to lunch to discuss this further.

2230 Knollwood Drive • Boulder Colorado 80302   Jane D. Martin
(303) 440-0517

1. How did you hear about our company?

2. Did the finished project meet your expectations?

3. Are there changes you would make if you could? If so, what would you change?

4. What would have improved your satisfaction with the final results?

5. We try to provide the best service possible to our clients. Please share your comments about our service in each of these areas. We want to know your opinions and your suggestions for improvement.

• How well did we deliver what we promised?

• How well did we communicate?

• How well did we respond to your needs and requests?

• Was our staff courteous? Can you suggest ways we could be more helpful to clients during projects?

FIGURE 8-2   *Client feedback questionnaire.*

• Can you suggest improvements to our project management system? Our contracts? Our billing system? Was this process clear to you during this project?

• Did you find our company hard to work with? If so, in what ways? How could we improve?

6. What did you like the most about this project or the experience of working with our company? May we quote you for our marketing?

7. What did you like least about this project?

8. May we photograph your home or office?

9. Is there anyone you know who could use our services?

10. Are you planning another design project we can help you with in the future?

We have enjoyed working with you. Thank you for your comments— we appreciate your suggestions for improving our service.

Thank you,

Jane D. Martin

FIGURE 8-2 *(continued)*

Sometimes the Personal Interview Is Best

Personal interviews take more time than mailing a questionnaire, but they will give you the best information about what clients really think. Couch your request for feedback in a way that helps clients be honest with you. You don't want to put clients on the spot and have them tell you only the good things. Demonstrate your professionalism by sharing your own critique of the project. Then ask for the client's comments on the project and suggestions for improvement.

One way to manage getting client evaluations is to do personal interviews mixed with your mailed survey. Commit to doing a personal interview every fifth job (or whatever frequency makes sense in your business).

But always do personal interviews after jobs that have not gone well. If you suspect the client isn't pleased, make the effort to talk it over. Getting clients' feelings aired and their suggestions for improvement will help you many times more than hearing positive comments from happy clients. Peter Miscovich explains his approach. "We don't use our questionnaire on a regular basis. For the most part we try to have a one-on-one debriefing with the client — to see whether we succeeded or how we failed. I think this is really important when a relationship goes bad. There is a real opportunity to secure the relationship if you are proactive. You need to go in, sit down, and find out what the issues are. Get everyone at the table and try to develop a solution — a way out of that bad scenario. The more personalized that approach is, the more successful it will be. Someone once told me and I'll quote them — 'clients aren't concerned with how much you know, they're concerned with how much you care.'"

MAKE COMPLAINTS CONSTRUCTIVE

Teach yourself to see complaints as marketing opportunities. A client who bothers to call and complain to you is a client who is still willing to work with you. The client you never hear from is the one who walks. Tell the client that you appreciate his/her willingness to tell you what is wrong — and mean it.

If possible, make sure that you are the first person that hears complaints. If you try to avoid them, realize that others will become the audience. Bad word-of-mouth reports circulating without your knowledge can undo much of your careful marketing.

Work through the complaint without being defensive. Most complaints come in over the phone. The constraints of telephone communication require extra effort to demonstrate to clients that you are listening and that you care about their problem.

It takes preparation to respond appropriately to an emotional complaint. If the person is angry, don't take it personally. Remind yourself that the client is angry at the situation, not at you. And that you have the power to change the situation.

Keep in mind these two basic steps to a positive outcome from complaints.

1. Understand and acknowledge the emotion in the client's complaint. Listen and show that you understand. It's important to respond sympathetically. Show that you care. Tell them that you are sorry they are upset and that you understand why they feel this way—that you would feel upset, too. Ask them to tell you what happened. Then ask what it will take to make them feel better about this situation.

Never respond to emotion with logic. You don't want to make the client feel petty or stupid for complaining. Logical problem-solving comes later, once the emotion is vented and released. And *never* fall into the swamp of arguing over who is at fault.

2. Do what the client asks to correct the problem. Many complaints are quite simple. The client can tell you what would make him/her happy. Giving your full attention to the client's complaint is a large part of the solution.

Other situations may be more complex. But, if you work through the emotion in the first step, you and the client can work together to solve the problem. Now you can both use logic to analyze the situation. Ask the client to team with you to find the right solution.

Aim for a win-win solution. But be willing to pay or spend extra time to correct this problem. Above all, you want the client to feel happy with the outcome and to be reassured of your sincere desire to please.

Fix the problem and then go beyond the expected to show clients that you care about their opinion of you. You'd like this person to end the encounter saying—Thanks! You really didn't have to do *that!*

Preventing Complaints Is Always the Best Strategy

Remember to take the time in the beginning to clarify all expectations—both in the finished design and the way you handle client contact, billing, and scheduling—to prevent complaints whenever possible.

- Take the time to make sure your clients understand how your business works and how this project will be managed.
- In design projects, there are always elements that you can't control. You have to rely on many people who aren't on your payroll. Make sure your clients understand this—without using it as an excuse.

- Always be clear that the project itself is under your control. Explain how you manage projects to diminish the risk of getting off schedule or budget. Get the client to make decisions with you. If you know certain choices may create delays or other problems, explain the pros and cons to the client and decide together.

JANE'S NOTE

Some of the best people who work for me are artists. A few of them, while very talented, have a history of not completing work on time. This habit can cause huge problems with clients if it comes as a nasty surprise at the end of the project. Clients must be told before the project and given the choice of using this artist or not. I tell them that I think the artist's talent is worth the wait, but I let the clients make the decision. And I keep them informed about the artist's progress.

I work with a woodworker who is so talented I believe his work will be in the Smithsonian someday. But his attitude is that a table doesn't really have to be finished for Christmas when, after all, these clients will cherish this table all their lives. The client, however, who has invited her entire family from Indiana for the holiday and is planning to serve dinner on this very table may not appreciate his logic.

YOUR CLIENT LIST IS VALUABLE

The payoff for achieving a reputation for quality and good service is loyal clients and a steady stream of referrals. Your satisfied clients are a source of referrals, repeat jobs, and continued good will through their word-of-mouth networks. So cherish and nurture this vital marketing resource. Your client list is the heart of your business.

Marketing to former clients is more cost efficient than marketing to new clients — you don't have to spend all that time convincing them of your value. New client acquisition is always important, but it requires a larger investment. In repeat business a higher percentage of your fee becomes profit.

Yet many service professionals neglect the chore of maintaining their client lists. Make it your priority to keep your client list up to date and to keep adding to it. And learn to use it effectively to keep your clients coming back.

You need an efficient system for keeping your client information ready to use in your marketing. Set up a client profile for each job and make sure you have this information before you leave the client at the end of the project.

Computer data base programs or contact management software now make this very easy. With computer software, you are able to create forms, enter and retrieve data, and link to files in word processing to personalize messages with names and addresses. You can also create reports to see how well you're doing in generating repeat business and referrals.

What Information Do You Need?

Capture the information you will need to follow up with clients. You will gradually learn the kind of information that you need to keep about your clients. Decide for your own business what additional information would be "nice to know." Try to record everything you know about your clients and their preferences while you're finishing each job. Don't count on remembering all these small details later. Keeping track impresses clients with your caring and recognition of their individuality. Everyone is flattered when others take care to know and remember them. Take pride in not letting former clients fade into an anonymous blur.

The nice-to-know categories of client information will vary greatly between commercial and residential clients—and by design specialty. The lists below are just springboards for your thinking.

1. *Get the basics first.*
   - Name and title.
   - Organization or business.
   - Address.
   - Telephone and fax numbers.
   - Source of referral.
   - Where the contact originated: public presentations, mailings, proposals or presentations, sales calls, and so on.
   - Description of all previous design jobs for this client.

2. *Nice-to-know categories for residential designers.*
   - Names of spouse and children; ages of children.
   - Who is the decision maker.
   - Sports and hobbies.
   - Likes and dislikes.
   - Personal interests.
   - Special issues or design needs—such as allergies or the demand for environmentally safe materials.

3. Nice-to-know categories for commercial designers.

- Name of contact person in the company.
- Names and titles of all company people involved in project.
- Name of decision maker.
- Size of company.
- Space standards for the industry.
- Technological needs.
- Organizational structure/needs.
- Competitors.
- Design needs or problems.
- Likes and dislikes.
- Names of spouses of key people.
- Personal interests of key people.

We recommend setting up a computerized client list. But if you haven't yet begun using computers in your business, keep hard copy client files. Create a form that records the client information you need and keeps track of contacts with the client. Keep this information together in one place. Make it easy to use. Set up a file of index cards or a three-ring binder — both methods make it easy to add or delete individual client profiles.

Your client file becomes the basis for periodic follow-up messages to clients. "I send a letter to my mailing list about four times a year," says B. J. Peterson. "I'll make it seasonal. I mail to clients, keeping up with clients from 20 years ago. I also mail to a select list of people I work with a lot: contractors, architects, landscape architects, and such. It's a select list; I don't send it to people I don't want to work with. More and more of my referrals are coming from these professional constituents. In the letter I might tell them about an interesting project I'm doing or send articles that have been printed about me. Several times I have sent the whole magazine because I was on the cover and had a ten-page article inside. You have to make the letter interesting; think about who the audience is and what would make them respond."

A good practice is to do follow-up checks on client satisfaction with design jobs. Checking with clients six months and twelve months after installation is proof to clients that you truly care how well the finished design works for them. Few service professionals carry follow-up this far. Doing this can help make your emphasis on service distinctive.

Sample Client List Form

Name of Client _____
Phone _____
Fax _____
Address _____
_____

Contact

Spouse

Children

Pets

Special Dates

Referred by

Description of Job

Comments _____
_____

Date _____

Staying in Touch with Your Client List

Send your client list information about your business — recent projects that might be of interest or new products and services that you're offering. This file could become the mailing list for a newsletter that keeps the name of your business in front of clients. For more ideas on staying in touch with clients, see the last section in *Chapter 5: Breaking the Ice with Prospective Clients.*

 1. Send out a customized letter promoting a specific service, perhaps offering a special service or discounted rate to "old friends."

 2. Use the deep knowledge you already have about these clients to offer design services tailored to their unique needs. This practice is the height of

targeted marketing—using your information to satisfy specific client needs. An example is sending congratulations when a former client's son graduates from high school and suggesting a consultation on redesigning his room as a guest room or home office.

3. Have small parties to celebrate a successful job or an award or to show new products or design ideas. Invite a group of clients to a warm, beautifully designed gathering (Figure 8-3).

4. Send holiday greetings and birthday cards to maintain contact with clients. This gesture keeps your name current with them. Make your communication unique to stand out from other services who may also remember these events (Figure 8-4).

5. Pick another holiday that gets less attention than Christmas and Hanukkah to send cards or a little gift: Halloween, Thanksgiving, or the first day of spring. Show your creativity and thoughtfulness— use your sense of style to remind clients that you're a good designer.

6. Send a special offer to clients and ask them to pass it along to a friend. This could be a coupon for free consultation or an invitation to a special event.

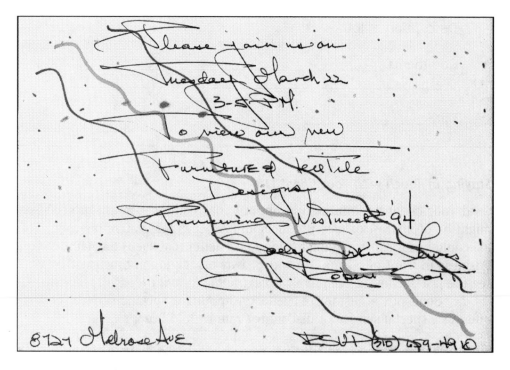

FIGURE 8-3   A hand-drawn invitation designed by Sally Sirkin Lewis.

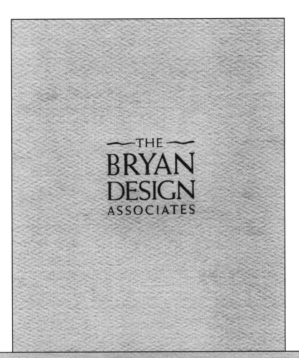

FIGURE 8-4 *The Bryan Design Associates Christmas card, which is personalized with a photograph of one of their projects. Photograph copyright © Hal Lott Photography. Card Design by David B. Waller, Jr.*

Ideas to Remember from This Chapter

- Quality is the client's perception of your design work and your service; this perception is formed by every detail of the client relationship and the design project.

- Customer service is what you do to influence the client's judgment of your business; good customer service requires putting the client's needs first.

- Knowing what your clients think about your business is the key to improving—develop a system for getting good client feedback.

- Your client list is one of your business's most valuable assets. Imaginative use of your client list becomes a competitive advantage.

CHAPTER

9

Forty Marketing Ideas to Get You Started

Focus Your Marketing for Better Results

1. Use positive words to refer to your business and yourself. Learn to feel comfortable using words such as award-winning, creative, efficient, skilled, prestigious, and professional to describe your design work. Use words that emphasize the value of the project to the client —words like investment, value, excellent, and extraordinary.

2. Stay in touch with old clients. Call your clients to say hello or write a warm handwritten note. Invite them to a party or an event in your studio. Send copies of recent publicity about your business. Keeping your name current in their minds increases your chance of referrals or another job from old clients.

3. Contribute consulting time to a charity. Offer a block of design consultation time as a contribution for a charity auction fundraiser. Make an attractive display for your auction item with prominent logo and some photographs. It's good publicity for your business and a contribution to a good cause. And the person who has the high bid for your consultation may become your next client.

4. Write a "how-to" design article for your local newspaper.   Home and lifestyle editors are always looking for material. List three or four possible topics and call the editor to check out interest. Demonstrate your expertise *and* get good publicity.

5. Join an organization to which prospective clients belong.   Pick an organization that interests you and brings you into contact with potential clients. This organization could be a home builder's association, the International Facility Management Association, the Junior Symphony Guild, or a tennis club. Be active and volunteer to meet people and to be well known in the organization.

6. Help educate the public about what designers do.   We need to educate every client about design and the benefits of working with a designer. Take every opportunity to speak about design services and to demonstrate your design knowledge.

7. Join ASID or IIDA referral services.   Don't overlook the obvious — list your name and business information with these referral services. These organizations want to support us, and they do a lot to promote the value of design to the public. These referral services can be a great source of leads.

8. Register at your local design center.   Clients often look to these centers to tell them who are good designers. The San Francisco chapter — ASID California North — has spearheaded a program in which designers can show three projects, their profile, and their photograph on a touch computer screen at the design center. The system is called Design Finder.

9. Speak on the radio on a design subject.   Talk radio stations are always looking for new material listeners want to hear. Pick a topic that is current and relevant — make it interesting. For example, talk about environmental issues from a design perspective.

10. Build a relationship with other designers to share resources and practices.   Build a peer network to share marketing ideas and resources. Networking can be done by phone, informal chats, or regular gatherings to exchange ideas. Create opportunities for co-op advertising and other joint marketing.

11. Organize a showcase room or house.   Organize a group of designers to sponsor your own showcase project. Plan your event as a benefit for hospice or another good cause. Take charge of the project and create good publicity while demonstrating your talent.

12. Get a testimonial. Many designers are reluctant to ask clients for testimonials. But satisfied clients are proud and flattered to help.

13. Send a series of 3 x 3 laminated cards with tips on decorating to your client list. Print a series of tips with your logo, address, and phone number. Send them monthly or quarterly. Send tips on home offices, different styles of throw pillows, or whatever.

14. Send cards for client birthdays and special events. The more personalized, the better. If you can send one for a child's graduation or the anniversary of opening their business, it's impressive. This gesture makes your clients feel special.

15. Always carry business cards. Both past and future clients need them. Give your card to someone who wants your phone number, even if it's just to schedule a future tennis game.

16. Figure out what makes you unique in design and develop it. Analyze your strengths as a designer. Talk to clients to find out what they value in you. Compare your work and client service to other designers to find the special value in what you do. Then promote it.

17. Exceed a client's expectations. Do something extra on each job — something that shows clients your sincere desire to please them. If there is a problem, fix it quickly. Make your solution even better than the original plan. Make sure these clients will rave about your service instead of complaining about problems.

18. Get feedback from clients. Get feedback by phone, letter, or in person. Ask what was good and bad about the project. Do they need more work done or know somebody who does?

19. Challenge your staff and contract workers to market for you. Supply the people with whom you work with business cards and marketing material they can share with potential clients. Share your marketing message and tell them what clients you hope to attract. Reciprocate by recommending their services to friends and colleagues.

20. Update or add to your portfolio, brochure, or marketing material. Make a commitment to do this every six months. It's far too easy to let this slide until you've got a presentation to make tomorrow, and you want to include your most recent project — but you've not yet gotten photographs.

21. Improve your communication skills: drawing and speaking. Keep working on your skills. Practice using drawings to demonstrate concepts to clients. Tape one of your speeches and take time to listen carefully, critiquing and thinking about how to improve. Take classes in drawing, art, and public speaking.

22. Read a marketing book or go to a seminar. You're already ahead — you're reading this book! Stay current on new thinking about marketing. Read up-to-date books and articles about marketing. Take a marketing seminar — find out when ASIDs Marketing by Design seminars will be offered in your area.

23. Know your strengths and weaknesses — promote the strengths and improve the weaknesses. Ask clients and colleagues to tell you your strengths and weaknesses — as a designer and as a marketer. Be proud of your strengths and market them. Learn ways to overcome or compensate for your weaknesses.

24. Start a research file with articles about clients and potential clients. Research clients and learn everything you can about their businesses. Keep files of clippings and material gathered about them. The more you know about them, the better you can meet their needs and gear your marketing to speak their language.

25. Think globally. Learn languages and customs. Be open to new possibilities and think how you can market globally. Talk to other businesses who are successful in international marketing and learn from their experiences.

26. Put a sign on the grounds of a current project or put your logo on your car. Let people know who you are and what you do. Be proud of your work and your business.

27. Use interns from local colleges to help with design, marketing, or graphics. Get help with your needs while giving a student valuable on-the-job experience. They'll also share new ideas and a fresh perspective. This generation is the source of future clients — learn how they think and what is important to them in design.

28. Whether you won the job or not, ask why. Most of us would rather forget it when we don't get the job, but asking nets valuable information about how both you and competitors are seen by clients. Ask clients to tell you why they hired you — you'll learn which of your business's benefits are most important to your clients.

29. Send holiday or end-of-project gifts. Or send a donation to a charity in the client's name. Gifts are always a cordial way to thank clients and maintain their good will. Be creative in thinking of unique and appropriate gifts.

30. Build good relationships and be courteous to your suppliers and trades people. Nurture your relationships with suppliers. Show your sincere appreciation for their help. Be loyal and supportive of their businesses. When someone does something extra to help you, send a thank-you note.

31. Computerize your current and prospective client lists. Take advantage of a slow time in your business to become computer literate. Transfer your card files to computer files—maybe with the help of one of those student interns. Invest in computer software that sets up mailing lists for you (see the list of software in Appendix B). Then enjoy the new flexibility in your client mailings and the ease of updating and maintaining your lists.

32. Take a weekend or day to focus solely on marketing. Try to do this twice a year. Review your mission. What worked in your last marketing plan and what did not? What new marketing methods would you like to learn about and try in your business?

33. Analyze your competition. List your competitors and write down their strengths and weaknesses. Estimate how much of the total design market each firm commands. Who is getting the jobs you want? What do they do differently? What can you learn from your competitors?

34. Put together a slide library. Take slides of projects. Organize these into job categories for quick retrieval when you want to show your work. Slides are useful for presentations, contests, and awards competitions.

35. Create a specific space in your office for all your marketing tools: brochures, resumes, photographs, and magazine reprints. Being organized will save a lot of time when you're on a deadline to get a marketing package together for an important client. Keeping marketing materials together also makes it easier to update all your materials at once and keep everything consistent.

36. Hold weekly marketing meetings in the firm so all employees understand your marketing goals and priorities. Show your staff that marketing is important to everyone in the firm. Brainstorm new marketing ideas—keep your staff motivated to keep learning and thinking about marketing. Share successes and emphasize marketing results.

37. Be on design student jury panels or career day panels, or be involved in community activities, professional activities, and seminars that can be good publicity.   Send out press releases for these events. Arrange to be interviewed about design training and the future of design. Be creative in planning activities and events and in creating good publicity.

38. As you work, think people, not projects.   Keep nurturing client relationships. Dream up a way to remind yourself of the relationship — clip pictures of your client to the client's boards along with your sketches. Make a list of what clients have told you matters most to them and tack it on the wall where you see it often.

39. Schedule time to keep up with the design industry.   Go to conventions and other industry events. Read design industry publications and know the current issues. Go to the design center frequently just to see what is new — familiarize yourself with new products and meet with reps to see their new lines.

40. Send useful information to clients.   Keep a record of business and personal interests of your clients. When you see an article or some research that matches the client's concerns, send a copy with a personal note. Your clients will be grateful for your attention, and they'll see you as a thoughtful and knowledgeable resource.

A

Starting Your Own Interior Design Business

A Checklist for Evaluating Your Entrepreneurial Skills

Personality and Background

1. *Do you really want to be a designer? Do you feel you are creative and talented?*

   Are you artistic? Can you visualize a completed project? For example, can you "snatch and grab" fabrics quickly for a project?

2. *Are you decisive? Willing to make decisions?*

   Your first choices are often the best. You need the confidence and the guts to stay with your instincts. There are many decisions in running a business. Your employees need to look to you for leadership.

3. *Do you know your weaknesses and are you willing to hire someone whose strengths complement your weaknesses?*

   Interior design is a business of many details: suppliers' costs, availability, backorders, cost to client of product and labor, your labor cost, comparative costs, and so on. Hire the help you need to ensure everything will be done well.

4. *Do you have good organizational skills?*

   You must be organized to run the business, relate well to your employees, market your services, and be a competent designer.

5. *Do you enjoy people?*

Do you find them fascinating and want to spend time with all kinds of people? Design is a business in which we get to know our clients very well. It is important to appreciate differences in peoples' attitudes and lifestyles.

6. *Will you do residential or commercial design or both?*

Do you enjoy the personal relationships with residential clients? Do you want to do small offices or design large offices?

7. *Can you be honest?* And *tactful?*

You have to have the guts to tell people what looks bad. This should be done tactfully. Instead of saying, "Your master bedroom is outdated and has no character," say: "Does this bed have sentimental value for you, or could we replace it with one that has more weight and fits the size of the room better?"

8. *Are you able to market?*

Will you ask for the job? If you get rejected, can you accept it and try harder for the next one?

9. *Do you have a basic ability in math ?*

It is necessary to estimate costs for window covering and carpeting jobs, to figure pricing and percentages. You have to be able to figure a project in different ways and make your estimates clear to clients.

10. *Do you have good communication skills?*

It is important to get your ideas across clearly to your clients and employees.

11. *Do you have a sense of self-worth and ability?*

You must have the confidence to charge for your time and services and have a positive attitude about your profession.

12. *Are you able to talk about money with clients?*

This skill is necessary to run a profitable business. Talking about money gets easier the more you do it.

13. *Are you willing to work hard?*

Some projects demand many hours and late nights. Interior design is a business that takes a lot of energy.

14. *Do you have a sense of humor?*

If you cannot laugh at circumstances or at yourself in this business, you may get overly frustrated or burn out.

15. *Are you flexible?*

The interior design market changes, and client needs change. There are always backorders, discontinues, or delays. Your time and attitude must be flexible for the client.

16. *Are you a person of integrity?*

Integrity is the key to a successful relationship with a client and the success of the business.

17. *Do you have the training? Are you willing to keep up with your training? To get the training and experience you need, you can*

- Go to school and get your degree in interior design.
- Work for another designer or store.
- Read design magazines and trade journals.
- Travel—even if you don't stay in fancy hotels, go and experience other places, from little towns to huge ones. Go to art museums, study the architecture. A designer is the sum of all experiences.
- Take adult education classes or professional organization classes.
- Develop a group of trusted design friends from all age groups. Stimulate and challenge each other. Use design peers as a sounding board for new ideas.
- Train students, use interns. It's fun to learn what the younger designers are thinking.
- Learn to draw or sketch. Sketching is great to help clients visualize the finished project.
- Be involved and attend your professional organizations.

Business Structure

1. *How do you want your business structured: sole proprietorship, corporation, or partnership? Have you met the legal requirements?*

A lawyer is helpful to explain the differences and to set up your business. Check with city, state, and federal governments to be sure you have complied with all legal requirements.

2. *Have you registered the name of your company and gotten a sales tax number for your state?*

   If you use a trade name or any name other than your first or last name, you must register it — with the Department of Revenue if you are a sole proprietor and with the Secretary of State if you are a Corporation. If you sell products, you will be required to have a sales tax license. There are fees for the license as well as for registering your name.

3. *Where will you work?*

   Are you going to have a home office or outside office? If you have a partner and are working from home, whose address will be the main office?

4. *Will you have a partner?*

   The decision to create a partnership is a big one, and much thought should go into it. How will the money be divided? Will you spend equal time? Will your hours be full time or flexible? Will it be a company that appreciates family time — a lifestyle other than the corporation — or will it be a total work company? Choose a partner who has goals similar to yours. Partnerships should include enjoying, respecting, and complementing each other's talents.

5. *Will you have employees?*

   You will need to pay social security and you may need to provide medical benefits. Is contract labor appropriate for your business? Which employees will have which responsibilities? You will need to set up a Wage Withholding Account for income tax withholding.

6. *Who will do your marketing?*

   Will you be in charge, will you have support help, or will an employee be in charge? The best situation is when everyone involved is marketing the business.

7. *Do you know where to get outside help?*

   Many Chambers of Commerce give assistance. Senior citizen's groups volunteer their expertise to start up companies.

Financial Requirements

1. *How do you get credit?*

   Will you buy or borrow money for your office equipment? Do you need credit? Do you need a Dun and Bradstreet number to get credit from suppliers?

2. *Have you assessed your risks?*

Do you need insurance? Many designers carry errors and omissions insurance. Know your legal responsibility as it applies to your type of design; for example, disability requirements in public spaces.

3. *How will you do your accounting?*

You can do the accounting yourself, use a computer software program, or hire a bookkeeper.

4. *Do you have adequate financing?*

How will you pay for inventory? Can you cover clients' purchases or do you need to have clients pay in full?

Establishing Your Office

1. *What will your office needs be?*

Phone. Obviously an essential purchase. How many lines do you need? Do you want call waiting? Where should the telephones be placed?

Answering Machine. It is important to have an appropriate message on the machine. Use your message as an opportunity to market. Answering services may be an alternative.

Copier. A must.

Fax. An essential as soon as you can afford it. It is such a time saver to communicate instantly in written form.

Computer. A wonderful asset for running your business as well as marketing. Great marketing programs, business programs and very sophisticated design programs are available.

Laser Printer. Prints with a professional look.

Modem. Allows your computer to connect with a worldwide network of phone lines.

Office Furniture. This may include desks, files, drawing tables, client seating, and a reception area. Your office or studio should be orderly, professional, and display some of your work. A library of resource books is helpful.

2. *Do your office supplies convey a consistent image?*

Make sure your proposals, letters of agreement, cards, and stationery are professional looking and appropriate to reach the clients you want.

Suppliers and Workrooms

1. *Where will you find your suppliers and workrooms?*

Ask other designers to refer their suppliers. You can do them a favor in return. Go to show houses and get business cards for suppliers and workrooms whose work you like. Public libraries often have lists of local artists. Develop your artists and craftspeople — they make you look good because of their uniqueness and quality. Keep records of your trades people — what they do, where they live, and their phone numbers.

2. *Where will you get your samples, line, and stock?*

Investigate access to samples through your local design center. If you are too far away from a design center, you will need to build an inventory of samples in your office. Commercial designers are normally given their samples.

APPENDIX
B
Tips for Using Technology

The Joy of Computers — Really!

Computer technology is a necessity for managing a small business efficiently. We know that there are still designers who haven't yet added computers to their office systems. Many people are still intimidated by them. But no one can afford to ignore the time-saving potential of computerizing financial management and marketing activities. Nor would we want to do without the creative tools of CAD and desktop publishing. Imagine a program that draws for you!

We advise you to invest in a computer system as soon as you start your business. It is one of the best investments you can make. We can't imagine trying to market effectively and run a design business without this electronic "staff" to help.

If you're a computer neophyte, get advice on what system will work best for you. We won't even try to explain the options — the choices are too numerous and computer needs too individual. Ask other designers what computer system they have and what software programs they use. Take time to be in the office, just watching how people use their computers. Then make a list of your questions and the things you would like your computer system to do. Locate a good computer consultant or a friend who is adept, and start researching what you want.

Work to overcome computer phobia. Observe and learn and experiment. Find your own way to understand computer systems and to appreciate all the things a computer can do to help you.

JANE'S NOTE

I had no computer knowledge when I started working on this book. But, since we were creating this book on a computer, it made sense to be able to store drafts on the computer and trade files as we worked. I was terrified in the beginning, but I decided I would try to learn. But I felt like my friend, Julie Stewart-Pollack, who said, "I thought when I died the tombstone would read— 'Here lies Julie, she never touched a computer.'"

I bought a Macintosh PowerBook and started trying to learn. The best thing I did was hire my 15-year-old neighbor, Tevis Morrow, to tutor me and set up my system. He was very skilled as well as patient and kind to me. It was fun to appreciate a computer from the eyes of a fifteen year old. Now I have After Dark, *my computer makes funny sounds, and I can play games in my spare time.*

What I found is that when I learn a little with the computer, I want to keep learning. I'm hoping to get my office fully computerized and stay up on the technology. I have a business program—MacAccounting. It has a client list that I plan to use for my marketing. What I have realized is the amount of time a computer can save a designer. Someday I will design a home via video-conference in Switzerland, Mexico, or China in less time and more efficiently than it takes to get design ideas and information to my clients here in Boulder.

How to Use Computer Technology Effectively

The many ways computers aid marketing are woven throughout the designers' stories included in this book. Computers boost your productivity, particularly when you work alone. Computer technology makes it easier to market your service—making more time for design.

Computer software programs can help you with the following often quite time-consuming aspects of marketing:

1. Managing and using your client list and your list of prospective clients. Contact management and data base programs allow you to capture all the information you need about clients and prospective clients. You can create data files customized to the needs of your specific business.

But the payoff for a computerized list is in list maintenance and use for mailing. You can update your lists continuously — and easily.

Your information stays current and useful. You can use these lists for mailings simply by merging the names and addresses with your marketing letters or other messages. The program prints personalized letters and envelopes for you.

2. Creating and customizing marketing materials. The word processing, desktop publishing, and drawing programs provide unlimited potential for creating excellent marketing tools. You can develop brochures, marketing packet enclosures, marketing letters, proposals, presentation graphics, and newsletters. All in your own office with your computer, the right software, and a good laser printer.

Add this capability to the innovative services now available from most copy centers and you have the potential for color copies, printing on many kinds of paper, and gorgeous special effects. The technology available for our use today is a gift of imagination. Make the time to get out and see what can be done.

3. Using CAD (computer aided design) systems for design projects. These programs are fast becoming the standard of the design world. This software takes over the time-consuming tasks of drafting and rendering.

4. Managing your business — accounting and financial management. These accounting and spreadsheet programs take over the routine work of managing your accounts and budgeting. They also allow you to create financial and monitoring reports that give you invaluable feedback about your marketing results. You can create reports that gather financial information from your electronic records and compile the figures into meaningful measures of profitability and return on marketing investment.

The key to business benefits from computer technology is to keep learning and using your imagination. We're fortunate to live in a time when the technological boundaries are stretching daily. Imagine "what if" — and there will soon be a computer program to help you complete your fantasy.

Computers are changing the way we do business. The technology allows small firms to compete successfully in some arenas with large firms in a service business like design. "I saw the vision years ago of what computers could do for me as a creative tool," says Gary Whitney. "I really pioneered the concept of using computers to bridge design and production. I can partner and create virtual corporations because of my CAD skills and my ability to modem and connect. The world is becoming a possible client."

Computer Software for Designers

This software list is by no means exhaustive. These are software programs designers mentioned to us and ones we currently use. The technology changes rapidly and is updated constantly.

1. Contact Manager Software

Mailing lists used to be a nightmare, but this software allows even a small company to keep its mailing list or contact list updated. The software organizes client names, business names, addresses, phone and fax numbers. You can group client names by business type or profession. You can group lists by zip codes.

These software programs are great for managing client and supplier lists. These programs are called contact managers because they can keep track of your contacts, record meetings, and note follow up tasks. Most programs have basic word processing capability, a telephone dialer (modem required), and a calendar to schedule meetings and phone calls.

ACT!

Symantec
175 West Broadway
Eugene, Oregon 97401
(800) 441-7234

Contact manager. The program tracks every contact, its status, and when and how to follow through. If you have a modem, you can auto dial. IBM/DOS, Windows, Macintosh.

Now Contact

Now Software, Inc.
921 S. W. Washington Street-500
Portland, Oregon 97205-2823
(503) 274-28000

Contact manager. The program tracks names, numbers, and addresses and provides a calendar. Macintosh.

2. Word Processing and Desktop Publishing Software

Word processing and desktop publishing provide the basic tools for creating your own marketing materials and for all communication with clients.

Word processing programs allow you to type, edit and print text; programs include such writing aids as a spelling checker and a thesaurus.

The following word processing software can be used with IBM/DOS, Windows, and Macintosh.

Word	*Microsoft*
WordPerfect	*Novell, Inc.*
Ami Pro	*Lotus Development Corp.*

Desktop publishing provides tools to create special layouts such as newsletters or brochures and to incorporate graphic design. We recommend using a laser printer with these programs to present a professional image.

CorelDRAW! *(Windows, Macintosh)*	*A&L/Corel*
QuarkXPress *(Windows, Macintosh)*	*Quark, Inc.*
Pagemaker *(Windows, IBM/DOS)*	*Aldus*

3. CAD Software

CAD programs enable the designer to draft floor plans, cabinet drawings, and renderings. The ability to use CAD software is becoming one of the new standards of the design industry. Many clients want this service.

DesignCAD	*American Small Business Computers, Inc.*
	One American Way
	Pryor, Oklahoma 74361
	(918) 825-4848

DesignCAD offers over 6,700 symbols: tables, chairs, showers, sinks, cabinets, people, plants, and accessories, and so on. IBM/DOS, Macintosh.

Roomer 3	*Hufnagel Software*
	P.O. Box 747
	Clarion, Pennsylvania 16214
	(814) 226-5600

This program includes scaled floor plans, furniture, and furnishings. IBM/DOS.

CAD Services Only	*CAD Ventures Inc.*
	14831 Franklin Ave.
	Tustin, California 92680
	(714) 838-CADD

This program does drafting, scanning and digitizing for converting paper drawings to CAD, renderings, and animation. IBM/Macintosh compatible.

AutoCAD *(Windows and IBM/DOS)*	*AutoDesk, Inc.*
AutoCAD LT *(Windows)*	*2320 Marinship Way*
AutoSketch *(Windows)*	*(415) 333-2234*

Floor Plan Plus	*Computer Easy*
	414 East Southern Avenue
	Tempe, Arizona 85282
	(602) 829-9614

The program provides a library of symbols for drafting furniture, finish materials, plants and architectural features. This company's sister program for Floor Plan Plus is Estimator Plus. Estimator Plus does estimating, bidding, and quotes.

4.   Data Base and Spreadsheet Software

Data base and spreadsheet programs can help you manage market research, budgeting, and cost estimates. These programs can save an incredible amount of time in the marketing planning process. Spreadsheets can calculate changes in cost factors and percentages instantly, allowing you to test alternative marketing strategies quickly and easily.

Lotus 1-2-3*(IBM/DOS, Windows)*	*Lotus Development Corp.*
Quattro Pro *(IBM/DOS, Windows, Macintosh)*	*Novell, Inc.*
Excel *(IBM/DOS, Windows, Macintosh)*	*Microsoft*

5.   Accounting and Financial Management Software

Accounting programs are great time savers that allow you more time to market and design. These programs automate the accounting process and offer a variety of report formats to help you manage your business finances.

Design Manager	*Franklin-Potter Associates, Inc.*
	3681 Cold Spring Creamery Road
	Doylestown, Pennsylvania 18901
	(800) 836-2999

This program provides an accounting package, inventory, electronic order processing, and payroll. It has a time keeping module that tracks time and billable and nonbillable expenses. IBM/DOS.

MacCounting   *Woodard and Associates, Inc.*
                                   21025 Bank Mill Lane
                                   Saratoga, California 95070
                                   (408) 867-5085

This program is accounting software specifically for interior designers—developed by interior designers. Macintosh.

Designers Business Tools   *Grafx Database Systems*
                                   5150 NW 73rd Way
                                   Ft. Lauderdale, Florida 33319
                                   (800) 659-4723

This software consists of five base modules: general ledger, accounts payable, accounts receivable, sales order/proposal, and purchase orders. IBM.

Design Age   *Design Age Computer Software*
                                   P.O. Box 410
                                   Ft. Collins, Colorado 80522
                                   (303) 224-9939

This program manages work-in-process and floor inventory plus accounting functions. IBM, Macintosh.

Designer's Business Choice   *Systems Integrated Solutions*
                                   1047 El Camino Road - Suite 203
                                   Menlo Park, California 94025
                                   (415) 324-1055

This program tracks clients, jobs, contracts, proposal forms, and invoices. It also prepares the bills and tells you your profit. IBM, Macintosh.

Quicken   *Intuit*
QuickBook   *P.O. Box 3014*
                                   Menlo Park , California 94025
                                   (415) 322-0573

Quicken is a personal finance program. Quickbook is accounting software for small businesses of five to fifty people. IBM/DOS, Windows, Macintosh.

Peachtree Accounting   *Peachtree Software*
                                            1505-C Pavilion Place
                                            Norcross, Georgia 30090
                                            (800) 247-3224

This program manages accounting for small to midsize businesses.
IBM/DOS, Windows, Macintosh.

6.   Electronic Phone Book

These software programs maintain lists of names, addresses, and phone
numbers of certain groups of people that can be entered into your computer
automatically. For example, Fortune 500 Prospector, published by Group of
San Francisco working with Fortune magazine, has a package of all of the key
executives of the Fortune 500 companies. This list would be a great help if
the list you bought was your target market.

References

Starting and Managing a Design Business

Berger, C. Jaye, *Interior Design Law and Business Practices*, Wiley, New York, 1994.

A valuable up-to-date explanation of critical legal issues in a design business. This book provides what you need to know to avoid legal problems.

Jones, Gerre, *How to Market Professional Design Services*, 2nd ed., McGraw-Hill, New York, 1983.

Introduction to marketing planning and techniques for design firms — presented in textbook style. More applicable to large architectural firms than small interior design businesses.

Kaderlan, Norman, *Designing Your Practice: A Principal's Guide to Creating and Managing a Design Practice*, McGraw-Hill, New York, 1991.

Guide to managing a design practice. Focus is on the larger firm: managing staff, providing leadership, group process, and organization structure and character. Presumes an established organization; not entrepreneurial. Good sections on working relationships with clients and planning, and appendix has worksheets for planning.

Knackstedt, Mary V., *The Interior Design Business Handbook*, Whitney Library of Design, New York, 1988.

This excellent resource covers the major issues in establishing and maintaining an interior design practice. The chapter on marketing is repeated and expanded in Knackstedt's *Marketing and Selling Design Services*.

Marcus, Bruce W., *Competing for Clients in the 90s: A Dynamic Guide to Marketing, Promoting & Building a Professional Services Practice*, Probus Publishing, Chicago, 1992.

Good resource on marketing for professional services as distinct from marketing products. Not written specifically for designers — probably more applicable to services like management consulting and medical or legal practices. The benefit of this book is that it is very current and contains detailed marketing advice for professionals.

Siegel, Harry, *A Guide to Business Principles and Practices for Interior Designers*, revised edition, Whitney Library of Design, New York, 1982.

A helpful resource for starting a design practice. Thorough treatment of legal structures and of pricing and managing design jobs — lots of useful forms and examples of contracts.

Stasiowski, Frank A., AIA, *Staying Small Successfully: A Guide for Architects, Engineers, and Design Professionals*, Wiley, New York, 1991.

Thorough discussion of the issues involved in maintaining a small design practice — includes planning, customer service, managing staff, and financial management.

Stasiowski, Frank A., AIA, *Starting a New Design Firm, or Risking it All!*, Wiley, New York, 1994.

Good resource for establishing and managing a design practice. More emphasis on organization and management than on marketing.

Marketing

Connor, Dick and Davidson, Jeff, *Getting New Clients*, 2nd ed., Wiley, New York, 1993.

Thorough discussion of marketing for professional service providers. Key techniques are creating demand and targeting specific clients, using direct mail and telephone follow-up.

Davidson, Jeff, *Marketing on a Shoestring: Low-Cost Tips for Marketing Your Products or Services*, 2nd ed., Wiley, New York, 1994.

Good marketing resource that focuses on marketing techniques requiring time rather than money.

Edwards, Paul and Edwards, Sarah, *Getting Business to Come to You*, Jeremy P. Tarcher, New York, 1991.

Source of marketing ideas for self-employed designers. Very practical and entrepreneurial — though more focused on marketing products than services.

Graham, John R., *Magnet Marketing*, Wiley, New York, 1991.

Good explanation of techniques designed to get the customer to feel the need for your service. More product-oriented than service-oriented; written for larger businesses.

Hawken, Paul, *Growing a Business*, Simon and Schuster, New York, 1987.

A clear and readable guide to starting *small* with small business and letting the business grow naturally.

Knackstedt, Mary V., *Marketing and Selling Design Services*, Van Nostrand-Reinhold, New York, 1993.

Though written primarily for large design firms, this marketing book has good specific advice for marketing interior design services.

Levinson, Jay Conrad, *Guerrilla Marketing: Secrets for Making Big Profits from Your Small Business*, Houghton-Mifflin Company, Boston, 1984.

Useful resource on leveraging limited marketing resources. Focuses more on product marketing. The emphasis is on advertising and publicity.

Morgan, Jim, *Marketing for the Small Design Firm*, Whitney Library of Design, New York, 1984.

Overview of marketing techniques for established design firms. Written by an architect, its main focus is architect practices. Contains interesting marketing profiles of design firms.

Putman, Anthony O., *Marketing Your Services*, Wiley, New York, 1990.

An excellent resource on marketing for professional services. More helpful in focusing your business and reaching the right clients than on how-to details on marketing techniques. Helpful exercises to guide you through marketing decisions.

Market Research

Breen, George and Blankenship, A. B., *Do-It-Yourself Marketing Research*, 2nd ed., McGraw-Hill, New York, 1982.

Practical step-by-step guide for doing simple market research. This book is good for small business because it assumes you are looking for the fastest and cheapest—as well as the best—way to answer your questions.

Fink, Arlene and Kosecoff, Jaqueline, *How to Conduct Surveys: A Step-by-Step Guide*, Beverly Hills, California, 1985.

Frigstad, David B., *Know Your Market: How To Do Low-Cost Market Research*, Oasis Press, Grants Pass, Oregon, 1995.

Detailed explanation of market research methods. Written for larger companies but has useful information for small businesses as well. Good presentation of primary research methods.

Direct Mail

Bly, Robert W., *Selling Your Services*, Henry Holt, New York, 1991.

A good primer on marketing and selling a service primarily through direct mail. The type of service discussed is more standardized than most design services so not all methods are applicable.

Rapp, Stan and Collins, Tom, *Maxi-Marketing*, New American Library, New York, 1988.

Expert advice on using targeted direct mail techniques to reach a specific group of clients.

Public Relations

Nolte, Lawrence W. and Wilcox, Dennis, *Effective Publicity: How to Reach the Public*, Wiley, New York, 1984.

Soderberg, Norman R., *Public Relations for the Entrepreneur and the Growing Business: How to Use Public Relations to Increase Visibility and Create Opportunities for You and Your Company*, Probus, Chicago, 1986.

Customer Service

Desatnick, Robert L., *Managing to Keep the Customer: How to Achieve and Maintain Superior Customer Service Throughout the Organization*, Jossey-Bass, San Francisco, 1987.

Wilson, Jerry R., *Word-of-Mouth Marketing*, Wiley, New York, 1991.

Detailed presentation of creating good customer service and using satisfied customers as part of your marketing. Written for large companies selling products, but useful information for any business.

Time Management

Allen, Jane Elizabeth, *Beyond Time Management*, Addison-Wesley, Reading, Massachusetts, 1986.

Lakein, Alan, *How to Get Control of Time and Your Life*, New American Library, New York, 1973.

A classic on managing your time and using your time for what is most important. Helpful exercises.

Mackenzie, R. Alec, *The Time Trap: Managing Your Way Out*, Amacom, New York, 1972.

Publishing Your Work

Adler, Elizabeth W., *Print That Works*, Bull Publishing, Palo Alto, California, 1991.

ASID, *How to Get Design Work Published: A Guide to Magazine Markets*, American Society of Interior Designers, Washington D.C.

Selling

Connor, Tim, *Soft Sell: The New Art of Selling, Self-Empowerment and Persuasion*, 2nd ed., Sourcebooks, Napierville, Illinois, 1994.

Good presentation of classic sales techniques with a contemporary slant. Focuses on the psychology of selling — the purpose behind the classic steps of selling. Lots of useful exercises to practice.

Laborde, Genie, *Influencing with Integrity*, Syntony Publishing, Palo Alto, California, 1987.

Peppers, Don and Rogers, Martha, *The One-to-One Future: Building Relationships One Customer at a Time*, Currency-Doubleday, New York, 1993.

Good orientation to the basics of collaborative selling.

Rackham, Neil, *Spin Selling*, McGraw-Hill, New York, 1988.

Willingham, Ron, *Integrity Selling*, Doubleday, New York, 1987.

Useful discussion of how to sell with integrity and with respect for the client.

Seminars

Shenson, Howard L., *How to Create and Market a Successful Seminar*, Everest House, New York, 1981.

Cross-Cultural Comunication

Axtell, Roger E., *Gestures: The Do's and Taboos of Body Language Around the World*, Wiley, New York, 1991.

Poyatos, Fernando, *Cross-cultural Perspectives in Nonverbal Communication*, Hogrefe, Lewiston, New York, 1988.

Design Publications

Architecture (AIA), Billboard Publications, 1515 Broadway–15th Floor, New York, New York 10036.

Architecture Record, McGraw-Hill, 1221 Avenue of the Americas, New York, New York 10020.

ASID Report, ASID Service Corporation, 608 Massachusetts Avenue N.E., Washington, D.C. 20026-6006.

Contract Design, Miller Freeman, Inc., 1515 Broadway–24th Floor, New York, New York 10036.

D&WC (Draperies and Window Coverings), L. C. Clark Publishing Co., 840 U.S. Highway One, Suite 330, North Palm Beach, Florida 33408-3878.

Elle Decor, Elle Publishing, L. P., 1633 Broadway, New York, New York 10019.

Interior Concerns Newsletter, Interior Concerns Environmental Resources, P.O. Box 2386, Mill Valley, California 94942.

Interior Concerns Resource Guide, Interior Concerns Environmental Resources, P.O. Box 2386, Mill Valley, California 94942.

Interior Design, Cahners Publishing Co., 249 West 17th Street, New York, New York 10011.

Interiors, BPI Communications, 1515 Broadway, New York, New York 10036.

Kitchen and Bath Business, Miller and Freeman, Inc., 600 Harrison Street, San Francisco, California 94107.

Kitchen and Bath Design News, KBC Publications, 2 University Plaza, Hackensack, New Jersey 07601.

Kitchen and Bath Specialist, Kasmar Publishing, P.O. Box 2638, Palm Desert, California 92255.

Lighting Design and Application, Illuminating Engineering Society, 120 Wall Street–17th Floor, New York, New York 10005.

Perspective, International Interior Design Association, 341 Merchandise Mart, Chicago, Illinois 60654.

Professional Office Design, NY Law Publishing Co., 111 Eighth Avenue, Suite 900, New York, New York 10011.

Progressive Architecture, Penton Publishing, 600 Summer Street, P.O. Box 1361, Stamford, Connecticut 06904.

Small Business Publications

Dun & Bradstreet Reference Book of American Business, Dun & Bradstreet, 299 Park Avenue - 24th Floor, New York, New York 10171.

Entrepreneur Magazine, Entrepreneur Magazine, 2392 Morse Avenue, Irvine, California 92714-6234.

In Business, J. G. Press, Inc., 419 State Avenue, Emmaus, Pennsylvania 18049-035.

Journal of Marketing, American Marketing Association, 222 South Riverside Plaza, Chicago, Illinois 60606.

Success Magazine, Lang Communications, 230 Park Avenue - 7th Floor, New York, New York 10169-0005.

Voice of Small Business, National Small Business Association, 1604 K Street N.W., Washington, D.C. 20006.

Design Associations

AIA	American Institute of Architects 1735 New York Avenue N.W. Washington, D.C. 20006 (202) 626-7300
ANSI	American National Standards Institute 11 West 42nd Street New York, New York 10036 (212) 642-4900
ASFD	American Society of Furniture Designers 521 South Hamilton Street Boston, Massachusetts 02109 (617) 884-4074

ASID   American Society of Interior Designers
            608 Massachusetts Avenue N.E.
            Washington, D.C. 20002
            (202) 546-3480

ASLA   American Society of Landscape Architects
            4401 Connecticut Avenue N.W., #500
            Washington, D.C. 20008
            (202) 686-2752

ASTM   American Society for Testing and Materials
            1916 Race Street
            Philadelphia, Pennsylvania 19103-1187
            (215) 299-5400

            Association of Registered Interior Designers of Ontario
            717 Church Street
            Toronto, Ontario, Canada M4W 2M5
            (416) 921-2127

BOMA   Building Owners and Managers Association
            1201 New York Avenue N.W., Suite 300
            Washington, D.C. 20005
            (204) 408-2662

            Color Association of the United States
            409 West 44th Street
            New York, New York 10036
            (212) 582-6884

CMG   Color Marketing Group
            4001 North 9th Street, Suite 102
            Arlington, Virginia 22203
            (703) 528-7666

FIDER   Foundation for Interior Design Education Research
            60 Monroe Center N.W.
            Grand Rapids, Michigan 49503
            (616) 458-0400

HFES   Human Factors and Ergonomics Society
            P.O. Box 1369
            Santa Monica, California 90406-1369
            (310) 394-1811

IALD   International Association of Lighting Designers
18 East 16th Street, Suite 208
New York, New York 10003-3193
(212) 206-1281

IDSA   Industrial Designers Society of America
1142-E Walker Road
Great Falls, Virginia 22066
(703) 759-0100

IDEC   Interior Design Educators Council
14252 Culver Drive, Suite A-331
Irvine, California 92714
(714) 551-1622

IES   Illuminating Engineers Society of North America
345 East 47th Street
New York, New York 10017
(212) 705-7926

IFDA   International Furnishing and Design Association
107 World Trade Center, P.O. Box 580045
Dallas, TX 75258-8045
(214)747-2406

IFMA   International Facility Management Association
1 East Greenway Plaza, Suite 1100
Houston, Texas 77046-0194
(713) 623-4362

IIDA   International Interior Design Association
341 Merchandise Mart
Chicago, Illinois 60654
(312) 467-1950

IREM   Institute of Real Estate Management
430 North Michigan Avenue
Chicago Illinois 60611
(312)329-6000

NAHB   National Association of Home Builders
15th and M Streets N.W.
Washington, D.C. 20005
(202) 822-0200

NCIDQ   National Council for Interior Design Qualification
50 Main Street
White Plains, New York 10606-1920
(914) 948-9100

NIOSH   National Institute for Occupational Safety and Health
4676 Columbia Parkway
Cincinnati, Ohio 45226
(513) 533-8225

NKBA   National Kitchen and Bath Association
687 Willow Grove Street
Hackettstown, New Jersey 07840
(201) 852-0033

OBD   Organization of Black Designers
300 M Street S.W., Suite N 110
Washington, D.C. 20024
(202) 659-3918

OSHA   Occupational Safety & Health Administration
200 Constitution Avenue N.W.
Washington, D.C. 20210
(202) 219-0478

SMPS   Society for Marketing Professional Services
99 Canal Center Plaza, Suite 320
Alexandria, Virginia 22314
(703) 549-6117

WA   Wallcovering Association
401 N. Michigan Ave.
Chicago, Illinois 60611
(312) 644-6610

WCMA   Window Covering Manufacturers Association
355 Lexington Avenue
New York, New York 10017
(212) 661-4261

Index

Action plan for marketing, 43, 44, 46,
  49–54. *See also* Marketing plan
Advertising, 37, 74, 86, 92, 94, 99, 115,
  118, 125, 126, 128, 147–150, 165,
  220
American Disabilities Act (ADA), 14, 45,
  154, 199
American Society of Interior Designers
  (ASID), 24, 95, 100, 104, 106, 114,
  132, 148, 169, 220, 222

Barriers to competition, 19
Benefits of design service, 10–12, 26, 27,
  29, 32, 44, 54, 56, 58, 62, 63, 66, 72,
  73, 75, 80, 84, 88, 92, 110, 122–124,
  127, 134, 142, 150, 154, 170, 173,
  180, 188–192, 220, 222, 233
Billing, 61, 211. *See also* Fees
Boards, 88, 127, 181, 184, 186, 224. *See
  also* Selling, sales presentations
Brochures, 25, 52, 78, 126, 132, 134,
  140–143, 153, 165, 188, 223, 233,
  235
Budgeting for marketing, *see* Marketing
  plan, budget
Building the designer–client relationship,
  see Marketing process
Business cards, 78–81, 85, 87, 98, 113,

128–132, 143, 164, 204, 221–223. *See
  also* Company graphics
Business name, 75, 127, 131, 234

CAD (computer-aided design software),
  123, 189, 231, 233, 235
Client follow-up, *see* Follow-up after jobs
Client interviews, 65, 133, 171–176, 210
  client profile records, 149, 212, 214
  needs assessments, 167
Client list, 106, 116, 154, 161, 221, 223,
  232
  using contact management software, 213.
  See also Computers
Client satisfaction, 134, 142–143, 196, 204,
  206, 207, 212, 214, 221. *See also*
  Customer service
  getting client feedback, 193, 197, 207,
  210, 218, 221
  knowing the client's expectations, 57,
  127, 174, 198, 200, 221
  understanding the client's perspective,
  44, 93, 170, 189
Closing the sale, 175, 189–192, 197,
  212–216, 218
Cold calls, 82, 155–157. *See also* Selling
Commercial interior design, 9–10, 59, 66,
  67, 68, 89, 95, 98, 117, 132, 134,

Commercial interior design *(cont,d)*
140, 148, 157, 172, 179, 191, 194,
198, 200, 213–214, 221, 226, 228
Community involvement as marketing, 84,
88, 92–94, 99, 105, 115–119, 155,
156, 159, 224
Company graphics, 127–132
Competition, 6, 18, 19, 21, 24–26, 44–45,
56–58, 61–62, 118, 122, 131, 142,
147, 148, 150, 158, 160, 180, 193,
197, 206, 222–223
Competitive advantage, how to achieve,
58, 160
Competitors, *see* Competition
Complaints, how to manage, 210–211
Computers, 123, 134, 143, 160–161,
181–182, 187, 213, 220, 223, 229,
231–238
 software, 123, 160, 213, 223, 229
 using computer technology for marketing, 187, 233
Consultants, help with marketing, 30, 123
Contract negotiation, *see* Negotiation
Credibility, establishing, 13, 20, 56–57, 89,
90, 96–99, 104, 115, 116, 122, 124,
125, 143, 147, 169, 193
Customer service, 20, 86, 197, 199–206,
218. *See also* Quality service

Data base, client, *see* Client list
Deposits, requiring, 67
Design associations, 24, 123. *See also*
American Society of Interior
Designers (ASID); International
Interior Design Association (IIDA)
Design centers, 220, 224, 230
Design competitions, 97, 104, 106, 117,
118, 124, 127, 134, 205, 216, 219, 223
Design specialty, 6, 12, 17, 24, 57, 77, 78,
84, 106, 115, 122, 124, 127, 134, 150,
213. *See also* Niche marketing
Desktop publishing software, 143, 160,
187–188, 231, 233–235. *See also*
Computers
Differentiating your design services, 26–27,
62
Direct mail marketing, 30, 49, 92, 102, 126,
145, 150, 152–155, 165
 mailing lists, 30, 152–155, 165, 223
 marketing letters, 152–156, 233

telephone follow-up, 76, 126, 154–158,
165

Endorsements from clients, *see*
Testimonials, how to get and use
Entertaining as a marketing method,
157–159, 176, 216
Evaluating marketing results, 49
Expert status as a designer, 89, 97, 106,
112, 115, 117, 118, 121–124, 160. *See
also* Credibility, establishing

Fact sheet on your design business, 142
Fees, 20, 25, 55–69, 75, 192, 205, 228. *See
also* Pricing your services
 design concept fee, 60, 62
 purchasing fee, 59
Fliers, 92, 116, 150, 159
Follow–up after jobs, 206–210
 client questionnaires, 145, 207, 210
Free consultation, 87, 155–157, 177–179,
216, 219

Gap in the market, *see* Market opportunity
Gifts, 88, 186, 204, 216, 223
Goals, *see* Marketing plan, goals
Guarantees, 184, 190, 204

Insider position in a market niche, 19, 23
International Interior Design Association
(IIDA), 24
Interviews, *see* Client interviews

Leads for marketing, 70, 71, 81–88, 90,
116, 151, 152, 156, 161, 172, 178,
179, 190, 197
Listening, how to improve, 68, 81, 114,
158, 167–169, 174–178, 181, 191,
195, 210
Logos, 113, 128, 131, 132, 147, 186, 204.
See also Company graphics

Mailing lists, *see* Direct mail marketing,
mailing lists
Market, understanding the, 12, 17, 18, 31,

37, 43, 44, 48, 52, 54, 56, 84, 90, 94, 96, 104, 128, 149, 151, 155, 159
Market opportunity, 13–16, 27, 192
Market research, 17, 21, 22, 25, 27, 30, 37, 43, 222, 224, 236
  primary, 22, 24–26
    focus groups, 22, 25, 30
    surveys, 22, 25
  questions, 17–22
  secondary, 22, 23
Market segmentation, 6
  market segment, 6, 9–11, 17, 20,
Market trends, 18, 22, 23, 45, 95–96, 151, 159, 160
Marketing information packets, 87, 117, 122, 125, 126, 132, 134–140, 143, 147, 149, 165, 233
  marketing packet enclosures, 134–140, 143, 233
Marketing materials, 27, 52, 125–165, 223, 233–234. *See also* Brochures; Direct mail marketing; Fliers; Marketing information packets; Newsletters; Photographs; Portfolios
Marketing message, importance of, 58, 69, 89, 99, 125–127, 132, 134, 143, 196, 221
Marketing methods, how to select, 29–31, 34, 37, 46, 49, 54, 89, 92, 125, 126, 152, 223
Marketing partnerships, *see* Professional relationships, use in marketing
Marketing plan, how to write and use, 28–54, 83, 179, 221, 223, 224, 236
  action plan, *see* Action plan for marketing
  budget, 29, 46, 48, 116,
    estimating marketing expenses, 46, 48, 50, 65, 105, 116
    estimating revenue, 37, 46, 49, 50, 63
    weighing costs and benefits, 29, 32, 54
  categories to include, 30, 33, 36, 46
  formats for planning, 28, 31, 34
    bubble diagram, 28, 31, 32, 38, 44,
    planning an outline, 28, 31–33
    writing a letter, 28, 34, 35, 52
  goals, 28, 30, 31, 34, 36, 38, 43–46, 49, 50, 53, 54, 83–85, 108, 223
  mission, *see* Mission
  strengths & weaknesses and opportunities & threats (SWOT), 34, 37, 44, 45, 54

Marketing process, building the designer–client relationship, 74, 90, 147, 166–169, 195, 218, 224
Marketing strategy, 34, 55, 104–105, 126, 160, 165, 179
Mission, 33, 35, 36, 38–42, 54, 84, 128, 223
  business mission, 38, 40
  personal mission, 38
Model homes, demonstrating design skills in, 97
Monitoring marketing results, 49, 233

Negotiation, 68, 192
Network for marketing, 70, 71, 81–86, 88, 179, 220
Networking, 71, 81–86, 88, 90, 220
Newsletters, 52, 96, 113, 150, 159–161, 204, 215, 233, 235
News media, 92, 116–119, 147, 149
Niche marketing, 5–27, 43, 57, 77, 78, 84, 90, 94, 106, 122, 124, 213

Objections, how to manage in selling, 155, 167, 190–193

Photographs, use in marketing, 97, 99, 106, 108, 109, 117, 119, 131–133, 140, 142, 148, 164, 181, 186, 188, 200, 219, 220, 223
Portfolios, 25, 78, 106, 110, 125, 126, 131–134, 165, 221
Postoccupancy evaluations, *see* Follow-up after jobs
Press releases, 31, 35, 37, 106, 117, 119, 120, 224
Pricing your services, 45, 55–60, 66, 69, 226. *See also* Fees
  fixed-fee pricing, 60
  percentage of cost pricing, 61
  pricing by square footage, 61
Professional ethics, 90, 116, 147, 196, 197
Professional image, 66, 79, 92, 126–128, 131–133, 147, 150, 165, 182, 197, 207, 230
Professional relationships, use in marketing, 70–82, 85–88, 220, 223
  joint ventures, 70–73, 75–77, 88

Professional relationships, use in marketing *(cont'd)*
  networking, *see* Networking
  reciprocal referrals, 71, 77–79, 88
Profit margin, 55, 62, 192. *See also*
  Marketing plan, budget
Project management, 60, 66, 182
  project budgets, 65, 76, 174, 192
  project estimates, 60, 61, 63, 65, 66, 69,
    157, 187, 190, 226, 236
Promotions, 37, 49, 84, 90, 92, 125,
  150–155, 165
Proposals, 29, 52, 57, 66, 69, 90, 145, 151,
  168, 172, 181, 186–190, 195, 237
  request for proposals (RFPs), 52
Prospective clients, 45, 49, 66, 77, 81, 84,
  86, 88, 89–93, 99, 110, 112, 115, 116,
  122, 124, 125, 126, 131, 133, 140,
  145, 147, 150–152, 155–161, 165,
  169, 172, 178, 220, 232
Publicity, 35, 73, 92, 97–101, 104–106,
  109–112, 116–119, 122, 124, 127, 128,
  147–150, 155, 159, 165, 204, 219,
  220, 224
Public relations, 37, 92, 118. *See also*
  Publicity
Public speaking, 37, 50, 92, 96, 97,
  110–117, 123, 124, 183, 222
Publishing, 29, 31, 35–37, 52, 67, 76, 85,
  92, 95–99, 104, 106, 108–110, 113,
  114, 117, 118, 124, 174–176, 187,
  188, 202, 214, 220, 222–224

Qualifying prospective clients, 68, 156,
  167, 171, 178, 179, 192, 195
Quality service, 45, 55, 56, 62, 72–75, 95,
  109, 110, 112, 116, 127, 128, 131–133,
  142, 145, 160, 175, 187, 192,
  196–200, 206, 212, 218, 230. *See also*
  Customer service

Referrals, 70–74, 77–88, 99, 161, 178, 179,
  192, 196, 197, 202, 204, 212–214,
  219, 220. *See also* Professional relationships, use in marketing
Reprints of publications, 108, 113, 127,
  145, 147, 164, 223. *See also*
  Publishing

Reputation, value of, 13, 19, 44, 57, 62, 71,
  76, 89, 94, 96, 97, 100, 106, 123,
  124, 187, 196, 197, 206, 212
Residential interior design, 9, 10, 12, 16,
  30, 36, 58, 59, 66, 73, 77, 78, 84, 89,
  94, 95, 98, 123, 148, 157, 169, 174,
  184, 213, 226

Saying thank you, importance of and how
  to, 80, 87, 143–145, 204
Selling, 29, 37, 44, 58, 62, 65, 66, 68, 72,
  74, 78, 79, 90, 92, 101, 113, 143, 148,
  151–154, 157, 161, 165, 166–195,
  199, 202, 206, 213, 228, 237
  closing, *see* Closing the sale
  qualifying, *see* Qualifying prospective
    clients
  sales presentations, 73, 78, 83, 90, 112,
    116, 123, 125, 151, 157, 167–169,
    172, 173, 176, 180–186, 189, 191,
    194, 233
Seminars, giving presentations for, 87, 96,
  97, 115–117, 123, 222, 224
Show houses, 97–105, 133, 149, 170, 172,
  179, 189, 220, 230
Special marketing events, 147, 216, 221
Staff, 18, 29, 30, 44, 48, 53, 72, 78, 79,
  117, 150, 151, 157, 180, 187, 202,
  221, 223, 231
Studio, 18, 92, 104, 116, 126–128, 150,
  165, 219, 229
Suppliers and work rooms, 86, 98, 223,
  225, 228, 230

Target clients, 6, 8, 18, 46, 56–58, 69, 84,
  90, 91, 97, 104, 105, 109, 124, 127,
  147, 149, 151, 154, 165, 180
  target client profile, 8–11, 149, 159, 212,
    220
    attitude and lifestyle characteristics, 9
    demographics, 9
    industry characteristics, 10
  target market, 84, 109, 149, 238
Teaching classes as marketing, 115, 119,
  124
Telephone follow-up, *see* Direct mail marketing, telephone follow-up
Terminology for marketing, 92

Testimonials, how to get and use, 20,
143–146, 154, 165, 221
Time management, 48, 50–54
Trade organizations, how to use in marketing, 92, 96, 115, 149, 154
advertising in trade organization directories, 148–149
trade shows, 24
Training in marketing, 115, 123, 202, 224, 227

Visibility, to target clients, 20, 43, 77, 89, 90, 94, 98, 124, 125

Word-of-mouth marketing, 70, 77, 81, 86–88, 151, 196, 210, 212. *See also* Networking; Professional relationships, use in marketing

Yellow pages, 148